CULTS AND BELIEFS
AT EDESSA

ÉTUDES PRÉLIMINAIRES
AUX RELIGIONS ORIENTALES
DANS L'EMPIRE ROMAIN

PUBLIÉES PAR

M. J. VERMASEREN

TOME QUATRE-VINGT-DEUXIÈME

H. J. W. DRIJVERS

CULTS AND BELIEFS
AT EDESSA

LEIDEN
E. J. BRILL
1980

H. J. W. DRIJVERS

CULTS AND BELIEFS
AT EDESSA

WITH 34 PLATES

LEIDEN
E. J. BRILL
1980

ISBN   90 04 06050 2

To Tonny and the children

CONTENTS

PREFACE

Years ago I conceived the plan of writing a monograph on pagan religion in Edessa, according to pious legend the first Christian kingdom in the world. The pressures of academic life, however, delayed the execution of this idea, except for some articles dealing with specific aspects. I am, therefore, very grateful to the Institute for Advanced Study at Princeton, U.S.A. and to the Faculty of its School of Historical Studies for giving me the opportunity of writing this book during the academic year 1977-78, which I spent in the stimulating scholarly atmosphere of the Institute. Discussions with permanent and visiting members were a great help and stimulus and will certainly be of lasting significance. I owe special thanks to Mrs Roxanne S. Heckscher, for correcting and improving the sometimes poor English of my first manuscript, and for her patience and devotion in typing the last draft.

I am greatly indebted to my colleagues in the Department of Semitic Studies of Groningen University, who took over my teaching and other duties during that year.

Many colleagues and friends helped me with advice and comments. I am especially grateful to Professor J. B. Segal of London University, for his help and companionship during a trip to Urfa. His publications aroused my interest in the subject and without them this book could not have been written.

I am greatly indebted to professor M. J. Vermaseren, who accepted this monograph for publication in the EPRO and gave much useful advice.

I would like to express my thanks to the staff of the University Library of Groningen University for all their help, and to Mrs A. Reinink-Sirag and Mrs J. Y. Horlings-Brandse, who typed the footnotes and the bibliography.

Most of all I am indebted to my wife, who has sustained me during many years with tolerance, interest, and love.

Groningen, October 5, 1978.

ABBREVIATIONS

AAAS	=	Annales archéologiques arabes de Syrie
AA	=	Archäologischer Anzeiger
AAL	=	Atti dell' (a.r.) accademia dei Lincei
AAS	=	Annales archéologiques de Syrie
AASOR	=	Annual of the American schools of Oriental research
AAW	=	*Die Araber in der Alten Welt*, 5 Vols, ed. F. Altheim - R. Stiehl, Berlin 1963-1969.
AAWG.PH	=	Abhandlungen der Akademie der Wissenschaften in Göttingen - Philologisch-historische Klasse
ADAJ	=	Annual of the department of antiquities of Jordan
AE	=	Année épigraphique
AfO	=	Archiv für Orientforschung
AHw	=	Wolfram von Soden. Akkadisches Handwörterbuch
AIPh	=	Annuaire de l'institut de philologie et d'histoire orientales
AJA	=	American journal of archaeology
AJP	=	American journal of philology
AKM	=	Abhandlungen für die Kunde des Morgenlandes
ANET	=	Ancient Near Eastern texts relating to the Old Testament
ANRW	=	Aufstieg und Niedergang der römischen Welt
AnSt	=	Anatolian studies
AO	=	Der alte Orient
AS	=	H. Seyrig, *Antiquités syriennes*, 5 Vols, Paris 1934-1966.
BAH	=	Bibliothèque archéologique et historique
BASOR	=	Bulletin of the American schools of oriental research
BCH	=	Bulletin de correspondance hellénique
BHTh	=	Beiträge zur historischen Theologie
BMB	=	Bulletin du musée de Beyrouth
BMC	=	British Museum Coins
BSOAS	=	Bulletin of the school of oriental and African studies
BSOS	=	Bulletin of the school of oriental studies
BZAW	=	Beihefte zur Zeitschrift für die alttestamentliche Wissenschaft
CAH	=	Cambridge ancient history
CAr	=	Cahiers archéologiques
CCDS	=	Corpus Cultus Deae Syriae
CH	=	Cahiers d'histoire
CIL	=	Corpus inscriptionum Latinarum
CIMRM	=	M. J. Vermaseren, *Corpus Inscriptionum et Monumentorum Religionis Mithriacae*, 2 Vols, The Hague 1956-1960.
CIS	=	Corpus inscriptionum Semiticarum
CRAI	=	Comptes rendus des séances de l'académie des inscriptions et belles lettres
CSCO	=	Corpus scriptorum Christianorum orientalium
DISO	=	C.-F. Jean - J. Hoftijzer, *Dictionnaire des inscriptions sémitiques de l'Ouest*, Leiden 1965.

EPRO	=	Etudes préliminaires aux religions orientales dans l'empire romain
FHG	=	Fragmenta historicorum Graecorum
HdO	=	Handbuch der Orientalistik
HUCA	=	Hebrew Union College Annual
IEJ	=	Israel exploration journal
IG	=	Inscriptiones Graecae
IGLS	=	Inscriptions grecques et latines de la Syrie
IGRR	=	Inscriptiones Graecae ad res Romanas pertinentes
ILS	=	Inscriptiones Latinae selectae
JA	=	Journal asiatique
JAOS	=	Journal of the American oriental society
JBL	=	Journal of biblical literature
JCS	=	Journal of cuneiform studies
JdI	=	Jahrbuch des (k.) deutschen archäologischen Instituts
JEOL	=	Jaarbericht van het vooraziatisch-egyptisch genootschap "Ex oriente lux"
JHS	=	Journal of Hellenic studies
JJS	=	Journal of Jewish studies
JNES	=	Journal of Near Eastern studies
JRS	=	Journal of Roman studies
JSS	=	Journal of Semitic Studies
JThS	=	Journal of theological studies
KAI	=	Kanaanäische und aramäische Inschriften
LIMC	=	Lexicon Iconographiae Mythologiae Classicae
MDOG	=	Mitteilungen der deutschen Orientgesellschaft
MFOB	=	Mélanges de la faculté orientale de l'université Saint Joseph
MH	=	Museum Helveticum
MIDEO	=	Mélanges de l'institut dominicain d'études orientales de Caire
MUSJ	=	Mélanges de l'université Saint Joseph
NovTest	=	Novum Testamentum
NumC	=	Numismatic chronicle and Journal of the (r.) numismatic society
NNM	=	Numismatic notes and monographs
OCPM	=	Oxford classical and philosophical monographs
OGIS	=	Orientis graeci inscriptiones selectae
Or	=	Orientalia
OrChr	=	Oriens Christianus
OrChrA	=	Orientalia Christiana analecta
PETSE	=	Papers of the Estonian theological society in exile
PO	=	Patrologia orientalis
PS	=	Patrologia Syriaca
PW	=	Pauly-Wissowa, Real-Encyclopädie der classischen Altertumswissenschaft
RA	=	Revue d'assyriologie et de l'archéologie orientale
RAC	=	Reallexikon für Antike und Christentum
RB	=	Revue biblique
RBNS	=	Revue belge de numismatique

REA	=	Revue des études anciennes
REG	=	Revue des études grecques
REJ	=	Revue des études juives
RES	=	Revue des études sémitiques
RevArch	=	Revue archéologique
RHPhR	=	Revue d'histoire et de philosophie religieuses
RHR	=	Revue de l'histoire des religions
RNum	=	Revue numismatique
RSO	=	Rivista degli studi orientali
RTP	=	*Recueil des tessères de Palmyre*, ed. H. Ingholt - H. Seyrig - J. Starcky, Paris 1955
SBAW.PPH	=	Sitzungsberichte der bayerischen Akademie der Wissenschaften - Philosophisch-philologische und historische Klasse
SC	=	Sources chrétiens
SDB	=	Supplément au dictionnaire de la bible
SEG	=	Supplementum Epigraphicum Graecum
StudSem	=	Studi Semitici
TRE	=	Theologische Realenzyklopädie
TU	=	Texte und Untersuchungen zur Geschichte der altchristlichen Literatur
UCPCP	=	University of California publications in classical philology
VigChr	=	Vigiliae Christianae
WVDOG	=	Wissenschaftliche Veröffentlichungen der deutschen Orientgesellschaft
WZKM	=	Wiener Zeitschrift für die Kunde des Morgenlandes
YCS	=	Yale classical studies
ZA	=	Zeitschrift für Assyriologie
ZDMG	=	Zeitschrift der deutschen morgenländischen Gesellschaft
ZE	=	Zeitschrift für Ethnologie
ZThK	=	Zeitschrift für Theologie und Kirche

BIBLIOGRAPHY

Aggoula, B., Remarques sur les inscriptions hatréennes II, *MUSJ* 47, 1972, 3-80.

Aimé-Giron, N., *Textes araméens d'Égypte*, Caire 1931.

Aland, B., Mani und Bardesanes. Zur Entstehung des Manichäischen Systems, *Synkretismus im syrisch-persischen Kulturgebiet*, hrsg. v. A. Dietrich, *AAWG.PH*, 96, 1975, 123-143.

Aland, B., Marcion, Versuch einer neuen Interpretation, *ZThK* 70, 1973, 420-447.

Alföldi, A., Apollo Pythius Aziz; *Vjestnik Hrv. Archeol. Društva* (N.S.), 1928, 223ff.

Alföldi, A., *Studien zur Geschichte der Weltkrise des 3. Jahrhunderts nach Christus*, Darmstadt 1967.

Al-Salihi, W., New Light on the Identity of the Triad of Hatra, *Sumer* 31, 1975, 75-80.

Altheim, F., *Niedergang der alten Welt* II, Frankfurt am Main 1952.

Amand, D., *Fatalisme et liberté dans l'antiquité grecque*, Louvain 1945.

Andrae, W. - P. Jensen, *Aramäische Inschriften aus Assur und Hatra aus der Parther Zeit*, MDOG 60, 1920.

Andrae, W. - H. Lenzen, *Die Partherstadt Assur*, *WVDOG* 57, Leipzig 1933.

Attridge, H. W. - R. A. Oden, *The Syrian Goddess (De Dea Syria) attributed to Lucian*, Texts and Translations 9, Missoula 1976.

Avi-Yonah, M., Mount Carmel and the God of Baalbek, *IEJ* 2, 1952, 118-124.

Avi-Yonah, M., Syrian Gods at Ptolemais-Accho, *IEJ* 9, 1959, 1-12.

Babelon, E., Numismatique d'Édesse en Mésopotamie, *Mélanges Numismatiques*, 2ème Série, Paris 1893, 209-296.

Babelon, J., *Impératrices syriennes*, Paris 1957.

Bailey, C. R., The Cult of the Twins at Edessa, *JAOS* 88, 1968, 342-344.

Balty, J. Ch., - J. Balty, Apamée de Syrie, archéologie et histoire I. Des origines à la Tétrarchie, ANRW II, 8, Berlin-N.Y. 1977, 103-134.

Baudissin, W. W., *Adonis und Esmun*, Leipzig 1911.

Baudissin, W. W., *Studien zur semitischen Religionsgeschichte* II, Leipzig 1878.

Bauer, W., *Rechtgläubigkeit und Ketzerei im ältesten Christentum*, BHTh 10, Tübingen 1934.

Baumstark, A., *Geschichte der syrischen Literatur*, Bonn 1922.

Beck, E., Ephräms Brief an Hypatios, *OrChr* 58, 1974, 76-120.

Beck, E., Ephräms Rede gegen eine philosophische Schrift des Bardaiṣan, *OrChr* 60, 1976, 24-68.

Beck, E., *Des heiligen Ephraem des Syrers Carmina Nisibina* I, II, *CSCO* 218-219, Script. Syri 92-93. CSCO 240-241, Script. Syri 102-103, Louvain 1961-1963.

Beck, E., *Des heiligen Ephraem des Syrers Hymnen contra Haereses*, CSCO 169-170, Script. Syri 76-77, Louvain 1957.

Beck, E., *Des heiligen Ephraem des Syrers Hymnen de Fide*, CSCO 154-155, Script. Syri 73-74, Louvain 1955.

Bedjan, P., *Homiliae S. Isaaci Syri Antiocheni* I, Par. 1903.
Bellinger, A. R. - C. B. Welles, A third-century contract of Sale from Edessa in Osrhoene, *YCS* 5, 1935, 95-154.
Bellinger, A. R., *Coins from Jerash*, 1928-1934, *NNM* 81, 1938, 29-31.
Bellinger, A. R., *The Eighth and Ninth Dura Hoards, NNM* 85, New York 1939, 16-28.
Bellinger, A. R., *Syrian tetradrachms of Caracalla and Macrinus, NS* 3, New York 1940, 50-57.
Berg, P.-L. van, *Corpus Cultus Deae Syriae* (CCDS), 2 vols. *EPRO* 28, Leiden 1972.
Betz, H. D., *Lukian von Samosata und das Neue Testament, TU* 76, Berlin 1961, 218-251.
Bevan, E. R., *The House of Seleucus*, 2 Vols, London 1902.
Beyer, K., Der reichsaramäische Einschlag in der ältesten syrischen Literatur, *ZDMG* 116, 1966, 242-254.
Bickell, G., (ed.), *S. Isaaci Antiocheni doctoris Syrorum opera omnia* I, II, Gissae 1873-1877.
Bidez, J., Les écoles chaldéennes sous Alexandre et les Séleucides, Volume offert à Jean Capart, *AIPh* 3, 1935, 41-89.
Bidez, J., Le philosophe Jamblique et son école, *REG* 32, 1919, 29ff.
Bidez, J. - F. Cumont, *Les mages hellénisés*, 2 vols., Paris 1938.
Bikerman, E., *Institutions des Séleucides*, Paris 1937.
Bivar, A. D. H. - S. Shaked, The Inscriptions at Shīmbār, *BSOAS* 27, 1964, 265-290.
Bonner, C., κεστὸς ἱμάς and the Saltire of Aphrodite, *AJPh* 70, 1949, 1-6.
Borger, R., Die Inschriften Asarhaddons, Königs von Assyrien, *AfO*, Beiheft 9, 1956, 53ff.
Bossert, H. Th., *Altsyrien*, Tübingen 1951.
Bounni, A., Nouveaux bas-reliefs religieux de la Palmyrène, *Mélanges K. Michalowski*, Warszawa 1966, 313-320.
Bounni, A., Nabû Palmyrénien, *Orientalia* 45, 1976, 46-52.
Bounni, A. - M. Saliby, Six nouveaux emplacements fouillés à Palmyre (1963-1964), *AAS* 15, 1965, 121-138.
Branden, A. v. d., *Histoire de Thamoud*, Beyrouth 1966.
Bresciani, E. - M. Kamil, *Le lettere Aramaiche de Hermopoli, AAL* 1966, Serie VIII, Vol. XII, fasc. 5.
Brock, S. P., Barnabas: ΥΙΟΣ παρακλησις, *JThS* 25, 1974, 93-98.
Brock, S. P., Review of Drijvers' Bardaiṣan of Edessa, *JSS* 1970, 115ff.
Broek, R. van den, *The Myth of the Phoenix according to classical and early Christian Traditions, EPRO* 24, Leiden 1972.
Brooks, E. W., (ed.), Severus of Antioch, *Selected Letters*, 2 vols, London 1902-1903.
Brown, P., Approaches to the religious Crisis of the third century A.D., *Religion and Society in the Age of St. Augustine*, London 1972, 74-93.
Brown, P., *The World of Late Antiquity*, from Marcus Aurelius to Muhammad, London 1971.
Bruneau, Ph., *Recherches sur les cultes de Délos à l'époque hellénistique et à l'époque impériale*, Paris 1970.
Brykczyński, P., Astrologia w Palmyrze, *Studia Palmyrenskie* VI, 1975, 47-109.

Buffière, F., *Les mythes d'Homère et la pensée grecque*, Paris 1956.
Burkitt, F. C., *Euphemia and the Goth with the Acts of Martyrdom of the Confessors of Edessa*, London 1913.
Burkitt, F. C., Appendix to mr. C. Winckworth's note, *JThS* 25, 1924, 403ff.
Burkitt, F. C., *Urchristentum in Orient*, Tübingen 1907.
Caquot, A., Chadrapha. À propos de quelques articles récents, *Syria* 29, 1952, 74-88.
Caquot, A., Critical review on Fahd's Le panthéon de l'Arabie Centrale, *Syria* 1970, 187-191.
Caquot, A., Inscriptions et graffites hatréens de Doura-Europos, *Syria* 30, 1953, 240-246.
Caquot, A., Nouvelles inscriptions araméennes de Hatra, *Syria* 29, 1952, 89-118.
Caquot, A., Nouvelles inscriptions araméennes de Hatra II, *Syria* 30, 1953, 234-246.
Caquot, A., Nouvelles inscriptions araméennes de Hatra III, *Syria* 40, 1963, 1-16.
Caquot, A., Sur l'onomastique religieuse de Palmyre, *Syria* 39, 1962, 231-256.
Castelus, K. O., Coinage of Rhesaena in Mesopotamia, *NNM* 108, 1946.
Chabot, J.-B., (ed.), *Michel le Syrien, Chronique de Michel le Syrien*, Paris 1899-1910.
Chabot, I.-B. - A. Vaschalde, *Iacobi Edesseni Hexaemeron seu in opus creationis libri septem*, CSCO 92-97, *Script. Syri* 44-48, Louvain 1928.
Chabot, J.-B., *Choix d'inscriptions de Palmyre*, Paris 1922.
Chad, C., *Les dynastes d'Émèse*, Beyrouth 1972.
Chantraire, H., *Freigelassene und Sklaven im Dienst der römischen Kaiser*, Studien zu ihrer Nomenklatur, Wiesbaden 1967.
Chapot, V., Antiquités de la Syrie du Nord, *BCH* 26, 1902, 161ff.
Chwolsohn, D. A., *Die Ssabier und der Ssabismus*, 2 vols., St. Petersburg 1856.
Clemen, C., *Lukians Schrift über die syrische Göttin*, AO 37, 3-4, Leipzig 1938.
Clermont-Ganneau, M., *Recueil d'archéologie orient.* VIII, 1924.
Collart, P. - J. Vicari, *Le sanctuaire de Baalshamin à Palmyre* I, Topographie et Architecture, Rome 1969.
Colledge, M. A. C., *Parthian Art*, Ithaca, New York 1977.
Colpe, C., Parthische Religion und parthische Kunst, *KAIROS* N.F. 17, 1975, 118-123.
Conteneau, G., *Manuel d'archéologie orientale*, Paris 1927-47.
Cook, A. B., *Zeus. A Study in Ancient Religion*, 3 vols, Cambridge 1914-1940.
Cowley, A., *Aramaic Papyri of the Fifth Century BC*, Oxford 1923.
Cross, F. M., An Aramaic Inscription from Daskyleion, *BASOR* 184, 1966, 7-10.
Cumont, F., *Études Syriennes*, Paris 1917.
Cumont, F., *Recherches sur le symbolisme funéraire des Romains*, Bibliothèque archéologique et historique 35, Paris 1966.
Cumont, F., Antiochus d'Athènes et Porphyre, *Mélanges Bidez*, Bruxelles 1934, 135-156.
Cumont, F., Les noms des planètes et l'astrolatrie chez les Grecs, *l'Antiquité Classique* 4, 1935.

Cumont, F., *Les religions orientales dans le paganisme romain*, 4ᵉ ed., Paris 1929.
Cumont, F., *La théologie solaire du paganisme romain*, *Mém. prés. par div. savants à l'Académie des Inscr.* XII, 2, 1913, 1-33.
Cumont, F., Le culte de Mithras à Edesse, *RevArch* 1888, 95-98.
Cumont, F., l'Aigle funéraire d'Hiérapolis et l'apothéose des empereurs, *Études Syriennes*, Paris 1917, 35-118.
Cumont, F., *Fouilles de Dura-Europos* 1922-1923, 2 Vols. Paris 1926.
Cureton, W., *Spicilegium Syriacum*, London 1855.
Cureton, W., *Ancient Syriac Documents relative to the earliest Establishment of Christianity in Edessa and the neighbouring Countries*, London 1864, reprint Amsterdam 1967.
Daux, G., Aigeai, site des tombes royales de la Macédoine antique, *CRAI* 1977, 620ff.
Debevoise, N. C., *A political History of Parthia*, Chicago 1938.
Degen, R., Altaramäische Grammatik, *AKM* 38, 1969.
Degen, R., Die aramäischen Inschriften aus Taimā' und Umgebung, *Neue Ephemeris f. Sem. Epigraphik* 2, 1974, 79-97.
Degen, R., Zur syrischen Inschriften von Birecik, *Neue Ephemeris f. Sem. Epigraphik* 2, 1974, 105-109.
Delcor, M., Une inscription funéraire araméenne trouvée à Daskyleion en Turquie, *Le Muséon* 80, 1967, 301-314.
Dentzer, J.-M., l'Iconographie iranienne du souverain couché et le motif du banquet, *AAAS* 21, 1971, 39-50.
Dhorme, E., *Les religions de Babylonie et d'Assyrie*, Paris 1945.
Dillemann, L., *Haute Mésopotamie orientale et pays adjacents*, Contribution à la géographie historique de la région du Vᵉ s. avant l'ère chrétienne au VIᵉ s. de cette ère, Paris 1962.
Dölger, F., *IXTHUS, Das Fischsymbol in Frühchristlicher Zeit*, Bd. I, Rom 1910.
Dohrn, T., *Die Tyche von Antiochia*, Berlin 1960.
Domaszewski, A. von, *Aufsätze zur römischen Heeresgeschichte*, repr. Darmstadt 1972.
Domaszewski, A. von, *Die Religion des römischen Heeres*, Trier 1895.
Downey, G., *A History of Antioch in Syria*, Princeton 1961.
Downey, S., A Preliminary Corpus of the Standards of Hatra, *Sumer* 26, 1970, 195-225.
Downey, S., *The Stone and Plaster Sculpture. Excavations at Dura-Europos*, *Monumenta Archaeologica* 5, Los Angeles 1977.
Drijvers, H. J. W., art. Bardesanes, TRE, (in print).
Drijvers, H. J. W., *Bardaiṣan of Edessa. Studia Semitica Neerlandica* VI, Assen 1966.
Drijvers, H. J. W., Bardaiṣan of Edessa and the Hermetica. The Aramaic Philosopher and the Philosophy of his Time. *Jaarbericht Ex Oriente Lux* 21, 1969-70, 190-210.
Drijvers, H. J. W., Bardaiṣan von Edessa als Repräsentant des syrischen Synkretismus in 2. Jahrhundert n. Chr., *Synkretismus in Syrisch-persischen Kulturgebiet*, ed. A. Dietrich, *AAWG.PH*, 96, 1975, 119ff.

Drijvers, H. J. W., *The Book of the Laws of Countries*, Dialogue on Fate of Bardaiṣan of Edessa, Assen 1965.

Drijvers, H. J. W., The Cult of Azizos and Monimos at Edessa, *Ex Orbe Religionum*, Festschrift G. Widengren, Vol. I, Leiden 1972, 355-371.

Drijvers, H. J. W., Edessa und das jüdische Christentum, *VigChr* 24, 1970, 4-33.

Drijvers, H. J. W., Die Götter Edessas, *Studien zur Religion und Kultur Klein-Asiens*, Festschrift F. K. Dörner, Leiden 1978, I, 264-283.

Drijvers, H. J. W., Hatra, Palmyra und Edessa. Die Städte der syrisch-mesopotamischen Wüste in politischer, kulturgeschichtlicher und religionsgeschichtlicher Beleuchtung, *ANRW* II, 8, Berlin-New York 1977, 799-906.

Drijvers, H. J. W., Das Heiligtum der arabischen Göttin Allat in westlichen Stadtteil von Palmyra, *Antike Welt* 7, 1976, 28-38.

Drijvers, H. J. W., Une main votive en bronze trouvée à Palmyre, dédiée à Ba'alshamên, *Semitica* 27, 1977, 105-116.

Drijvers, H. J. W., Mani und Bardaisan. Ein Beitrag zur Vorgeschichte des Manichäismus. *Mélanges H. Ch. Puech*, Paris 1974, 459-469.

Drijvers, H. J. W., De matre inter leones sedente. Iconography and Character of the Arab goddess Allât, *Hommages à M. J. Vermaseren*, Vol. I, *EPRO* 68, Leiden 1978, 331-351.

Drijvers, H. J. W., Mithra at Hatra? Some remarks on the Problem of the Irano-Mesopotamian Syncretism, *Acta Iranica, Textes et Mémoires* Vol. IV, *Etudes Mithraiques*, Leiden-Téhéran-Liège 1978, 151-186.

Drijvers, H. J. W., A New Sanctuary at Palmyre, *Archaeology* 31, 1978, fasc. 3, 6of.

Drijvers, H. J. W., *Old Syriac (Edessean) Inscriptions*, Leiden 1972.

Drijvers, H. J. W., Rechtgläubigkeit und Ketzerei in ältesten syrischen Christentum, *Symposium Syriacum* 1972, *OrChrA* 197, Roma 1974, 291-310.

Drijvers, H. J. W., *The Religion of Palmyra*, Iconography of Religions XV 15, Leiden 1976.

Drijvers, H. J. W., Some New Syriac Inscriptions and Archaeological Finds from Edessa and Sumatar Harabesi, *BSOAS* 36, 1973, 1-14.

Drijvers, H. J. W., Spätantike Parallelen zur altchristlichen Heiligenverehrung unter besonderer Berücksichtigung des syrischen Stylitenkultes, *Aspekte frühchristlicher Heiligenverehrung*, Oikonomia 6, Erlangen 1977.

Drijvers, H. J. W., Theory Formation in Science of Religion and the Study of the History of Religions, in: Th. P. van Baaren - H. J. W. Drijvers, *Religion, Culture and Methodology*, Religion and Reason 8, The Hague-Paris 1973, 57ff.

Dunand, F. - et al., *Mystères et syncrétismes*, Paris 1975.

Dunand, F. - P. Lévèque, *Les syncrétismes dans les religions de l'antiquité*, *EPRO* 46, Leiden 1975.

Dunand, M., *Le Musée de Soueida*, Paris 1934.

Dunand, M., Nouvelles inscriptions, *RB* 1932, 399-416.

Dunant, C., Nouvelle inscription caravanière de Palmyre, *MH* 13, 1956, 216-223.

Dunant, C., Le sanctuaire de Baalshamin à Palmyre III, Les Inscriptions, Rome 1971.

Dupont-Sommer, A., "Bêl et Nabû, Šamaš et Nergal" sur un ostracon araméen inédit d'Eléphantine, *RHR* 128, 1944, 28-39.

Dupont-Sommer, A., Le Psaume 50 et son origine essénienne, *Semitica* 14, 1964, 25-62.

Dupont-Sommer, A., David et Orphée, *Institut de France* 1964, no. 20.

Dupont-Sommer, A. - L. Robert, *La déesse de Hiérapolis Castabala* (Cilicie), Paris 1964.

Dussaud, R., *Les Arabes en Syrie avant l'Islam*, Paris 1907.

Dussaud, R., Melqart, *Syria* 25, 1946-48, 205-230.

Dussaud, R., Notes de mythologie syrienne 2, Azizos et Monimos parèdres du dieu solaire, *RevArch* 1903, I, 124ff.

Dussaud, R., Nouveaux textes égyptiens d'exécration contre les peuples syriens, *Syria* 21, 1940, 170-182.

Dussaud, R., *La pénétration des Arabes en Syrie avant l'Islam*, Paris 1955, passim.

Dussaud, R., Peut-on identifier l'Apollon barbu de Hiérapolis de Syrie ? *RHR* 126, 1943, 128-149.

Dussaud, R., Le Temple de Jupiter Damascénien, *Syria* 3, 1922, 219-250.

Dussaud, R., Temple et cultes de la Triade Héliopolitaine à Ba'albeck, *Syria* 23, 1942-43, 33-77.

Dussaud, R., *Topographie historique de la Syrie antique et mediévale*, Paris 1927.

Duval, R., *Histoire politique, religieuse et littéraire d'Edesse jusqu'à la première croisade*, Paris 1892, reprint A'dam 1975.

Ehlers, B., Kann das Thomasevangelium aus Edessa stammen ? Ein Beitrag zur Frühgeschichte des Christentums in Edessa, *NovTest* 12, 1970, 284-317.

Eilers, W., *Sinn und Herkunft der Planetennamen*, SBAW.PPH 1975, 5, München 1976.

Eissfeldt, O., *Tempel und Kulte syrischer Städte in hellenistisch-römischer Zeit*, AO 40, Leipzig 1941.

Excavations (The) at Dura-Europos. Preliminary report 1-9 season, New Haven 1929-1952. Final reports I-VIII, New Haven 1947-1967.

Eynde, C. v. d., (ed.), Commentaire d'Ishodad de Merv sur l'ancien testament, *CSCO* 126, *Script. Syri* 67, Louvain 1950.

Eynde, C. v. d., (ed.), Commentaire d'Ishodad de Merv sur l'ancien testament, *CSCO* 229-230, *Script. Syri* 96-97, Louvain 1962-63.

Fahd, T., *Le panthéon de l'Arabie Centrale à la veille de l'Hégire*, Paris 1968.

Fauth, W., Art. Simia, *PW*, Suppl. XIV, 1974, 679-701.

Festugière, A. J., *Antioche païenne et chrétienne*. Libanius, Chrysostome et les moines de Syrie, Paris 1959.

Février, J. G., *La religion des Palmyréniens*, Paris 1931.

Février, J. G., Un aspect du Dioscurisme chez les anciens Sémites, *JA* 229, 1937, 293-299.

Fiey, J., *Jalons pour une histoire de l'église en Iraq*, CSCO, Subs. 36, Louvain 1970.

Fiey, J., Ma'in, général de Sapor II, confesseur et évêque, *Le Muséon* 84, 1971, 437-452.

Fitz, J., *Les Syriens à Intercisa*, Coll. *Latomus* 122, 1972.

Fitzmyer, J. A., *The Aramaic Inscriptions of Sefîre*, Rome 1967.

Fleischer, R., *Artemis von Ephesos und verwandte Kultstatuen aus Anatolien und Syrien*, EPRO 35, Leiden 1973.

Frankfort, H., *Kingship and the Gods*, Chicago 1948.

Frisch, P., *Die Inschriften von Ilion*, Inschriften griechischer Städte aus Kleinasien 3, Bonn 1975.

Frye, R. N. - J. F. Gilliams - H. Ingholt - C. B. Welles, Inscriptions from Dura-Europos, *YCS* 14, 1955, 127-213.

Funk, F. X., (ed.), *Constitutiones apostol.*, Paderborn 1905.

Furlani, G., *Sur le stoïcisme de Bardesane d'Édesse*, Archiv Orientální IX, 1937, 347-352.

Gabriel, F., *l'Antica società beduina*, Roma 1959.

Gadd, C., The Harran inscriptions of Nabonidus, *AnSt* 8, 1958, 35-92.

Gadd, C., *The Stones of Assyria*, London 1936.

Gawlikowski, M., *Recueil d'inscriptions palmyréniennes, provenant de fouilles syriennes et polonaises récentes à Palmyre*, Paris 1974.

Gawlikowski, M., *Monuments funéraires de Palmyre*, Warszawa 1970.

Gawlikowski, M., Nouvelles inscriptions du Camp de Dioclétien, *Syria* 47, 1970, 313-325.

Gawlikowski, M., À propos des reliefs du temple des Gaddê à Doura, *Berytus* 18, 1969, 105-109.

Gawlikowski, M., Le Temple d'Allat à Palmyre, *RA* 1977, 253-274.

Gawlikowski, M., *Le temple palmyrénien*, Warszawa 1973.

Gebhardt, O. von, *Die Akten der edessenischen Bekenner Gurjas, Samonas und Abibos*, TU 37, 2, Leipzig 1911.

Gesche, H., Kaiser Gordian mit dem Pfeil in Edessa, *Jahrb. f. Num.* 19, 1969, 47-77.

Gese, H. - M. Höfner - K. Rudolph, *Die Religionen Altsyriens, Altarabiens und der Mandäer*, Stuttgart 1970.

Ghirshman, R., *Parthes et Sassanides*, Paris 1962.

Gibson, M. D., (ed.), *The Commentaries of Isho'dad of Merv*, Vol. IV, *Horae Sem.* X, Cambridge 1913.

Gilliam, J. G., Jupiter Turmasgades, *Actes du IX Congrès Intern. d'études sur les frontières romaines*, Köln-Wien 1974, 309-314.

Glueck, N., *Deities and Dolphins. The Story of the Nabataeans*, New York 1965

Goldstein, J. A., The Syriac Bill of Sale from Dura-Europos, *JNES* 25, 1966, 1-16.

Goossens, G., *Hiérapolis de Syrie*. Essai de monographie historique, Louvain 1943.

Greenfield, J. C., Standard Literary Aramaic, *Actes du premier congrès Intern. de Linguistique Sémitique, Paris 1964*, The Hague-Paris 1974, 280-289.

Greenfield, J. C., The Dialects of Early Aramaic, *JNES* 37, 1978, 93-99.

Greenfield, J. C., The Marzeah as a social Institution. *Acta Ant. Acad. Scient. Hung. XXII*, 1-4, 1974, 451-455.

Grelot, P., *Documents araméens d'Egypte*, Paris 1972.

Grimal, P., *Dictionnaire de la mythologie grecque et romaine*, Paris 1958.

Guidi, I. - E. W. Brooks - I.-B. Chabot, Chronica Minora I, II, III, *CSCO* 1-6, *Script. Syri* 1-6, Louvain 1903-1907.

Guillaumont, A., Genèse 1, 1-2 selon les commentateurs syriaques, *In Principio*. Interprétations des premiers versets de la Genèse, Paris 1973, 115-132.
Hadley, R. A., Royal Propaganda of Seleucus I and Lysimachus, *JHS* 94, 1974, 50-65.
Hajjar, Y., *La Triade d'Héliopolis-Baalbek*. Son cult et sa diffusion à travers les textes littéraires et les documents iconographiques et épigraphiques, 2 Vols, *EPRO* 59, Leiden 1977.
Hallier, L., *Untersuchungen über die Edessenische Chronik*, *TU* 9, 1, Leipzig 1892.
Hallo, W., On the antiquity of Sumerian litterature, *JAOS* 83, 1963, 167-176.
Halsberghe, G. H., *The Cult of Sol Invictus*, *EPRO* 23, Leiden 1972.
Hanslik, R., Apollo Pythius Azizus und sein Kult, *VigChr* 8, 1954, 176-181.
Harnack, D., Parthische Titel, vornehmlich in den Inschriften aus Hatra. Ein Beitrag zur Kenntnis des parthischen Staates, in: F. Altheim - R. Stiehl, *Geschichte Mittelasiens im Altertum*, Berlin 1970, 492-549.
Harris, J. R., *Boanerges*, Cambridge 1913.
Harris, J. R., *The Cult of the Heavenly Twins*, Cambridge 1906.
Haussig, H. W., (ed.), *Wörterbuch der Mythologie*, Stuttgart 1961.
Heidel, A., *The Babylonian Genesis*, Chicago Ill. 1942.
Hengel, M., *Judentum und Hellenismus*, Tübingen 1969.
Henninger, J., *Über Lebensraum und Lebensformen der Frühsemiten*, Köln-Opladen 1968.
Henninger, J., *Les fêtes de printemps chez les Sémites et la pâque israélite*, Paris 1975.
Henninger, J., Über Sternkunde und Sternkult in Nord- und Zentral Arabien, *ZE* 79, 1954, 82-117.
Henninger, J., Zum Problem der Venussterngottheit bei den Semiten, *Anthropos* 71, 1976, 129-168.
Herrmann, W., Yarik und Nikkal und der Preis der Kutarat-Göttinnen, *BZAW* 106, Berlin 1968.
Hill, G. F., *BMC, Arabia*, London 1922.
Hillers, D. R., "MŠKN'" "temple" in inscriptions from Hatra, *BASOR* 206, 1972, 54-56.
Hjärpe, J., *Analyse critique des traditions arabes sur les Sabéens Ḥarraniens*, Diss. Uppsala 1972.
Hoenn, K., *Artemis*. Gestaltwandel einer Göttin, Zürich 1946.
Hoffmann, G., *Opuscula Nestoriana*, Kiel 1880.
Hoffmann, G., *Auszüge aus syrischen Akten persischer Märtyrer*, *AKM* 73, 1880 (reprint 1966).
Hohl, E., Das Ende Caracallas, *Miscellanea Academica Berolinensia*, Berlin 1950, 276-293.
Hörig, M., *Dea Syria*. Studien zur religiösen Tradition der Fruchtbarkeitsgöttin in Vorderasien, *AOAT* 208, 1979.
Hornbostel, W., *Sarapis*. Studien zur Überlieferungsgeschichte, den Erscheinungsformen und Wandlungen der Gestalt eines Gottes, *EPRO* 32, 1973.
Hrozny, B., *Inscriptions cunéiformes de Kultépé* I, Prague 1952.

Ingholt, H., Inscriptions and Sculptures from Palmyra I, *Berytus* 3, 1936, 83-127.

Ingholt, H., *Parthian Sculptures from Hatra*, Orient and Hellas in Art and Religion, *Mémoirs of the Conn. Acad. of Art and Sciences* 12, New Haven 1954.

Jamme, A., Safaitic Vogué 402, *JNES* 31, 1972, 16-21.

Jansma, T., Project d'édition du "Ketâbâ derêš melle" de Joḥannân Bar Penkayê, *l'Orient Syrien* 7, 1963, 87-106.

Jensen, P., Nik(k)al in Harran, *ZA* 11, 1896, 293ff.

Jones, A. H. M., *The cities of the Eastern Roman Provinces*, 2e ed., Oxford 1971.

Jones, L. W., The Cult of Dacia, *UCPCP* 9, 8, 1929, 285ff.

Kádár, Z., *Die Kleinasiatisch-syrischen Kulte zur Römerzeit in Ungarn*, *EPRO* 2, Leiden 1972.

Kaegi, W., The fifth-century Twilight of Byzantine Paganism, *Classica et Mediaevalia* 27, 1966, 243-275.

Kammerer, A., *Petra et la Nabatène*, Paris 1929.

Kaufmann, S. A., *The Akkadian Influences on Aramaic*, *Assyriological Studies* 19, Chicago 1974.

Kirsten, E., Edessa, *RAC* IV, 1959, 552-597.

Klugkist, A. C., Pagane Bräuche in den Homilien des Isaak von Antiocheia gegen die Wahrsager, *OrChrA* 197, Roma 1974, 353-364.

Klijn, A. F. J., *Edessa, de stad van de Apostel Thomas*, Baarn 1962.

Kraeling, C. H., *Gerasa*. City of the Decapolis, New Haven 1938.

Krencker, D. - W. Zschietschmann, *Römische Tempel in Syrien*, Berlin-Leipzig, 1938.

Krzuzanowski, A., Trésor de monnaies palmyréniennes trouvé à Alexandrie, *Actes du 8ème Congrès int. de Num. New York-Washington 1973*, Paris-Bâle 1976, 327-332.

Lacroix, L., Copies de Statues sur les monnaies de Séleucides, *BCH* 73, 1949, 158-175.

Lacroix, L., *Les réproductions de statues sur les monnaies grecques*. La Statuaire archaïque et classique, *Bibl. de Liège*, facs. 116, Liège 1949.

Lagarde, P. de, *Gesammelte Abhandlungen*, Leipzig 1866.

Lambert, W. G., Nabonidus in Arabia, in: *Proceedings of the fifth Seminar for Arabian Studies held at the Oriental Institute, Oxford, 22nd and 23rd Sept. 1971*, London 1972, 53-65.

Lambert, W. G., A Catalogue of Texts and Authors, *JCS* 16, 1962, 59-77.

Lammens, H., Le culte des bétyles et les processions religieuses chez les Arabes préislamites, *l'Arabie Occidentale avant l'Hégire*, Beyrouth 1928, 100-179.

Lamy, Th., *Sancti Ephraemi Syri Hymni et Sermones II, IV*, Mechliniae 1886, 1902.

Landersdorfer, P. S., Die Götterliste des mar Jacob von Sarug in seiner Homilie über der Fall der Götzenbilder. Ein religionsgeschichtliches Dokument aus der Zeit des untergehenden Heidentums, *Programm des Kgl. Gymnasium im Benediktiner Kloster Ettal für das Schuljahr 1913/14*, München 1914.

Langdon, S., (bearb.), *Die Neubabylonische Königsinschriften*, Vorderasiatische Bibliothek IV, Leipzig 1912.

Laroche, E., Koubaba, déesse anatolienne, et le problème des origines de Cybèle, *Elements orientaux dans la religion grecque ancienne, Colloque de Strasbourg 1958*, Paris 1960, 113-128.

Leipolt, J., Frühes Christentum im Orient, *HdO* 8, 2, Leiden 1961, 3-42.

Lenzen, H. J., Ausgrabungen in Hatra, *AA* 70, 1955, 334-375.

Leroy, J., Mosaiques funéraires d'Edesse, *Syria* 34, 1957, 306-342.

Leroy, J., Nouvelles découverts archéologiques relatives à Edesse, *Syria* 38, 1961, 159-169.

Levi della Vida, G., "El" Padrone della terra, *RSO* 21, 1945-46, 247-248.

Levy, I., Cultes et rites syriens dans le Talmud, *REJ* 42, 1901, 186ff.

Levy, J., Naḥ et Rušpan, *Mélanges R. Dussaud* I, Paris 1939, 273-275.

Lewy, H. - J. Lewy, The God Nusku, *OrNS* 17, 1948, 146-159.

Lewy, H., *Chaldaean Oracles and Theurgy*. Mysticism, Magic and Platonism in the Later Roman Empire, Le Caire 1956.

Lewy, J., The late Assyro-Babylonian cult of the moon and its culmination at the time of Nabonidus, *HUCA* 19, 1945-46, 405-491.

Lidzbarski, M., *Ephemeris für semitische Epigraphik* I, Giessen 1902.

Lipiński, E., *Studies in Aramaic Inscriptions and Onomastics*, Leuven 1975.

Littmann, E. - D. Meredith, Nabataean Inscriptions from Egypt, *BSOAS* 16, 1954, 211-246.

Littmann, E., *Syria*, Division IV, Section B, *Syriac Inscriptions*, inscr. 16B and 65, Leyden 1934.

McCown, C. C., The Goddesses of Gerasa, *AASOR* 13, 1931-32, 129-166.

McDowell, R. H., *Stamped and inscribed objects from Seleucia on the Tigris*, Ann Arbor 1935.

Magie, D., *Roman Rule in Asia Minor*, 2 Vols, Princeton 1950.

Magne, J., Seigneur de l'univers ou David-Orphée, *Revue de Qumran* 34, 1977, 189-196.

Marcadé, J., *Au Musée de Délos*. Étude sur la sculpture hellénistique en ronde bosse découverte dans l'île, Paris 1969.

Maricq, A., BDR D NḤY: dans l'inscription de Serrin, Classica et Orientalia, Extrait de *Syria* 1955-1962, Paris 1965, 141-144.

Maricq, A., La Chronologie des dernières années de Caracalla, *Syria* 34, 1957, 297-302.

Martin, P., Discours de Jacques de Saroug sur la chute des idoles, *ZDMG* 29, 1875, 107-147.

Mellinghoff, F., Ein Relief aus Palmyra. Untersuchungen zu seiner geschichtlichen Einordnung und Deutung in: Altheim-Stiehl, *AAW* V 2, Berlin 1969, 58-164.

Menasce, P. de, Autour d'un texte syriaque inédit sur la religion des Mages, *BSOS* 9, 1937-39, 587-601.

Merlat, P., Observations sur les castores Dolichéniens, *Syria* 28, 1951, 229-249.

Merlat, P., *Orient, Grèce, Rome*, un exemple de syncretism? Les "castores" dolichéniens, *Éléments orientaux dans la religion grecque ancienne*, Paris 1966, 77-94.

Merlat, P., *Répertoire des inscriptions et monuments figurés du culte de Jupiter Dolichenus*, Paris 1951.

Mesnil du Buisson, R. du, De Shadrafa, Dieu de Palmyre, à Baꜥal-shamîn, dieu de Hatra, aux IIe et IIIe siècle après J.-C., *MUSJ* 38, 1962, 143-160.

Mesnil du Buisson, R. du, Le bas-relief du combat de Bêl contre Tiamat dans le temple de Bêl à Palmyre, *AAAS* 26, 1976, 83-111.

Mesnil du Buisson, R. du, Un bilingue araméen-grec de l'époque Parthe à Doura-Europos, *Syria* 19, 1938, 147-152.

Mesnil du Buisson, R. du, *Inventaire des inscriptions palmyréniennes de Doura-Europos*, Paris 1939.

Mesnil du Buisson, R. du, *Les tessères et les monnaies de Palmyre*, Paris 1962.

Michalowski, K., *Palmyre. Fouilles polonaises I-V*, Warszawa 1960-1966.

Milik, J. T., *Dédicaces faites par les dieux* (Palmyre, Hatra, Tyr) et des thiases sémitiques à l'époque romain, Bibl. archéol. et hist. 92, Paris 1972.

Milik, J. T., Les papyrus araméens d'Hermoupolis et les cultes syro-phéniciens en Égypte perse, *Biblica* 48, 1967, 546-621.

Millar, F., The Background to the maccabean Revolution: Reflections on Martin Hengel's "Judaism and Hellenism", *JJS* 29, 1978, 1-21.

Millar, F., Paul of Samosata, Zenobia and Aurelian: the church, local culture and political allegiance in third-century Syria, *JRS* 61, 1971, 1-17.

Mitchell, C. W., *S. Ephraim's Prose Refutations of Mani, Marcion, and Bardaisan*, 2 Vols, London 1912-1921.

Monneret de Villard, U., *Le Leggende orientali sui magi Evangelici*, Roma 1952.

Monnot, G., Sabéens et idolâtres selon 'Abd al-Jabbar, *MIDEO* 12, 1974, 13-48.

Mørkholm, O., *Antiochus IV of Syria, Classica et Mediaevalia*, Diss. VIII, Køpenhavn 1966.

Mouterde, R., Cultes antiques de la Coelésyrie et de l'Hermon, *MUSJ* 36, 1959, 53-84.

Mouterde, R., Dea Syria en Syrie, *MUSJ* 25, 1942-43, 137-142.

Mouterde, R., La *Statio ad Dianam* du *Portorium* de Syrie près le Golfe d'Aqaba, *CRAI* 1954, 482-487.

Mundle, I., Dea Caelestis in der Religionspolitik des Septimius Severus und der Julia Domna, *Historia* 10, 1961, 228-237.

Murray, Ch., The Christian Orpheus, *CAr* 26, 1977, 19-27.

Murray, R., *Symbols of Church and Kingdom*. A Study in Early Syriac Tradition, Cambridge 1975.

Naster, P., Les monnaies d'Edesse rélèvent-elles un dieu 'Elul?, *Revue belge de numismatique* 114, 1968, 5-13.

Naveh, J., Remarks on Two East Aramaic Inscriptions, *BASOR* 216, 1974, 9-11.

Neusner, J., *A History of the Jews in Babylonia* I. The Parthian Period, Leiden 1965.

Newell, E. T., *The coinage of the Western Seleucid Mints from Seleucus I to Antiochus III*, NS 4, New York 1941.

Newell, E. T., *Coinage of the Eastern Seleucid Mints*, New York 1940.

Newell, E. T., Late Seleucid Mints in Ake-Ptolemais and Damascus, *NNM* 84, 1939.

Nilsson, M. P., *Geschichte der griechischen Religion* I, II. München 1950-1955.

Nock, A. D., Sarcophagi and Symbolism, *AJA* 50, 1946, 140-170 = *Essays on Religion and the Ancient World* II, Cambridge, Mass. 1972, 606-641.

Noiville, J., Le culte de l'étoile du matin chez les Arabes pré-islamitiques, *Hespéris* 8, 1928, 363-384.

Nyberg, H. S., Questions de cosmogonie et de cosmologie Mazdéennes, *JA* 214, 1929, 193-310.

Oden, R. A., *Studies in Lucian's De Syria Dea, Harvard Semitic Monographs* 15, 1977.

Oppenheim, A. L., *Ancient Mesopotamia*, Chicago, 1964.

Ortiz de Urbina, I., *Patrologia Syriaca*, Roma 1965.

Parke, H. W. - P. E. W. Warnell, *The Delphic Oracle*, Oxford 1956.

Parrot, A., *Malédictions et violations de Tombes*, Paris 1939.

Paulovics, St., *Laureae aquincenses*, Budapest 1944.

Pearson, B. A., *Religionssyncretism in Antiquity*, essays in conversation with G. Widengren, Missoula 1975.

Perdrizet, P., A Propos d'Atargatis 1. Le sein d'Atargatis, *Syria* 12, 1931, 267-273.

Perkins, A., *The Art of Dura-Europos*, Oxford 1973.

Peters, T. E., The Nabateans in the Hawran, *JAOS* 97, 1977, 263-277.

Peterson, E., Die geheimen Praktiken eines syrischen Bischofs, *Frühkirche, Judentum und Gnosis*, Freiburg 1959, 333-345.

Phillips, G., *The Doctrine of Addai, the Apostle*, London 1876.

Philonenko, M., David-Orphée sur une mosaique de Gaza, *RHPR* 1967, 355-357.

Picard, Ch., Sur l'Orphée de la fontaine monumentale de Byblos, *Misc. Jerphanion* I, Roma 1947.

Picard, Ch., Une Atargatis méconnue à Leptis Magna, *RA*, Sér. 6, Tome 37, 1951, 231-233.

Picard, Ch., Sur l'Atargatis-Derkétô des Thermes d'Aphrodisias en Carie, *Hommages J. Bidez et F. Cumont, Collection Latomus* II, 257-264.

Picard, Ch., Les castores "conservatores" assesseurs du Jupiter Dolichenus, *RHR* 109, 1934, 73-82.

Pigulevskaja, N., *Les villes de l'état iranien aux époques parthe et sassanide*, Paris-La Haye 1963.

Pirenne, J., Aux origines de la graphie syriaque, *Syria* 40, 1963, 101-137.

Pirenne, J., La religion de Hiérapolis de Syrie au début de notre ère à la lumière des documents récemment exhumés à Hatra, *Sacra Pagina* I, Leuven 1959, 288-299.

Places, E. des, *Oracles chaldaïques*, Paris 1971.

Pognon, H., *Inscriptions mandaites des coupes de Khouabir*, Paris 1899.

Pognon, H., *Inscriptions sémitiques de la Syrie, de la Mésopotamie et de la région de Mossoul*, Paris 1907.

Poidebard, A., *La trace de Rome dans le désert de Syrie*, Paris 1934.

Pomponio, F., *Nabû*. Il culto e la figura di un dio del Pantheon babilonese ed Assiro, *Stud. Sem.* 51, Roma 1978.

Ponsich, M., Une mosaique d'Orphée, *Bulletin d'Archéologie Marocaine* 6, 1966, 479-481.

Porada, E., Syrian seal impressions on tablets dated in the time of Hammurabi and Samsa-Iluna, *JNES* 16, 1957, 192-203.

Porten, B., *Jews of Elephantine and Arameans of Syene*. Aramaic texts with transl., Jerusalem 1974.

Porten, B., *Archives from Elephantine*. The life of an ancient Jewish Military Colony, Berkeley-Los Angeles 1968.

Prentice, W. K., *Syria: Greek and Latin Inscriptions, Northern Syria*, Leiden 1907.

Quasten, J., *Patrology I-III*, Utrecht 1950-1963.

Quispel, G., *Makarius, das Thomasevangelium und das Lied von der Perle*, Leiden 1967.

Rahmani, I. E., *Studia Syriaca IV*, documenta de antiquis haeresibus, primo edidit etc., In Seminario Scharfensi de monti Libano 1909.

Rahner, H., *Griechische Mythen in Christlicher Deutung*, Zürich 1957.

Rehm, A., *Didyma*, Vol. II, *Die Inschriften*, Berlin 1958.

Reinink, G. J., Die Textüberlieferung der Gannat Bussame, *Le Muséon* 90, 1977, 103-175.

Rengen, W. van, l'Epigraphie grecque et latine de Syrie. Bilan d'un quart de siècle de recherches épigraphiques, *ANRW* II, 8, 1977, 31-53.

Rey-Coquais, J.-P., *Arados et sa pérée aux époque grecque, romaine et byzantine*, *BAH* 97, Paris 1974.

Rey-Coquais, J.-P., Inscriptions grecques d'Apamée, *AAAS* 23, 1973, 39-84.

Ricci, S. de, Bulletin épigraphique de l'Égypte romain, *Archiv f. Papyrusf.* 2, 1903.

Ridder, A. de, Catalogue de la collection de Clerq III, Paris 1904.

Robert, L., *Études anatoliennes*, Paris 1937.

Röllig, W., Erwägungen zu neuen Stelen König Nabonids, *ZA* 56, 1964, 218-260.

Ronzevalle, S., La couronne ("Nemara?") d'Atargatis à Délos, *MUSJ* 22, 1939, 10-121.

Ronzevalle, S., Jupiter Héliopolitain Nova et Vetera, *MUSJ* 21, 1937, 3-181.

Ronzevalle, S., Les monnaies de la dynastie de ʿAbd-Hadad et les cultes de Hiérapolis-Bambycé, *MUSJ* 23, 1940, 3-82.

Rosenfield, J. M., *The Dynastic Arts of the Kushans*, Los Angeles 1967.

Rosenthal, F., *Die aramaistische Forschung*, Leiden 1939.

Ross Taylor, L., *The Divinity of the Roman Emperor*, Middleton, 1931.

Rostovtzeff, I. M., *Caravan Cities*, Oxford 1932; reprint New York 1971.

Rostovtzeff, I. M., The Caravan-Gods of Palmyra, *JRS* 1932, 107-116.

Rostovtzeff, I. M., Le Gad de Doura et Seleucus Nicator, *Mélanges R. Dussaud*, Paris 1939, 281-295.

Rostovtzeff, I. M., Hadad and Atargatis at Palmyra, *AJA* 1933, 58-63.

Rostovtzeff, I. M., Progonoi, *JHS* 55, 1935, 56-66.

Rijckmans, G., *Les religions arabes préislamiques*, 2e ed., Louvain 1951.

Sachau, E., Edessenische Inschriften, *ZDMG* 36, 1882, 142-167.

Safar, F. - M. A. Mustafa, *Hatra. The City of the Sun God*, Baghdad 1974.

Sanders, G. N., Art. Gallos, *RAC* 8.

Sauvegarde des antiquités du lac du Barrage de l'Euphrate, Damascus 1973.

Scher, A., *Theodorus bar Koni Liber Scholiorum* I, II, *CSCO, Script. Syri* 19, 26, Louvain 1910-1912.

Schlumberger, D., Descendants non-méditerranéens de l'art grec, *Syria* 37, 1960, 131-166; 253-318.

Schlumberger, D., *l'Orient hellénisé*, Paris 1970.

Schlumberger, D., *La Palmyrène du Nord-Ouest*, Paris 1951.

Schlumberger, D., Le prétendu dieu Gennéas, *MUSJ* 46, 1970-71, 209-222.

Schnabel, P., *Berossos und die babylonisch-hellenistische Literatur*, Leipzig 1923.

Segal, J. B., *Edessa*. "The Blessed City". Oxford 1970.

Segal, J. B., *Edessa and Harran*. An inaugural Lecture, London 1963.

Segal, J. B., The Jews of North Mesopotamia before the Rise of the Islam, *Sepher Segal*, Jerusalem 1965, 32-63.

Segal, J. B., New mosaics from Edessa, *Archaeology* 12, 1959, 150-157.

Segal, J. B., Pagan Syriac monuments in the Vilayet of Urfa, *Anat. Stud.* 3, 1953, 97-120.

Segal, J. B., The Sabian Mysteries. The Planet Cult of Ancient Harran, in: Bacon, E., (ed.), *Vanished Civilizations*, London 1963, 201-220.

Segal, J. B., Some Syriac Inscriptions of the 2nd-3rd century A.D., *BSOAS* 16, 1954, 13-31.

Seyrig, H., Bas-relief des dieux de Hiérapolis, *Syria* 49, 1972, 104-108.

Seyrig, H., Bêl de Palmyre, *Syria* 48, 1971, 85-114.

Seyrig, H., Cachets d'archives publiques de quelques villes de la Syrie romaine, *MUSJ* 23, 1940, 85-107.

Seyrig, H., Le culte du Soleil en Syrie à l'époque romaine, *Syria* 48, 1971, 337ff.

Seyrig, H., Les dieux armés et les Arabes en Syrie, *Syria* 47, 1970, 77-112.

Seyrig, H., Un ex-voto au dieu Bétyle, *Mémorial Jean de Menasce*, Louvain 1974, 87-90.

Seyrig, H., Le monnayage de Hiérapolis de Syrie à l'époque d'Alexandre, *RNum* VIᵉ Série, 13, 1971, 11-21.

Seyrig, H., Les tessères palmyréniennes et le banquet rituel, *Mémorial Lagrange*, Paris 1940, 51-58.

Seyrig, H. - R. Amy - E. Will, *Le temple de Bêl à Palmyre*, 2 Vols., *BAH* 83 Paris 1975.

Sourdel, D., *Les cultes du Hauran à l'époque romaine*, Paris 1952.

Soyez, B., *Byblos et la fête des Adonies*, EPRO 60, Leiden 1977.

Starcky, J., La civilisation nabatéenne, État des questions, IX Congrès Intern. d'archéologie classique, *AAAS* 21, 1971, 79-86.

Starcky, J., Deux inscriptions palmyréniennes, *MUSJ* 38, 1962, 123-139.

Starcky, J., Edesse et l'Orient chrétien, *Bible et Terre Saint* 119, 1970, 4-7, 24.

Starcky, J., "Genneas" (l'inscription), *Syria* 26, 1949, 248-257.

Starcky, J., Review E. Littmann, Nabataean Inscriptions from Egypt II, *Syria* 32, 1955, 150-157.

Starcky, J., Pétra et la Nabatène, *SDB* VII, Paris 1966, 886-1017.

Starcky, J., Relief dédié au dieu Munʿim, *Semitica* 22, 1972, 57-65.

Starcky, J., Un relief palmyrénien dédié au dieu Ilahay, *Mélanges Biblique A. Robert*, Paris 1957, 370-380.

Starcky, J., Le temple nabatéen de Khirbet Tannur. A propos d'un livre récent, *RB* 75, 1968, 206-235.

Starcky, J., Stèle d'Elahagabal, *MUSJ* 49, 1975-1976, 503-520.

Stark, J. K., *Personal Names in Palmyrene Inscriptions*, Oxford 1971.

Stern, H., Orphée dans l'art paléochrétien, *CAr* 23, 1977, 1-16.

Stern, H., La mosaique d'Orphée de Blanzy-les-Fismes, *Gallia* 13, 1955, 41-77.

Stocks, H., Studien zur Lukians "De Syria Dea", *Berytus* 4, 1937, 1-40.

Strong, H. A. - J. Garstang, *The Syrian Goddess*, London 1913.
Strugnell, J., The Nabataean Goddess al-Kutbâ᾿ and her sanctuaries, *BASOR* 156, 1959, 29-36.
Stucky, R. A., Figures apolliniennes grecques sur des tessères palmyréniennes, *Syria* 48, 1971, 135-141.
Stucky, R. A., Prêtres syriens II, Hiérapolis, *Syria* 53, 1976, 127-140.
Studemund, G., *Anecdota varia graeca musica metrica grammatica*, Berlin 1886.
Syria, Publications of the Princeton University Archaeological Expedition to Syria in 1904-1905 and 1909, IIIA, Leiden 1907-1949.
Tallquist, K., *Akkadische Götterepitheta*, Studia Orientalia 7, Helsingfors 1938.
Tardieu, M., Pour un phénix gnostique, *RHR* 183, 1973, 117-142.
Taylor, G., *The Roman Temples of Libanon*, Beyrouth 1967.
Teixidor, J., Notes Hatréennes, *Syria* 41, 1964, 273-284.
Teixidor, J., *The Pagan God*. Popular Religion in the Greco-Roman Near East, Princeton 1977.
Teixidor, J., Reflexiones sobre el Zoroastro siriaco, *OCP* 28, 1962, 181-185.
Teixidor, J., in: J. T. Milik - J. Teixidor, New Evidence on the North-Arabic Deity Aktab-Kutbâ, *BASOR* 163, 1961, 22-26.
Thureau-Dangin, F., *Rituels accadiens*, Paris 1921.
Timpe, D., Die Bedeutung der Schlacht bei Carrhae, *Museum Helveticum* 19, 1962, 102-129.
Trujillo, I., *The Ugaritic Ritual for a sacrificial meal honoring the good Gods*, Ph. Diss. Johns Hopkins Univ. 1973.
Tscherikower, V., *Die hellenistischen Stadtegründungen von Alexander dem Grossen bis auf die Römerzeit*, Philologus Suppl. 19, Leipzig 1927.
Turcan, R., Cybèle et la déesse syrienne: à propos d'un relief du Musée de Vienne (Isère), *REA* 53, 1961, 45-54.
Turcan, R., *Les religions de l'Asie dans la vallée du Rhône*, EPRO 30, Leiden 1972.
Vandenhoff, B., Die Götterliste des mar Jacob von Sarug in seiner Homilie über der Fall der Gotzenbilder, *OC* 5, 1915, 234-262.
Vattioni, F., Appunti dulle iscrizioni siriache antiche, *Augustinianum* 11, 1971, 433-446.
Vööbus, A., *Syriac and Arabic Documents regarding Legislation relative to Syrian monasticism*, PETSE 11, Stockholm 1960.
Vööbus, A., *A History of Asceticism in the Syrian Orient* I, II, CSCO, Subs. 14, 17, Louvain 1958-1960.
Wagner, J., *Seleukeia am Euphrat/Zeugma*, Beih. z. *TAVO*, Reihe B10, Wiesbaden 1976.
Wagner, J., Vorarbeiten zur Karte "Ostgrenze des römischen Reiches" im Tübinger Atlas des Vorderen Orients, Akten des XI. Intern. Limes-kongresses, 669-703.
Walker, J., The Coins of Hatra, *NumC* 18, 1958, 167-172.
Weissbach, F. H., *Die Keilinschriften der Achämeniden*, Vorderasiatische Bibliothek 47, Leipzig 1911.
Welles, C. B., The Gods of Doura-Europos, *Festschrift F. Altheim* II, Berlin 1969, 50-65.

Welles, C. B., The Population of Roman Dura, *Studies in Roman Economic and Social History of Allan Chester Johnson*, Ed. by P. R. Coleman-Norton, Princeton 1951.

Welles, C. B., *Royal Correspondence in the Hellenistic Period*, New Haven 1934.

Wellhausen, J., *Reste arabischen Heidentums*, 3e ed. Berlin 1961.

Winckworth, C., On Heathen Deities in the Doctrine of Addai, *JThS* 25, 1924, 402-403.

Widengren, G., *Iranisch-semitische Kulturbegegnung in parthischer Zeit*, Köln 1960.

Will, E., Art parthe et art grec, *Études d'archéologie classique* II, Paris 1959, 125-135.

Will, E., Aspects du culte et de la légende de la grande mère dans le monde grec, *Élements orientaux dans la religion grecque ancienne*, Paris 1966, 95-111.

Will, E., Les castores dolichéniens, *MUSJ* 27, 1947-48, 23-36.

Will, E., *Le relief cultuel gréco-romain*. Contribution à l'histoire de l'art de l'empire romain, Paris 1955.

Will, E., Le relief de la tour Kithot et le banquet funèbre à Palmyre, *Syria* 28, 1951, 70-100.

Winnett, F. V. - W. L. Reed, *Ancient Records from North Arabia*, Toronto 1970.

Wiseman, D. J. (ed.), *Peoples of the Old Testament Period*, Oxford 1973.

Wolski, J., Les Parthes et la Syrie, *Acta Iranica* V, 1976, 395-417.

Wright, W., *The Chronicle of Joshua the Stylite*, Cambridge 1882.

Wrzésniowski, A., The figure of Orpheus in Early Christian Iconography, *Archeologia* 21, 1970, 112-123.

Wuthnow, H., *Die semitischen Menschennamen in griechischen Inschriften und Papyri des Vorderen Orients*, Leipzig 1930.

Xella, P., Il mito di Šḥr e Šlm. Saggio sulla mitologia ugaritica, *Studi Semitici* 44, Roma 1973.

Yadin, Y., Symbols of Deities at Zinjirli, Carthage and Hazor, *Essays in Honor of Nelson Glueck. Near Eastern Archaeology in the twentieth Century*, ed. J. A. Sanders, New York 1970, 199-231.

Zaehner, R. C., *Zurvan*. A Zoroastrian Dilemma, Oxford 1955.

INTRODUCTION

The history of Edessa in the field of religion is still virtually unwritten, although much attention has been given to different aspects of this 'blessed city' in Northern Mesopotamia. It is especially known as the first Christian kingdom in the world—if credence is given to the rather legendary story of King Abgar's conversion—and as the cradle of Syriac-speaking Christianity.[1] It is mainly for this reason that historiography has paid close attention to all questions connected with the origins and later developments of Christian belief at Edessa and in most cases silently passed by other forms of religion existing in the first centuries A.D., or mentioned them only as background for the new belief. The first modern history of Edessa, written at the end of the nineteenth century by Rubens Duval, devotes only a few pages to pagan religions and this situation was fundamentally the same in 1959 when E. Kirsten's article, "Edessa", appeared in *RAC*.[2] In a certain sense J. B. Segal's *Edessa 'The Blessed City'*, which appeared in 1970, forms an exception to this practice; Segal, through many years of research at Edessa, made important finds of mosaics and inscriptions, and his book gives new insights at various points. It does not, however, offer a systematic description of pagan cults and beliefs at Edessa compared to other cities in Syria and Mesopotamia.[3] J. Teixidor's *The Pagan God, Popular Religion in the*

---

[1] See W. Bauer, *Rechtgläubigkeit und Ketzerei im ältesten Christentum*, *BHTh* 10, Tübingen 1934, 7ff.; Drijvers, Rechtgläubigkeit und Ketzerei im ältesten syrischen Christentum, *Symposium Syriacum 1972*, Orient. Christ. *Analecta* 197, Roma 1974, 291ff.; Drijvers, Hatra, Palmyra und Edessa, Die Städte der syrisch-mesopotamischen Wüste in politischer, kulturgeschichtlicher und religionsgeschichtlicher Beleuchtung, *ANRW* II, 8, Berlin-New York 1977, 895f.; Eusebius, *H.E.*, I, 13 is the oldest record of Abgar's conversion which is repeated in enlarged form in the *Doctrina Addai*, ed. G. Phillips, London 1876.

[2] R. Duval, Histoire politique, religieuse et littéraire d'Édesse jusqu'à la première croisade, *JA huitième série* 18, 1891, 87-133; 201-278; 381-439; 19, 1892, 5-102; E. Kirsten, Edessa, *RAC* IV, 1959, 562ff.; see R. Duval, *Histoire d'Édesse*, reprint A'dam 1975, 74-80: Le paganisme à Édesse.

[3] J. B. Segal, *Edessa*. 'The Blessed City', Oxford 1970, 43-61.

Greco-Roman Near East (Princeton, 1977) hastily surveys paganism at Edessa, but does not deal extensively with it either.[4] Works by F. C. Burkitt, J. Leipoldt, A. Vööbus, G. Quispel, A. F. J. Klijn, R. Murray, *et al.*, concentrate so exclusively on the origins of Christianity at Edessa and the supposedly special characteristics of Syrian theology, that they are completely silent on pagan religion or make only some general remarks on astrology as the main form of pagan superstition.[5]

If, however, a reliable sketch can be drawn of pagan religion at Edessa and its main structures and characteristics, a solid foundation will have been laid for the study of the most important cultural and social change in the Near East—at least in a major city in that area—in Late Antiquity, i.e., the gradual decline of pagan religion and the rise and victory of Christianity.[6] Both existed side by side for centuries, and both are main components in the dynamic process of religious changes during these centuries. Moreover, a history of pagan religion at Edessa might be an excellent paradigm of religious institutions and practices in a Syrian city in Greco-Roman times which exercised a certain influence on Roman paganism. This 'Syrian religion in the imperial age was a collection of singularly complex beliefs, into which in the course of a very long history there had come a combination of the most diverse elements,' as F. Cumont once characterized it.[7] The same scholar, in Chapter V of his famous book on Oriental religions in Roman paganism—still the starting-point for most work done in this field—[8]

---

[4] J. Teixidor, *The Pagan God*. Popular Religion in the Greco-Roman Near East, Princeton 1977, 146-151: Paganism at Edessa.

[5] F. C. Burkitt, *Urchristentum im Orient*, Tübingen 1907; J. Leipoldt, *Frühes Christentum im Orient*, *HdO* 8, 2, Leiden 1961, 3ff.; A. Vööbus, *A History of Asceticism in the Syrian Orient* I, *CSCO Subs.* 14, Louvain 1958; A. F. J. Klijn, *Edessa, de stad van de apostel Thomas*, Baarn 1962; G. Quispel, *Makarius, das Thomasevangelium und das Lied von der Perle*, Leiden 1967; R. Murray, *Symbols of Church and Kingdom*. A Study in Early Syriac Tradition, Cambridge 1975.

[6] *cf.* P. Brown, *Religion and Society in the Age of Saint Augustine*, London 1972, 9-21; *idem*, *The World of Late Antiquity*. From Marcus Aurelius to Muhammad, London 1971, 49ff.

[7] F. Cumont, *CAH* XI, 643.

[8] F. Cumont, *Les religions orientales dans le paganisme romain*, Paris 1929, 95-124.

gave a brief survey of what he considered to be the diverse
elements of these complex beliefs and the various levels on which
they manifest themselves. Edessa may afford a single case on which
his views can be checked. As is well-known, these are marked out
by a sharp distinction between popular beliefs and practices and
priestly theological reflection culminating in the supreme role of
the sun in religious and philosophical reflections and systems.
Especially this last-named component of Syrian religion would
have exercised a deep influence on Roman religion from the middle
of the third century A.D. on.[9]

The cultural pattern of Edessa had much in common with other
cities in or near the Syrian-Mesopotamian desert. Its history, beginning with its foundation by Seleucus I Nicator in 303/2 B.C. or
even earlier, is best known during Roman times when, especially
in the first two centuries A.D. and the first half of the third century,
Edessa played a certain role in the relations between Romans and
Parthians.[10] In the same period Palmyra became prosperous
through its caravan trade, providing luxury goods to the Roman
West; Hatra, situated near the site of ancient Assur, became a
well-known religious center in the North of the Mesopotamian
desert; and Dura-Europos provides a good example of life and
culture in a military post at the border between the Imperium
Romanum and the state of the Parthians. I. M. Rostovtzeff once
characterized such cities as caravan-cities; although this name does
not precisely characterize the function of all of them, the main
point is that their cultural and social pattern is more or less the
same.[11] The language spoken by the majority of the population is
Aramaic with its different dialects. We may assume, moreover,
that Greek was in use at least among the upper classes of society
and for administrative purposes. The epigraphical evidence confirms this fact: besides inscriptions written in one of the variants

---

[9] F. Cumont, *La théologie solaire du paganisme romain, Mém. prés. par
div. savants à l'Acad. des inscr.* XII, 2, 1913; *cf.* H. Seyrig, Le culte du Soleil
en Syrie à l'époque romaine, *Syria* 48, 1971, 337ff. for a criticism of Cumont's
views.

[10] See Drijvers, *ANRW* II, 8, 869ff.: Edessa und Rom in ihren gegen-
seitigen Beziehungen.

[11] I. M. Rostovtzeff, *Caravan Cities*, Oxford 1932; reprint N.Y. 1971.

of the already long-existing Aramaic cursive script, there occur
bilingual ones—at least at Palmyra—and purely Greek ones. So
Edessa yields a number of ancient Syriac inscriptions besides some
rare Greek ones; Hatra's inscriptions are nearly all Aramaic except
some Latin ones dating from the city's last years when a Roman
garrison defended it against the Sassanides; the bulk of the inscriptions and graffiti from Dura-Europos is Greek, but Palmyrene
and even Hatrene ones occur; at Palmyra most inscriptions are
Aramaic or bilingual, and we find texts resembling in their script
the Syriac inscriptions from the North of Mesopotamia.[12] The best
explanation for this variety in scripts assumes that the common
Aramaic cursive, in use in Syria and Mesopotamia for centuries,
developed into locally different variants when in Roman times the
autochthonous language became more and more used as a written
language. This whole area has in common the language—the spoken
as well as the written one—as one of the main components of its
culture.[13]

The situation in the field of art is fundamentally the same.
Since Rostovtzeff's studies the art of Palmyra like that of Doura-
Europos and Hatra and—we may add—of Edessa is commonly
called Parthian art because of several common features, the most
important of which is that figures are everywhere shown in frontal
view, the so-called frontality. Leaving aside the vigorous discussions on the origin of this special art which in all likelihood has
nothing to do with Parthia and Parthian artistic traditions, it
should be stated that this art only appears in the cities edging the
Syrian-Mesopotamian desert and seems to be restricted to that
area. Its first expressions go back to the beginning of our era;
remains from earlier times, as found, e.g., at Palmyra, represent
Oriental Hellenistic art that developed in Mesopotamia after

---

[12] Drijvers, Une main votive en bronze trouvée à Palmyre, dédiée à
Baʿalshamên, *Semitica* 27, 1977, 106f.

[13] We are still in need of a thorough investigation of the various languages
in the Near East in Roman times, their mutual relations and social implica-
tions; see: F. Millar, Paul of Samosata, Zenobia and Aurelian: The Church,
Local Culture and Political Allegiance in Third-Century Syria, *JRS* 61, 1971,
1-17; *idem, JJS* 29, 1978, 3ff.: Greek and Native Cultures in the Syrian
Region.

Alexander the Great.[14] Besides frontality—and closely related to it—the static and hieratic character of this art should be stressed. It is not dynamic and narrative like Greek art; rather it represents human beings and deities devoid of dramatic tension and without any causal connection. Nearly all sculptures are two-dimensional and are primarily meant to be decorative adjuncts to architecture. Especially in Palmyrene art there are reliefs of gods and goddesses in procession, one beside the next, with no apparent relatedness. This may reflect more a religious atmosphere characterized by a cumulation of divine beings than a tendency towards theological system-building which gives every deity its appropriate place and function in a well-considered conception.[15] This formal resemblance between works of art from Palmyra, Hatra, Edessa and Dura-Europos is substantially paralleled in the field of religion: deities which tradition assigns to the cults practiced at Edessa occur, e.g., at Palmyra, Hatra or Doura-Europos. This affords the opportunity of comparing certain phenomena at Edessa with related conceptions at other places in Syria or Mesopotamia. In a sense writing the history of pagan religion at Edessa is setting up a paradigm of what religion and religious practice may mean in a Syrian city during Greco-Roman times. All these cities had a more or less mixed population according to the proper names which occur: autochthonous Aramaeans mingled with Arab desert dwellers, Macedonians and people with Iranian names, and although the exact proportions between groups may differ in various cities, cultural influences from different origin are to be expected.[16] Syrian religion as a combination of the most diverse elements has some-

---

[14] cf. H. Seyrig, Remarques sur la civilisation de Palmyre, *Syria* 21, 1940, 328-337 = *AS* 3, 115-124; for a discussion of the different theories see Drijvers, *ANRW* II, 8, 86off.; M. A. R. Colledge, *Parthian Art*, Ithaca, N.Y. 1977, 138ff.: 'Parthian' art. See also C. Colpe, Parthische Religion und parthische Kunst, *KAIROS* N.F. 17, 1975, 118-123; S. Downey, *The Stone and Plaster Sculpture. Excavations at Dura-Europos, Monumenta Archaeologica* 5, Los Angeles 1977, 277ff.

[15] cf. Drijvers, *The Religion of Palmyra, Iconography of Religions* XV, 15, Leiden 1976, 9ff.

[16] A case-study is C. B. Welles, The Population of Roman Dura, *Studies in Roman Economic and Social History in Honor of Allan Chester Johnson*, ed. by P. R. Coleman-Norton, Princeton 1951, 251-274.

thing to do with influence of diverse cultures which were amalgamated in the Syrian area.

For the various reasons, briefly sketched before, religion and religious practice in the cities of Syria and Mesopotamia during Greco-Roman times show a common pattern with local variants exactly as in the field of language, art and population. Until now only the religion of Palmyra has been systematically described, and this description will stand in need of correction as long as excavations yield new material relevant to religion.[17] The various cults of Dura-Europos have not been systematically dealt with, but the main lines of its religious history are indicated in an important article by C. Bradford Welles based on all preliminary reports of excavations.[18] Various aspects of religion at Hatra are dealt with in different articles and books, but the state of the excavations at that city and the way its results are published leads us to suppose that it will take a long time before a coherent picture can be drawn of religion at that pre-Muslim Mecca.[19] Other regions in Syria and the religions practiced there have been covered in various books and articles that all afford important comparative information; in this context Hierapolis-Mabbug, and Heliopolis-Baalbek should especially be mentioned.[20] Dealing in this way with all questions connected with religion at Edessa, and giving a description as

---

[17] For the most recent developments see Drijvers, Das Heiligtum der arabischen Göttin Allat im westlichen Stadtteil von Palmyra, *Antike Welt* 7, 1976, 28-38; M. Gawlikowski, Le Temple d'Allat à Palmyre, *RA* 1977, 253-274; Drijvers, A New Sanctuary at Palmyra, *Archaeology* 31, 1978, Fasc. 3, 6of.

[18] C. B. Welles, The Gods of Dura-Europos, *Festschrift F. Altheim* II, Berlin 1969, 50-65.

[19] F. Safar - M. A. Mustafa, *Hatra*. The City of the Sun God, Baghdad 1974 might be considered a preliminary report of all foregoing campaigns; *cf.* Drijvers, *ANRW* II, 8, 828ff.: Hatras Religion als synkretistische Erscheinung; *idem*, Mithra at Hatra? Some remarks on the Problem of the Irano-Mesopotamian Syncretism, *Acta Iranica, Textes et mémoires* IV, *Études mithriaques*, Leiden-Téhéran-Liège 1978, 151-186; B. Aggoula is preparing a history of Hatrene religion.

[20] For Hierapolis see now R. A. Oden, *Studies in Lucian's De Syria Dea*, *Harvard Semitic Monographs* 15, 1977; for Heliopolis Y. Hajjar, *La triade d'Héliopolis-Baalbek*. Son culte et sa diffusion à travers les textes littéraires et les documents iconographiques et épigraphiques. 2 Vols. *EPRO* 59, Leiden 1977.

precise as possible, forms a starting-point for a more systematic treatment of various aspects of pagan religion in Syria and Meso-potamia in Greco-Roman times.[21]

Main topics in this field are the formation of the various panthea and the contribution of different cultures and areas to them; the grouping of deities into dyads and triads and the cult of a young god (dieu-fils); the supposed Iranian influence on Syrian religions which was especially emphasized by F. Cumont; and the contribu-tion of Syrian cults to Roman paganism with the spread of Syrian soldiers, slaves and merchants in the Empire.

According to the statements of several Syriac authors pagan beliefs and practices persisted for many centuries and were still alive even when Christianity won the victory and functioned as a state religion in the Syrian area belonging to the Byzantine Em-pire.[22] Especially during the first centuries A.D. paganism, Judaism and Christianity in all their different forms co-existed side by side at Edessa sharing with each other a common culture and the means that culture provided to express various religious conceptions.[23] It should be pointed out that all different religions and cultural traditions used the same language, i.e., the local Aramaic dialect, called Syriac, which also was used to express philosophical ideas stemming from Hellenistic traditions. One of the oldest products of Syriac literature, Bardaisan's Dialogue de Fato, also called the

---

[21] O. Eissfeldt, *Tempel und Kulte syrischer Städte in hellenistisch-römischer Zeit*, AO 40, Leipzig 1941 is long overdue; J. Teixidor, *The Pagan God. Popular Religion in the Greco-Roman Near East*, Princeton 1977 only deals with certain aspects of pagan religion.

[22] *cf.* P. S. Landersdorfer, Die Götterliste des Mar Jacob von Sarug in seiner Homilie über den Fall der Götzenbilder. Ein religionsgeschichtliches Dokument aus der Zeit des untergehenden Heidentums, *Programm des Kgl. Gymnasiums im Benediktinerkloster Ettal für das Schuljahr 1913/14*, München 1914; B. Vandenhoff, Die Götterliste des Mar Jacob von Sarug in seiner Homilie über den Fall der Götzenbilder, OC 5, 1915, 234-262; A. C. Klugkist, Pagane Bräuche in den Homilien des Isaak von Antiocheia gegen die Wahrsager, *Orient. Chr. Anal.* 197, Roma 1974, 353-369; most of these statements are referred to in Drijvers, Die Götter Edessas, *Studien zur Religion und Kultur Kleinasiens, Festschrift F. K. Dörner*, Leiden 1978, 264-283; and will be published as a corpus in the *Göttinger Orientforschungen*. See for the Byzantine Empire as a whole Walter E. Kaegi, The fifth-century Twilight of Byzantine Paganism, *Classica et Mediaevalia* 27, 1966, 243-275.

[23] See Drijvers, Edessa und das jüdische Christentum, *VigChr.* 24, 1970, 4-33.

Book of the Laws of Countries, deals with philosophical problems, on Fate and Free Will rooted in Stoic tradition.[24] Thus we cannot detect a hellenized upper class using Greek as distinct from the common folk speaking a local dialect.[25] It seems that hellenistic traditions, at least at Edessa and perhaps in other places too, wore a local dress. That may provide an explanation—or at least a partial answer—for the persistence of classical culture in Syria into Muslim times. There was a continuous tradition without sudden changes or ruptures. Pagan cults gradually disappeared from public life in the cities; sometimes temples were destroyed intentionally by public order, or transformed into churches; but still in the fifth century an Edessene bishop showed the temple of Venus (i.e., the Dea Syria) in his city to a nun coming from Gaul to the Near East in search of relics.[26]

This complex situation of the co-existence of different religious traditions sharing a common culture raises the question of mutual dependence and influence already touched upon at the beginning of this chapter. A condition that should be fulfilled in trying to answer this question is a structural description, as precise as possible, of Edessa's pagan cults and beliefs. They are culturally determined expressions of the 'varieties of religious experience.' The study of the developments of and changes in these religious experiences, insofar as historical sources allow us access to knowledge of them, is the main task of the history of religion as a branch of the history of culture.[27] A short survey, therefore, of Edessa's history and cultural characteristics should precede the description and analysis of the sources for the study of its pagan religion, since these sources are not isolated pieces of evidence but components of Edessa's historical legacy.

---

[24] Drijvers, *The Book of the Laws of Countries*. Dialogue on Fate of Bardaiṣan of Edessa, Assen 1965; *idem, Bardaiṣan of Edessa, Studia Semitica Neerlandica* VI, Assen 1966, 76ff.

[25] *cf.* P. Brown, Approaches to the religious Crisis of the third Century A.D., *Religion and Society in the Age of St. Augustine*, London 1972, 85f.

[26] Éthérie, Journal de Voyage (Itinerarium Aetheriae), *SC* 21, 1948, 19.

[27] *cf.* Drijvers, Theory Formation in Science of Religion and the Study of the History of Religions, in: Th. P. van Baaren - H. J. W. Drijvers, *Religion, Culture and Methodology, Religion and Reason* 8, The Hague-Paris 1973, 57ff.; P. Brown, *Religion and Society in the Age of St. Augustine*, 18ff,

CHAPTER ONE

EDESSA'S HISTORY AND CULTURE

Edessa, like many other cities, was founded by Seleucos I Nicator in 303 or 302 B.C. The diadochos garrisoned the already long-existing citadel with Macedonian soldiers and transformed it into a Greek polis.[1] The older settlement does not occur in cuneiform sources, but it doubtless must have existed there considering the convenient situation of Edessa. It is situated 85 kms. east of the Euphrates at a junction of roads which connects it with Nisibis and Singara—more to the east—and leads from there to India and China. This is the ancient silk road, along which the luxury products of the Far East used to be transported to the Roman west.[2] This road passes by Edessa, crosses the Euphrates at Birtha Makedonopolis, and leads to the Seleucid cities in western Syria, among which Antioch was the most important. Another road leads from Edessa northwards to Armenia.[3] A limestone mountain range extends to the north of the city protecting it from that side and providing its abundance of water. The plain of Harran stretches to the southeast of the city and is protected on that side by the citadel. (Pl. I). Most likely Seleucus gave this new city the name of the ancient Macedonian capital because, like Macedonian Edessa,

---

[1] V. Tscherikower, *Die hellenistischen Städtegründungen von Alexander dem Grossen bis auf die Römerzeit*, *Philologus* Suppl. 19, Leipzig 1927, 51-58; 82ff.; A. H. M. Jones, *The Cities of the Eastern Roman Provinces*, 2nd ed. Oxford 1971, 216-222. For Edessa's history see R. Duval, *Histoire politique religieuse et littéraire d'Édesse*; E. Kirsten, Edessa, *RAC* IV, 552-597; J. B. Segal, *Edessa. 'The Blessed City'*, Oxford 1970; Drijvers, *ANRW* II, 8, Berlin 1977, 863-896.

[2] R. Dussaud, *Topographie historique de la Syrie antique et mediévale*, Paris 1927, 449; L. Dillemann, *Haute Mésopotamie orientale et pays adjacents*. Contribution à la géographie historique de la région du Ve s. avant l'ère chrétienne au VIe s. de cette ère, Paris 1962, 147ff., 299; see the maps 148, 178, 190ff.: Les routes et le commerce.

[3] *cf.* Plutarch, *Crassus* XXII, 3; Tacitus, *Annal.* XII, 12-13; cf. Dillemann, *Haute Mésopotamie*, 188f.

a name which is connected with a root meaning 'water,' [4] it, too, had a plentiful water supply. From long in the past Aramaean influence was rather strong in this area and, as at Harran, we may assume an Aramaean substratum in Edessa's culture.[5] Very little is known of Edessa's history in Seleucid times. Antiochus IV Epiphanes had bronze coins struck at Edessa on which the name of the city is called Antiochia Kallirhoe; following his reign it resumed the name Edessa.[6] The autochthonous designation of the pre-Seleucid place was Orhai which survives in modern Urfa.

When, through internal conflicts and Roman intrigues, the Seleucid Empire collapsed, Edessa acquired a certain independence which the Parthians tolerated. A dynasty of Arab stock reigned over the city and the surrounding region from about 132 B.C. on. The second king was called ʿAbdu bar Masʿur, and other real Arab names, like Bakru, Abgar and Maʿnu, are most frequent in the list of kings as handed down in the Syriac chronicle of Dionysios of Tellmahre.[7] The Arab part of Edessa's population must have been considerable; Plinius (N.H. VI, 117) and Tacitus (Ann. XII, 12) mention its inhabitants simply as *Arabes*. In this connection the designation *Arabes* denotes the semi-nomadic population of the Syrian and Mesopotamian desert who made their living from their flocks and from camel-breeding. Often they settled down in the cities and small villages, like nowadays. Thus these Arabs formed

---

[4] cf. Appian, *Syr.* 57; Steph. Byz. *s.v. Edessa*; Eusebius, *Chronicon*, 127, 368f. (ed. Helm); on the exact location of Macedonian Edessa vide G. Daux, Aigeai, site des tombes royales de la Macédoine antique, *CRAI* 1977, 620ff.

[5] cf. J. Lewy, The late Assyro-Babylonian Cult of the Moon and its Culmination at the Time of Nabonidus, *HUCA* 19, 1945-46, 421ff.; in this area Mesopotamian Aramaic originated, cf. S. A. Kaufmann, *The Akkadian Influences on Aramaic, Assyriological Studies* 19, Chicago 1974, 8ff.; J. C. Greenfield, The Dialects of Early Aramaic, *JNES* 37, 1978, 95.

[6] E. Babelon, Numismatique d'Édesse en Mésopotamie, *Mélanges Numismatiques*, 2-ème série, Paris 1893, 211f.; *BMC, Seleucid Kings of Syria*, 41; according to E. T. Newell, *The Coinage of the Western Seleucid Mints*, N.Y. 1941, 53-56 Antiochus I had Bronze coins struck at Edessa during the first Syrian war with Egypt.

[7] cf. A. Baumstark, *Geschichte der syrischen Literatur*, Bonn 1922, 274; see A. R. Bellinger - C. B. Welles, A Third-Century Contract of Sale from Edessa in Osrhoene, *YCS* 5, 1935, 142-154; the Chronology of Edessa; Segal, *Edessa*, 15, n. 3; for some corrections regarding the end of the local dynasty see Drijvers, *ANRW* II, 8, 882f., Anm. 339.

a considerable part of Palmyra's population and, it appears, even the bulk of Hatra's inhabitants.[8]

That Plinius and Tacitus mention the Arabs from Edessa gives indication of Edessa's involvement in Roman politics and of Rome's interference in the affairs of this city and of northern Mesopotamia in general. This area and the highlands of Armenia were, from a military point of view, of extreme importance to Rome in its permanent struggles with the Parthians. Consequently, in the course of these struggles the kings or phylarchs of Edessa tried to maintain a certain independence from both Great Powers of that time, often with success. King Abgar I Piqa, however, was slain by Sextilius, legatus of L. Licinius Lucullus, when, in 69 B.C. Lucullus made war against the Armenian King Tigranes, who got aid from Abgar. Here we get the first indication of relations between Edessa and Armenia which was to last for a long time. Abgar I's successor, Abgar II (68-53), managed during negotiations with Pompeius in 64 B.C. to keep his reign and independence mainly because he helped Afranius, legatus of Pompeius, when he lost his way and suffered from hunger and cold.[9] The same King Abgar II played a part in Crassus' defeat in 53 B.C., although he cannot be blamed for that. The Parthians put an end to his reign in the same year and this may be considered an indication that Abgar virtually was on the side of the Romans. From that time on Parthia's influence at Edessa became stronger. It sometimes was called 'Daughter of the Parthians'; whether, as is often stated, Parthian influence on Edessa's culture can, in fact, be ascertained, remains to be seen.[10] The Parthians dominated Meso-

---

[8] cf. R. Dussaud, *La pénétration des Arabes en Syrie avant l'Islam*, Paris 1955, *passim*; H. Seyrig, Les dieux armés et les Arabes en Syrie, *Syria* 47, 1970, 77-112; the strong Arab influence at Hatra appears from the many Arab proper names and typical Arab cults, cf. Drijvers, Mithra at Hatra?, *Acta Iranica, Textes et mémoires* IV, *Études mithriaques*, 1978, 166ff.

[9] Plutarchus, *Crassus* 21; *Cassius Dio* XXXVII, 5, 5; XL, 20, 1; cf. Duval, *JA* 1891, 129, n. 2; N. Pigulevskaja, *Les villes de l'état iranien aux époques parthe et sassanide*, Paris-La Haye 1963, 57.

[10] W. Cureton, *Ancient Syriac Documents relative to the earliest Establishment of Christianity in Edessa and the neighbouring Countries*, London 1864, 41, 97, 106; B. Ehlers, Kann das Thomasevangelium aus Edessa stammen? Ein Beitrag zur Frühgeschichte des Christentums in Edessa, *NovTest.* 12,

potamia ever since the battle at Harran-Carrhae, but a designation
like 'Daughter of the Parthians' indicates dependence on, as well
as independence of the Parthians; most daughters want to go
their own way! All subsequent events in Edessa's political history
may indeed be adduced as arguments for the fact that maintaining
its independence between Rome and Parthia was the main aim of
Edessa's kings. When in 47-48 A.D. Rome interfered in the conflicts between Gotarzes and Meherdates, the rival candidates for
the Parthian throne, and supported Meherdates' case, Abgar of
Edessa pretended to assist the inexperienced Meherdates, but in
fact, made him lose time in Armenia and afterwards deserted him.
Abgar thus gave the impression to both rivalling parties that he
supported their cases and could maintain a rather independent
position between them.[11] King Abgar VII's (109-116) attitude
towards the Roman Emperor Trajan during his campaign against
the Parthian King Chosroes in 114-116 A.D. is understandable
only if we accept with certainty that Edessa's independence was
Abgar's main aim. Dio Cassius (LXVIII, 18) explicitly states this.
First the Edessene king supported Trajan and received the emperor
as a guest into his city and palace; in the year 116 he took part in
the Parthian revolt against Trajan, when the emperor—for unknown and mysterious reasons—undertook his long march to the
Persian Gulf. The Roman General Lusius Quietus was ordered to
repress the rebellion in Northern Mesopotamia and during this
campaign he took Edessa and destroyed it (*Cassius Dio* LXVIII,
30, 2).[12] After an interregnum of two years, during which time the
Romans directly reigned over the city, Hadrian made the Parthian
Prince Parthamaspates, together with Ialud(r), a descendant of the
local dynasty, kings of Edessa in 118 A.D. The Roman emperor

1970, 294f.; on the relations between Parthia and Syria in general see
J. Wolski, Les Parthes et la Syrie, *Acta Iranica* V, 1976, 395-417; D. Timpe,
Die Bedeutung der Schlacht bei Carrhae, *Museum Helveticum* 19, 1962,
102-129.

[11] Tacitus, *Ann.* XI, 10; XII, 11, 13, 14; N. C. Debevoise, *A Political
History of Parthia*, Chicago 1938, 172f.; Pigulevskaja, *Les villes de l'état
iranien*, 66ff.

[12] *Cassius Dio* LXVIII, 18, 21; see Drijvers, *ANRW* II, 8, 872-875 for a
discussion of all problems connected with Trajan's campaign and its
chronology.

felt obliged to do something for his predecessor's favorite, whom the Parthians did not want as their king after Trajan's death. Hadrian pursued friendly and peaceful relations with all the kings and toparchs of the various Mesopotamian cities; in Spartian's words: "toparchas et reges ad amicitiam invitavit," and "a Meso-potamiis non exegit tributum quod Traianus imposuit.[13] That policy surely was a stimulus for the pro-Roman party at Edessa, but the pro-Parthian party did not lose its influence.

Directly after the accession of Marcus Aurelius and Lucius Verus, the Parthians went out on a campaign against the Romans; they conquered Edessa and put a puppet king Wa'el bar Sharu on the throne, who reigned for two years from 163-165. The Edessene King Ma'nu VIII bar Ma'nu took refuge with the Romans. Only numismatic evidence exists for Wa'el's reign: bronze coins with his bust and name in Syriac script, and on the reverse, the Parthian King Vologoses III. When the Romans took counter-measures, Avidius Cassius reconquered Edessa after the inhabitants had destroyed the Parthian garrison and opened the city gates (Lucian, *Quomodo hist.*, 22; Procopius, *De Bello Persico*, II, 12, 29).[14] Ma'nu's monarchy was restored and from that time on Edessa and surround-ing Osrhoene was a client-state of the Romans as appears from the coins struck at the city.

After Ma'nu's death in 177, his son Abgar VIII the Great suc-ceeded him (177-212). His policy towards the Romans was the same as that followed by his predecessors. The Parthian King Vologoses IV, together with the kings of Hatra, Adiabene and Abgar, supported the case of Gaius Pescennius Niger, one of the candidates for the imperial purple after the reigns of Publius Helvius Pertinax and Marcus Didius Julianus. Niger's strongest opponent was Septimius Severus, who made two campaigns in the Near East to fight his adversaries in the years 195 and 197. During his second campaign

---

[13] Historia Augusta, *Vita Hadriani* 13, 17; 21, 12; cf. Babelon, *Mélanges numismatiques*, 219.

[14] Babelon, *Mélanges numismatiques* 222ff.; Hill, *BMC, Arabia*, xcvff. and 91f.; J. B. Segal, Pagan Syriac Monuments in the Vilayet of Urfa, *Anat. Studies* 3, 1953, 97ff.; P. Naster, Les monnaies d'Édesse révèlent—elles un dieu 'Elul?, *Revue belge de Numismatique* 114, 1968, 5ff.; Debevoise, *History of Parthia*, 246.

Severus created the province of Osrhoene which was administered
by a Roman procurator. Abgar VIII was left with the city of
Edessa and lost the surrounding region. From that time on he
calls himself Lucius Aelius Septimius Abgar or Lucius Aelius
Aurelius Septimius Abgar which is the legend on some of his coins.[15]
During Abgar's reign Edessa's cultural life prospered. The Aramaean
philosopher Bardaisan lived at his court and Bardaisan's work
may be one of the reasons for Edessa being called 'the Athens of
the East.' In what exists of his philosophical and religious treatises
we find an authentic Edessene tradition of classical philosophy and
learning which must have existed long before him and surely continued after Bardaisan's death in 222.[16] Abgar was also famous for
his building activities and the two columns still standing on Edessa's
citadel may date from his time.[17] The story of his conversion to
Christianity, which is deduced from a remark in Bardaisan's
Dialogue de Fato (. . . when king Abgar came to the faith, he ordered
that every man who emasculated himself, i.e., in honour of Tar'ata,
should have his hand chopped off. . . .), combined with the report
in the *Doctrina Addai* on the conversion of a King Abgar should be
considered apocryphal.[18]

King Abgar VIII died in 212 and was succeeded by his son
Abgar IX Severus, who reigned till 213. In that year Caracalla
summoned the Edessene king and his sons to Rome, where they
were murdered; in January of the next year the emperor made
Edessa a Roman colony. In April 217 Caracalla was murdered near
Edessa, just as he had left the city in order to make a visit to the

---

[15] Babelon, *Mélanges numismatiques*, 255; for the province of Osrhoene
see *CIL* XII, 1856 = *Dessau* I, 1353; Drijvers, *ANRW* II, 8, 878.

[16] *cf*. G. Furlani, Sur le stoicisme de Bardésane d'Édesse, *Archiv Orientálni*,
9, 1937, 347-352; Drijvers, Bardaiṣan of Edessa and the Hermetica. The
Aramaic Philosopher and the Philosophy of his Time, *Jaarbericht Ex Oriente
Lux* 21, 1969-70, 190-210; Drijvers, *Bardaiṣan of Edessa*, 60-95; *idem*,
ANRW II, 8, 887; *cf*. D. Amand, *Fatalisme et liberté dans l'antiquité grecque*,
Louvain 1945, 229ff.

[17] Segal, *Edessa*, Pl. 9 and 29a; one of these columns bears a Syriac inscription in honor of Queen Salmath, *cf*. Drijvers, *Old-Syriac (Edessean)
Inscriptions*, Leiden 1972, No. 27 (Pl. IV).

[18] Kirsten, *Edessa*, 570 reaffirms a contrary opinion, int. al. based on
Julius Africanus, who calls Abgar VIII a ἱερὸς ἀνήρ.

famous Moon Temple of Harran (*Cassius Dio*, LXXIX, 5, 4; *Antoninus Caracalla*, VI, 6; cf. *Herod.* IV, 13, 3).[19] It is certain that life at Edessa underwent no substantial changes when the city was transformed into a *colonia Romana*. Our sources, scanty as they may be, do not show a major modification in the cultural pattern. People continued writing their inscriptions, building their tombs and venerating their gods. All mosaics bearing a year in the Syriac inscription, date from the time when Edessa was a colony. Where Syriac remained in use as written language, Roman rule did not touch common life nor the life of the upper class of the society, as the mosaics from the tombs of the well-to-do families demonstrate. It may be noted that Dionysios of Tell-Mahre's Chronicle mentions a king Ma'nu IX, who may have reigned for twenty-six years; of this king we do not possess numismatic evidence, so that, if there had been a King Ma'nu IX at all, he was only nominal king without effective power. Edessa remained a Roman colony and Severus Alexander even changed its name into Colonia Metropolis Edessenorum during his campaign against the Parthians in 231.[20] Relations between this emperor and the Edessenes were close, but after Alexander's death, Edessene soldiers in the Roman army, dissatisfied with his successor, started a rebellion and tried to make their own commander emperor (*Herod.* VI, 7, 8; VII, 1, 9-10). This action of the Osrhoene archers attests to the influence of soldiers from the Syrian area which was especially strong in and after the time of Elagabal and the empresses of Syrian origin.[21]

From the time of the Emperor Gordianus III (238-244) we have numismatic evidence of an Edessene King Abgar; he is also mentioned in the Syriac Chronicle of Michael the Syrian, who quotes

---

[19] cf. Bellinger-Welles, A Third-Century Contract of Sale, 152f.; A. Maricq, La chronologie des dernières années de Caracalla, *Syria* 34, 1957, 297-302 = *idem, Classica et Orientalia*, Paris 1965, 27-32; E. Hohl, Das Ende Caracallas, *Miscellanea Academica Berolinensia*, Berlin 1950, 276-293; Drijvers, *ANRW* II, 8, 878-880.

[20] cf. Babelon, *Mélanges numismatiques*, 274ff.

[21] cf. J. Babelon, *Impératrices syriennes*, Paris 1957, *passim*; I. Mundle, Dea Caelestis in der Religionspolitik des Septimius Severus und der Julia Domna, *Historia* 10, 1961, 228-237, esp. 237.

Jacob of Edessa. This king Abgar X Severus was expelled from his reign in the time of Philippus Arabs in 248, when the Edessenes revolted against Roman rule, and this year marks the factual end of the local Edessene dynasty.[22] As a Roman colony Edessa shared in all turmoils and wars in the eastern part of the Empire, especially from the middle of the third century on. Valerianus was defeated and taken captive near Edessa by Shapur I in 259, and later the Sassanides occupied the city for a short time. Afterwards the Romans recaptured it.[23] In all likelihood the Palmyrenes took the city for a while in the course of Queen Zenobia's campaigns and even earlier in the time of King Odainath.[24] This situation came to an end, however, in 272, when Aurelianus captured Palmyra and put an end to Queen Zenobia's reign.

When Diocletianus reorganized the empire and the army, he divided northern Mesopotamia into two provinces, Osrhoene and Mesopotamia. Edessa functioned as the capital of Osrhoene, but its role in politics ended as the frontier to the east protected the empire for nearly another two-hundred years, and made impossible any independent policy of these small buffer-states between the Roman and Sassanide Empires.[25]

Edessa's very function as a buffer-state, and its geographical situation in northern Mesopotamia, make it an interesting example of what, culturally-speaking, was going on in that area of the Near East. From its foundation as a Seleucid city on the site of an older settlement, till Byzantine times, we must evaluate its manifold

---

[22] H. Gesche, Kaiser Gordian mit dem Pfeil in Edessa, *Jahrb. f. Num.* 19, 1969, 47-77; cf. Michael Syrus, *Chronique*, ed. J.-B. Chabot, Paris 1899, Vol. I, 120 (transl.); Vol. IV, 77-78 (Syriac text); *cf.* X. Loriot, *ANRW* II, 2, 768f., n. 822 and 823 and Drijvers, *ANRW* II, 8, 882f. and n. 339.

[23] *Zonaras* XII, 23; cf. D. Magie, *Roman Rule in Asia Minor*, 2 Vols. Princeton 1950, 707f.; A. Alföldi, *Studien zur Geschichte der Weltkrise des 3. Jahrhunderts nach Christus*, Darmstadt 1967, 148ff.; 210ff.; cf. Drijvers, *ANRW* II, 8, 884, n. 341.

[24] cf. *FHG* IV, 187, Fr. 11: *Exc. De Leg, Gent. ad Rom.* p. 25; *H. A. Vita Gallieni* 12, 1; *Zosimus* I, 39; Segal, *Edessa* 110; Drijvers, *ANRW* II, 8, 884, n. 342.

[25] A. Poidebard, *La trace de Rome dans le désert de Syrie*, Paris 1934, 129-152; Dillemann, *Haute Mésopotamie*, 105ff.; cf. J. Wagner, Vorarbeiten zur Karte 'Ostgrenze des römischen Reiches' im Tübinger Atlas des Vorderen Orients, *Akten des XI. Internationalen Limeskongresses*, 669-703.

influences and traditions. The main components are: an Aramaic substratum composed of an autochthonous culture, religion and language—as can be expected in northern Mesopotamia; Hellenistic traditions of religion, administration and learning brought in by the Seleucids; strong Arab influence from the population of the desert which partly settled at Edessa; and some Parthian-Iranian influence which made itself felt all around and in the Syrian desert. It mainly can be detected, e.g., in habits of dressing and costume, and in the use of Parthian loan-words in the Syriac language.[26] Culture, however, is not a kind of chemical process during which different components are mingled or synthesized, or which, in the course of scientific research can be undone. Culture always functions as an organic unity, and if we speak of components of culture we mean that the various aspects of a given culture are apt to be interpreted in the context of different cultures; in other words, people coming from the Greek-speaking cities in the West, or from another city in Syria or Mesopotamia, or from the Syrian desert living under the tent, could recognize life and religion at Edessa as something familiar to them: Edessene culture was poly-interpretable.[27] Being poly-interpretable it could be approached from different sides, from various cultural backgrounds, without losing its basic identity. What is usually called syncretism as a cultural entity is not a mingling of different elements into a strange cocktail, but simply this poly-interpretable character of a syncretistic culture which still functions as a unity. The word assimilation would, in fact, be a better designation for the cultural process usually phrased as syncretism.[28] A culture assimilates other elements to its own

[26] G. Widengren, *Iranisch-semitische Kulturbegegnung in parthischer Zeit*, Köln 1960, 25ff.; F. Altheim - R. Stiehl, *AAW* I, 1964, 623-638; D. Harnack, Parthische Titel, vornehmlich in den Inschriften aus Hatra. Ein Beitrag zur Kenntnis des parthischen Staates, in: F. Altheim - R. Stiehl, *Geschichte Mittelasiens im Altertum*, Berlin 1970, 492-549; (cf. the critical remarks by R. Schmitt, *WZKM* 67, 1975, 85ff.); H. Seyrig, Armes et costumes iraniens de Palmyre, *Syria* 18, 1937, 4-31.

[27] cf. Drijvers, Edessa und das jüdische Christentum, *VigChr.* 24, 1970, 4-33; *idem*, Bardaiṣan von Edessa als Repräsentant des syrischen Synkretismus im 2. Jahrhundert n. Chr., *Synkretismus im syrisch-persischen Kulturgebiet*, ed. by A. Dietrich, *AAWG.PH*, 96, 1975, 119ff.

[28] cf. in general F. Dunand et al., *Mystères et syncrétismes*, Paris 1975: F. Dunand - P. Lévèque, *Les syncrétismes dans les religions de l'Antiquité*,

tradition and pattern, but does not mingle or mix everything together. Religious traditions which tend to be very traditional and
do not easily change are especially appropriate for demonstrating
this assimilation process.

Edessa's history, closely related to its geographical situation in
northern Mesopotamia, where it was open to various influences,
makes 'The Blessed City' an excellent example of this cultural
assimilation, especially in the field of religion. In its study, the
existing sources will show this more in detail.

EPRO 46, Leiden 1975; Birger A. Pearson, *Religious Syncretism in Antiquity*.
Essays in Conversation with Geo Widengren, Scholars Press, Missoula 1975.

CHAPTER TWO

THE SOURCES FOR THE STUDY
OF EDESSA'S RELIGION

Modern Edessa is a crowded town in a remote province of Turkey. Its name Urfa echoes original Urhai, as the city is called in Syriac sources.[1] As is often the case with cities that have continuously been occupied till modern times, the remains from ancient times have for the greater part disappeared, and archaeological research on what remains of the past cannot be done because of modern buildings and houses constructed at the antique site. Edessa's citadel is virtually the only spot where excavations can be performed, but this task is still waiting. Therefore all archaeological finds in and around Urfa are due to pure luck and accident. It may be assumed that, especially during the past hundred years, much that had been preserved from antiquity—purposely or unintentionally—has been destroyed by the inhabitants. The nineteenth-century German orientalist, E. Sachau, complained even then that the local population used to destroy the Syriac inscriptions in the ancient tombs and elsewhere, and since his time the number of inhabitants has substantially increased so that the ancient cave-tombs of Edessa's cemeteries have been changed into the slums of modern Urfa.[2] For this reason archaeological and epigraphical material connected with Edessa's pagan religion is, in fact, very limited.

In addition to archaeological remains and epigraphical evidence our sources consist of coins struck at Edessa which sometimes bear

---

[1] The etymology of Urhai is unknown, *cf.* Segal, *Edessa*, p. 2; Drijvers, *ANRW*, II, 8, 866; Urhai occurs in almost all Syriac sources dealing with Edessa's history; Edessa occurs only in Ephrem Syrus and in the Acts of Sharbel, ed. W. Cureton, *Ancient Syriac Documents relative to the earliest Establishment of Christianity in Edessa*, reprint Amsterdam 1967, 41; *cf.* Duval, *Histoire d'Édesse*, 21ff.

[2] *cf.* E. Sachau, Edessenische Inschriften, *ZDMG* 36, 1882, 143; Drijvers, Some New Syriac Inscriptions and Archaeological Finds from Edessa and Sumatar Harabesi, *BSOAS* 36, 1973, 2f.

representations from the field of religious iconography, and of information recorded by Syriac Christian authors which deal with pagan practice. Each of these four categories poses its own specific problems, which should now be dealt with.

Inscriptions

Due to fieldwork done by E. Sachau, H. Pognon, F. Cumont, J. B. Segal, et. al., seventy Old-Syriac inscriptions are now known.[3] Sixty-eight were published together in a small *corpus* in 1972; one was published in 1973 and another belongs to an unpublished stele in the museum of Urfa representing a man in Parthian dress and armed with a long sword.[4] They nearly all come from Urfa or the surrounding area and represent the language and script current in that region during first centuries A.D. The oldest one, a funerary text, is recorded in the tower of the old citadel in Birecik which dates from 6 A.D.;[5] the last dated one is from 277/78 A.D. so that they roughly cover three centuries. For practical and theoretical reasons the term Old-Syriac is used as a designation for the inscriptions from that period and which have several features in common.[6] The language of the inscriptions, as well as the script, stands mid-way between Official Aramaic—the language of the chancelleries of the Achaemenid Empire which functioned as a paradigm for later literary Aramaic—and later Syriac, which is an

---

[3] All publications listed in Drijvers, *Old-Syriac (Edessean) Inscriptions*, ed. with an Introduction, Indices and a Glossary, Leiden 1972; see also F. Vattioni, Appunti sulle iscrizioni siriache antiche, *Augustinianum* 11, 1971, 433-446.

[4] The one published in 1973 dates from A.D. 224 and belongs to a mosaic, see Drijvers, Some New Syriac Inscriptions, 12-14 and Pl. XI-XII (read ʿbdt instead of ḥdt in line 5); the stele will be shortly published by the present author.

[5] Drijvers, *Old-Syriac Inscriptions*, No. 1; *cf.* R. Degen, Zur syrischen Inschrift von Birecik, *Neue Ephemeris für Semitische Epigraphik* 2, 1975, 105-109, who rightly reads dʿwydlt instead of dʿwydnt in line 3.

[6] In fact the only reason for calling these inscriptions Syriac is that they originate in the same area in which Syriac later evolved as an East Aramaic dialect; *cf.* F. Rosenthal, *Die aramaistische Forschung*, Leiden 1939, 195ff.

Drijvers, *Old-Syriac Inscriptions*, XII-XIII; Th. Nöldeke had already enumerated all the linguistic characteristics of these inscriptions in a review of H. Pognon, *Inscriptions sémitiques de la Syrie, de la Mésopotamie et de la région de Mossoul*, Paris 1907, *ZA* 21, 1908, 151-161.

East-Aramaic dialect.[7] Of these seventy inscriptions forty-three
have a funerary character, among which nine belong to mosaics
on the floors of cave-tombs. These funerary texts yield some information about conceptions of life and death, but in most cases
their contribution to our knowledge of Edessa's history consists
only in making known some proper names. Proper names, in fact,
constitute about forty-percent of the total number of different
words occurring in all Old-Syriac inscriptions. Many of these names
also appear in the inscriptions of Palmyra, Hatra, Dura-Europos
and Nabataea, or have parallels in South-Semitic nomenclature.
The proper names, which are mainly theophorous ones, may increase
our knowledge of the religious feeling of the people of Edessa and
of the cults practiced by them, insofar as their theophorous elements
reflect existing beliefs. Often, however, they may be purely traditional, conventional and stereotype, as most of our usual proper
names are. It seems to me doubtful that all parents naming their
new-born son John are aware that they express with this very
name that they begot their son through God's grace. On the one
hand, proper names are "formules de dévotion, des documents sur
la piété"; [8] on the other hand, if proper names are used as confirmation of religious beliefs, more evidence about this devotion is
required. Often it is advisable to use their theophorous elements
only as additional arguments for a certain cult or belief. In this
study proper names will be dealt with in this way; they may offer
additional evidence for a certain cult, but the very existence of this
cult cannot be deduced from mere theophorous proper names.
Besides the inscriptions ancient Syriac literature yields a good
many proper names which will be dealt with in the same way. How

---

[7] cf. K. Beyer, Der reichsaramäische Einschlag in der ältesten syrischen
Literatur, ZDMG 116, 1966, 242-254; J. C. Greenfield, Standard Literary
Aramaic, Actes du Premier Congrès International de Linguistique Sémitique
Paris 1964, The Hague-Paris 1974, 280-289, esp. 289; J. Pirenne's views on
the origin of the Syriac script as expressed in: Aux origines de la graphie
syriaque, Syria 40, 1963, 101-137 are in need of a thorough revision in the
light of unpublished Palmyrene cursive inscriptions, cf. Drijvers, Une main
votive en bronze trouvée à Palmyre, dédiée à Baʿalshamên, Semitica 27,
1977, 106f., and n. 2.

[8] A. Caquot, Sur l'onomastique réligieuse de Palmyre, Syria 39, 1962,
255.

traditional name-giving is, however, can be concluded from pagan proper names, like, e.g., Šarbel (i.e., Bel is sovereign) of Christian priests in later centuries.[9]

Twenty-four inscriptions originate from Sumatar Harabesi, situated in the Tektek mountains about a hundred kilometres southeast of Urfa and about forty-five kilometres northeast of Harran. It has many sweetwater wells and is therefore a center for the shepherds with their flocks and herds. Some of them have settled there and in fact there now exists a small beduin village even with a school and a gendarmerie post. The first person who recorded archaeological remains and inscriptions at this place is H. Pognon, who visited it in 1901 and 1905.[10] J. B. Segal spent several days there in 1952, recorded new inscriptions and revised the known ones. He especially discovered some larger inscriptions on top of the so-called central mount which refer to the cult of Marelahê, "The Lord of the Gods" who was worshipped at Sumatar during the second century A.D. and in all likelihood also before and after that period. Segal related some buildings situated around this central mount to the planet-worship of the so-called Sabians of Harran. Mediaeval Islamic authors report on these Sabians as a crypto-pagan sect who were merely nominal Muslims but in fact they followed the traditional planet-worship of this area.[11] Cults practiced at Sumatar and Edessa and elsewhere in this region during the first centuries A.D. and earlier represent an earlier phase of the same conceptions and cult. B. Aggoula constructed political and religious bonds between Sumatar Harabesi and its

---

[9] This may, however, be due to the name of the famous martyr Sharbel; but cf. names like Barba'šamên and many Greek ones in Syriac transcription e.g. Demetrios, Dionysios etc. see E. Littmann, Syria, Division IV, Section B, Syriac Inscriptions, Leyden 1934, inscr. 16B and 65.

[10] H. Pognon, Inscriptions sémitiques de la Syrie, de la Mésopotamie et de la région de Mossoul, Paris 1907, 23-38.

[11] J. B. Segal, Pagan Syriac Monuments in the Vilayet of Urfa, Anat. Studies 3, 1953, 107ff.; idem, The Sabian Mysteries. The Planet Cult of Ancient Harran, in: E. Bacon (ed.), Vanished Civilizations, London 1963, 201-220. For the Sabians see: D. A. Chwolsohn, Die Ssabier und der Ssabismus, 2 Vols. St. Petersburg 1856; J. Hjärpe, Analyse critique des traditions arabes sur les Sabéens Ḥarraniens, Diss. Uppsala 1972 (with bibliography); G. Monnot, Sabéens et idolâtres selon 'Abd al-Jabbar, MIDEO 12, 1974, 13-48.

cult of Marᵉlahê and the city of Hatra, on which the Sumatar area
would be dependent after 200 A.D.[12] Therefore the cult of "The
Lord of the Gods" as attested at Sumatar requires a thorough re-
investigation in its whole cultural and religious context.

Of the three remaining Syriac inscriptions one is a honorific
text inscribed on one of the columns on the Citadel mount; it is
dedicated to a Queen Šalmat and dates most likely from the beginning of the third century A.D.[13] (Pl. IV) The other is to be read
on a fragmentary relief now at Istanbul, which mentions "our
Lord" and is probably a dedicatory relief to a god entitled "our
Lord".[14] The last one is inscribed on a stele found in the temple of
Hadad and Atargatis at Dura-Europos; it is a so-called memento-
text of a certain Vologases who wants to be remembered "before
the god." [15] (Pl. XXIII). Which deity is meant with "the god"
remains to be seen. A bilingual inscription in Greek and Palmyrene,
and another in Palmyrene only, are found over the entrance to the
upper storey of a tomb-tower standing near the ruins of a monastery
called Deyr Yakup, some kilometres south of Urfa. In the wall of
this tomb-tower is a relief of a reclining figure like those which
are to be seen in the walls of some tomb-towers at Palmyra. The
inscription records the name of "Amaššemeš wife of Šardu bar
Ma'nu." The tomb-tower and script of the inscriptions underline
the close cultural relations between Edessa and Palmyra.[16] Strictly
speaking, it is incorrect to consider the script Palmyrene; it is an
Edessan local variant of the Aramaic cursive of that period which
mostly resembles the script in use at Palmyra. At Palmyra, on
the other hand, inscriptions are found written in an old-Syriac

---

[12] B. Aggoula, Remarques sur les inscriptions hatréennes II, *MUSJ* 47,
1972, 33ff.; 47ff.

[13] Drijvers, *Old-Syriac Inscriptions*, No. 27; Segal, *Edessa*, Pl. 29a.

[14] Drijvers, *Old-Syriac Inscriptions*, No. 28; Segal, *Edessa*, Pl. 14a;
J. Leroy, Mosaiques funéraires d'Edesse, *Syria* 34, 1957, 337ff.

[15] Drijvers, *Old-Syriac Inscriptions*, No. 63 gave a new reading of this
inscription; first published by C. C. Torrey in: *The Excavations at Dura-
Europos. Preliminary Report of Third Season*, New Haven 1932, 68-71.

[16] *cf.* Pognon, *Inscriptions sémitiques*, 103-105; J. Pirenne, Aux origines
de la graphie syriaque, *Syria* 40, 1963, 109-115; J. Starcky, Édesse et
l'Orient chrétien, *Bible et Terre Sainte* 119, March 1970, 5; for the relief of the
reclining figure see Segal, *Edessa*, Pl. 39b.

ductus.[17] The same holds true for a Greek inscription on a relief
found at Urfa and now in the Urfa Museum. It yields the proper
name Zabdibolos, which is most common at Palmyra but may also
occur at Edessa. The relief represents two male figures wearing
swords and most likely in Parthian dress. It is not clear if it is a
funerary stele or a dedicatory relief; in the latter case Zabdibolos
may be the donor and the two figures may represent deities or
meritorious citizens, although that is less likely (Pl. VIII).[18] In
any case, the type of relief surely does not occur at Palmyra, although the name Zabdibolos points in that direction; it is another
sign of the mixed culture present in and on the edge of the Syrian
desert. Other indications of this cultural mixture are one Greek
and three Hebrew tomb inscriptions near tomb-caves in the cemetery of Kirk Mağara near Urfa. The Greek inscription too commemorates Jews, who bear Greek, Hebrew and Iranian names.[19]

Archaeologica

Archaeological remains of a purely religious character are very
rare at modern Urfa due to the circumstances described above.
Most of what has been preserved has a funerary character. On the
one hand funerary sculpture and decorations of tombs may express
some fundamental views on life and death, and as such may be
interpreted in a religious context; on the other hand, this sculpture
and decoration is so traditional and stylized that it conveys no
precise conceptions but only a kind of general climate and spiritual
atmosphere. In other words the symbolic meaning of many symbols
has become obscured and is not intelligible to everyone looking at
them. In his well-known review of F. Cumont, *Recherches sur le
symbolisme funéraire des Romains* A. D. Nock comments: "nor was
there any necessary correlation between ornament and ritual"; and
"In spite of local variations there is a massive unity in this sepulchral art; but is it not a unity of cultural inheritance and to some

---

[17] *cf.* Drijvers, Une main votive en bronze trouvée à Palmyre, 106f.

[18] Segal, *Edessa*, 30 n. 5, Pl. 14b.

[19] Pognon, *Inscriptions sémitiques*, 78ff.; Segal, *Edessa*, Pl. 31a: Jewish
inscription in Greek; Segal, The Jews of North Mesopotamia before the
Rise of the Islam, *Sepher Segal*, Jerusalem 1965, 32-63; J. Neusner, *A History
of the Jews in Babylonia* I. The Parthian Period, Leiden 1965, 166-169.

extent of feeling rather than a unity of belief?"[20] At Edessa we come across these local variations of widespread themes in sepulchral art. The most impressive part of this funerary art consists of ten mosaics which once decorated the floors of cave-tombs. Today nearly all must be considered lost except for one complete mosaic in the Istanbul Museum and some fragments in the Urfa Museum and elsewhere.[21] They are: the so-called mosaic of Zenodora; that of Aptuha, now at Istanbul; that of Belai bar Gusai; the "Family Portrait" mosaic (Pl. XIII); the "Funerary Couch" mosaic (Pl. XVII); the "Tripod" mosaic (Pl. XIV); the "Phoenix" mosaic (Pl. XVI); the "Orpheus" mosaic (Pl. XV); the "Animal" mosaic; and the "Four Pointed Stars" mosaic.[22] Fragments of the "Animal" mosaic are to be seen in the Urfa Museum and in a private house in that city. J. B. Segal gave a religious interpretation to the Phoenix mosaic representing the famous bird standing on top of a stele which is supported by a kind of socle, and to the Orpheus mosaic. This last one pictures the singer playing the lyre and surrounded by various animals. Segal connects it with the cult of Nebo, who at Hierapolis is identified with the Thracian singer and magian according to the Apology of Pseudo-Melito.[23] It should be noted that the inscriptions on these mosaics only give names and dates.

The "Funerary Couch" mosaic conveys a theme which is also attested in the rare reliefs in two tombs near Edessa and one at Kara Köpru north of Edessa (Pl. XVIII, XIX).[24] This motif of the "repas funéraire" occurs very often in the sepulchral art of

---

[20] A. D. Nock, Sarcophagi and Symbolism, *AJA* 50, 1946, 149 and 170 = *Essays on Religion and the Ancient World* II, Cambridge, Mass. 1972, 617 and 641.

[21] The fragments in the Urfa Museum belong to the so-called Animal Mosaic, see Segal, *Edessa*, Pl. 18-20; there is one fragment on view in the Louvre No. AO 22917.

[22] cf. Segal, *Edessa*, Pl. 1, 2, 3, 16b, 17a, b, 18, 19, 20, 43, 44; J. Leroy, Mosaiques funéraires d'Édesse, *Syria* 34, 1957, 306ff.; *id.*, Nouvelles découvertes archéologiques relatives à Édesse, *Syria* 38, 1961, 159ff.; Drijvers, *Old-Syriac Inscriptions*, No's 44-51; *idem*, Some New Syriac Inscriptions, 12-14.

[23] Segal, *Edessa*, 51f.; see Ch. III, p. 94, 189ff.

[24] cf. Segal, *Edessa*, Pl. 25a, b; Pognon, *Inscriptions sémitiques*, 179ff.; Pl. XI.

Palmyra and is also attested elsewhere.[25] Since Segal labels this
representation a "ritual banquet," whereas Seyrig, et al., stress the
purely profane meaning of this sepulchral motif, it should be
reinvestigated. The other items of funerary art which have been
preserved represent portraits of male and female personages—
winged victories decorating the arcosolia in the cave-tombs, and
a winged victory standing near the altar in a mourning attitude,
on view in the Urfa Museum (Pl. VI). They should be considered
motifs of sepulchral art traditional all over the Near East and the
Roman Empire to which no precise meaning can be given.[26]

Several funerary steles on view in the Urfa Museum, and originating from Zeugma on the Euphrates, represent an eagle, or a
basket for wool, or a combination of both themes (Pl. IX, X, XI,
XII).[27] F. Cumont interpreted the eagle as an "aigle funéraire"
which would symbolize the apotheosis of the dead.[28] In dealing
with the religious meaning of the eagle and its cult in the religion
of Edessa we will also have opportunity to give attention to these
funerary steles.

Two reliefs in the Urfa Museum are of special interest. One is a
representation of Hadad and Atargatis, the gods of Hierapolis, and
the famous *semeion* between them (Pl. XXII).[29] Since the cult of

---

[25] H. Seyrig, Le repas des morts et le "banquet funèbre" à Palmyre, *AAS*
1, 1951, 32-41 = *AS* IV, 208-215; E. Will, Le relief de la tour Kithot et le
banquet funéraire à Palmyre, *Syria* 28, 1951, 70-100; *cf.* J. M. Dentzer,
l'Iconographie iranienne du souverain couché et le motif du banquet, *AAAS*
21, 1971, 39-50.
[26] A tomb from Roman times at 'Anab al-Safinah on the upper course
of the Euphrates that has been excavated by a Syrian expedition, is decorated
by six victories, among them one in a mourning attitude, and four winged
lion-griffins; see: *Sauvegarde des antiquités du lac du barrage de l'Euphrate*,
Damascus 1973, 10, no. 9; in addition it may be mentioned that the same
tomb has yielded some Syriac inscriptions.
[27] *cf.* the list in J. Wagner, *Seleukeia am Euphrat/Zeugma*, Beih. z. *TAVO*,
Reihe B 10, Wiesbaden 1976, 112ff. and Pl. 6; 157ff.; 175ff. and Pl. 29-38;
40-44; 51-53.
[28] F. Cumont, *Études syriennes*, Paris 1917, 41ff.; Cumont considered the
basket a 'ciste mystique ... un élément essentiel des cérémonies secrètes
dans plusieurs cultes orientaux', p. 49.
[29] First published by Drijvers, Die Götter Edessas, *Studien zur Religion und Kultur Kleinasiens, Festschrift F. K. Dörner*, Leiden 1978, 276ff.,
Pl. CV.

Atargatis is also attested by literary sources and proper names, this relief has a special importance. A relief of a female triton may be referred to the same cult, where fish, and especially dolphins, played a role (Pl. XXI).[30] A sculptured bloc at the same museum which was clearly intended to support a statue, but which later was reused as a trough, shows two goats on the front side (Pl. XX). Since animals like sheep and rams usually belong to the iconography of Hermes Heliopolitanus and related deities, they may be interpreted in this way. This would give an indication of the cult of a "dieu-fils" at Edessa.[31] A relief of a winged lion-griffin with female head belongs to the traditional thematics of Near-Eastern art to which no exact meaning can be ascribed since they occur in various contexts (Pl. VII). Two charming reliefs of an embracing couple, the man completely nude and the woman partly dressed, are clearly intended for decorative purposes, as one is the reverse of the other (Pl. V). This is the whole known legacy from antique times in the field of representational art. Some lucky finds may add something, but since excavations on important sites in the city are impossible, expectations are rather dim.[32]

Also at Sumatar Harabesi very little has been saved. One cave, which H. Pognon visited, shows reliefs of male persons and symbols related to the cult of Marelahê.[33] On the central mount two reliefs are carved in niches: one of them pictures the god of Sumatar; the other is most likely a local magnate whose figure in relief was ordered by the same god (Pl. XXIV, XXV, XXVI, XXVII).[34] In addition, Sumatar yielded two eagle reliefs (Pl. XXX), a funerary

---

[30] Segal, *Edessa*, Pl. 15a; *cf.* N. Glueck, *Deities and Dolphins.* The Story of the Nabataeans, N.Y. 1965, 315ff.

[31] *cf.* H. Seyrig, Questions héliopolitaines, *AS* V, 100ff.; Y. Hajjar, *La triade d'Héliopolis-Baalbek* II, 507ff.

[32] One should add a relief from Urfa published by V. Chapot, Antiquités de la Syrie du Nord, *BCH* 26, 1902 and Fig. 6 (a drawing), representing eight masks of Greek divine figures.

[33] Pognon, *Inscriptions sémitiques*, 23ff.; *cf.* Segal, *Anat. Studies* 3, 1953, 102ff.: Pognon's Cave; J. T. Milik, *Dédicaces faites par des dieux* (Palmyre, Hatra, Tyr) et des thiases sémitiques à l'époque romaine, Paris 1972, 348ff.; Drijvers, Die Götter Edessas, 272ff.

[34] Segal, *Edessa*, Pl. 40b, 41; Drijvers, *Old-Syriac Inscriptions*, No's 13-16 (with literature).

stele of three women (Pl. XXXI) and one other fragmentary relief of a male person.[35] A headless male statue, recorded by J. B. Segal, seems to have disappeared.[36] An altar without any inscription or pictorial representation, seen at Sumatar in May 1977, is another sign of the important religious function of this place in antiquity. From the viewpoint of religious history the reliefs on the central mount, the symbols in the cave, and the reliefs with eagles form —together with the recorded inscriptions—our main documentation about the cult of Mar^elahê at Sumatar Harabesi.

Coins

The first comprehensive survey of Edessa's numismatics was done by E. Babelon, who described all coins which were struck at Edessa.[37] His views were, for the greater part, adopted by F. Hill, who published the Greek coins from Arabia, Mesopotamia and Persia in the British Museum Collections in 1922.[38] Since that time no new survey has been published, although material has substantially increased. Especially the excavations at Dura-Europos yielded many coins struck at Edessa, and were published by A. R. Bellinger.[39] Babelon and Hill assumed that coinage at Edessa started with Antiochus IV Epiphanes (175-164 B.C.), who had bronze coins struck at Edessa which, like in many other cities, had on the reverse side a representation of Zeus aetophoros.[40] These coins bear witness to Antiochus' veneration of the god of heaven, and for this reason caused the bitter enmity of the Jews towards

---

[35] Drijvers, Some New Syriac Inscriptions and Archaeological Finds from Edessa and Sumatar Harabesi, *BSOAS* 36, 1973, 1-14.

[36] Segal, *Edessa*, Pl. 13a; *idem, Anat. Studies* 3, 1953, Pl. XI, 1.

[37] E. Babelon, Numismatique d'Édesse en Mésopotamie, *Mélanges numismatiques*, 2ème série, Paris 1893, 209-296, Pl. III-VIII.

[38] G. F. Hill, *BMC, Arabia, Mesopotamia and Persia*, London 1922, xciv-cvii. 91-118, Pl. XIII-XVII.

[39] A. R. Bellinger, *The Eighth and Ninth Dura Hoards*, NNM 85, N.Y. 1939, 16-28; *id., Syrian Tetradrachms of Caracalla and Macrinus*, NS 3, N.Y. 1940, 50-57; *id., The Excavations at Dura-Europos, Final Report* VI, *The Coins*, New Haven 1949, Nos. 1393-1497.

[40] Babelon, Numismatique d'Édesse, 211ff.; Hill, *BMC, Arabia* xcivff.; *cf.* O. Mørkholm, *Antiochus IV of Syria, Classica et Mediaevalia*, Diss. VIII. København 1966, 127.

this Seleucid king.[41] E. R. Newell, however, assigned to Edessa some bronze coins struck during the reign of Antiochus I (280-261 B.C.)—of special importance to this king in his wars against the Syrian rebels and the invading armies of Ptolemy. There he assembled his forces to attack his enemies in Syria. These coins, outstanding for the thickness of their flans and the unusual arrangement of the inscriptions, show the bust of Antiochus I and the head of Athena wearing a crested Corinthian helm.[42]

From the viewpoint of the history of religions coins struck at Edessa under the reign of Wa'el bar Sharu are interesting. They show on the obverse the bust of Wa'el with his name and title in Syriac. The reverse bears the representation of a "Temple with pediment seen in three-quarters perspective; two columns in front, and steps leading up to it; within, a cubic cult-object on a base supported by two curved legs; in pediment, a star; inscription on right and left downwards; wreath-border." (Pl. XXXIII, 1).[43] This temple can be identified as the sanctuary of a local god, especially as it reappears on imperial issues of Edessa on which it is the characteristic sign of the city. On tetradrachms of Caracalla and Macrinus the shrine with pediment is usually pictured between the legs of an eagle on the reverse of the coins, or the same representation is to be seen beneath the eagle.[44] A tetradrachm of Elagabalus (219-222) (Pl. XXXIV, 5, 6), and another of Severus Alexander, (222-235) (Pl. XXXIV, 7) show the same reverse with eagle and shrine with pediment between its legs.[45] Bronze coins of Severus Alexander show on the reverse a small pedimental shrine within a larger edifice indicated by two columns supporting

---

[41] cf. M. Hengel, *Judentum und Hellenismus*, Tübingen 1969, 503ff.; F. Millar, The Background to the Maccabean Revolution: Reflections on Martin Hengel's "Judaism and Hellenism", *JJS* 29, 1978, 12ff.

[42] E. T. Newell, *The Coinage of the Western Seleucid Mints from Seleucus I to Antiochus III*, NS 4, N.Y. 1941, 53-56.

[43] Hill, *BMC, Arabia*, p. 91, Pl. XIII, 7; cf. Babelon, Numismatique d'Édesse, 223, no. 3.

[44] Bellinger, *The Syrian Tetradrachms*, 50-57, Nos. 134-151, Pl. X, 15, 16, 17, Pl. XI.

[45] Bellinger, *The Syrian Tetradrachms*, Nos. 152-155 and Pl. XII, 1, 2, 4, 5.

an arch.[46] Other bronzes of the same emperor bear a Tyche holding
the temple with pediment in her right hand (Pl. XXXIV, 4;
XXXIII, 4).[47] Bronze coins of Gordianus (238-244) bear a bust of
Tyche on the reverse; before it is a pedestal on which stands a
statue of Aquarius (?); usually but not invariably the little temple
with pediment is to be seen between bust and pedestal (Pl.
XXXII, 3, 4; XXXIV, 1, 2).[48]

It can therefore not be doubted that this shrine with pediment
represents a local temple of some importance. Syrian tetradrachms
of Caracalla and Macrinus that were struck at Hierapolis show a
lion, the characteristic animal of the Dea Syria of that place; and
those originating from Harran bear a crescent, the sign of the
famous moon god Sin of Harran, or the head of an ox.

The bronze coins of Wa'el with this shrine and pediment bear a
Syriac inscription which may identify the temple. Unfortunately
the texts on different coins show a considerable variation so that
no sure reading is possible. Hill, like E. Babelon, proposed with
great hesitation to read '*lh* '*lwl*—god of Elul; Elul might be the
name of one of the Babylonian months.[49] Although more coins of
this type have shown up since that time, the readings are not at
all clear so that the only conclusion might be: "Il convient donc
en conclusion de ne pas accepter comme une verité établie, ainsi
qu'on l'a fait, la modeste suggestion d'Ern. Babelon et en atten-
dant une possibilité de lecture plus certaine, il faut retenir sa discré-
tion,....[50]

The Tyche of Edessa is pictured on the coins of the city from the
time of Caracalla on. The type is patterned after the famous work
of Eutychides of Sicyon made for the city of Antioch about the

---

[46] Babelon, Numismatique d'Édesse, 279, no. 76; Hill, *BMC, Arabia*,
cvii, Pl. L, 17; *The Excavations at Dura-Europos, Final Report* VI, *The
Coins*, no. 1471, p. 143.

[47] Bellinger, *Eighth and Ninth Dura Hoards*, 16-28, Nos. 23, 45, 47, 48;
cf. Hill, *BMC, Arabia*, cvii and Pl. L, 16; Bellinger, *Syrian Tetradrachms*,
51, Pl. XI, 7.

[48] Hill, *BMC, Arabia*, cvi; Bellinger, *Eighth and Ninth Dura Hoards*, 27;
idem, Syrian Tetradrachms, Pl. XI, 9.

[49] Babelon, Numismatique d'Édesse, 224-225; Hill, *BMC, Arabia*, xcvif.

[50] P. Naster, Les monnaies d'Édesse révèlent-elles un dieu 'Elul?, *Revue
belge de Numismatique* 114, 1968, 13.

beginning of the third century B.C.[51] The types occurring in the coinage of Edessa show much variety of detail, especially in the times of Elagabalus and Severus Alexander. Tyche holds a branch, or fruits, or ears of corn, or temple with pediment, or simply an uncertain object; before her stands a flaming altar, or a rearing serpent; behind her a cornucopia is to be seen, or another altar; in the field sometimes there are two or four eight-pointed stars (Pl. XXXIII, 4; XXXIV, 2, 4).[52] It is not unlikely that the city goddess of Edessa, the local *Gad*, has some links with the local cult of Atargatis, who can function as a Tyche, either, e.g., at Palmyra and Dura-Europos. In particular the eight-pointed stars which are special features of the Dea Syria as Venus star, point in that direction.[53]

As already stated above some coins of Gordianus III show on their reverse the bust of Tyche and before her a small figure on a pedestal. The same figure on a pedestal is found on coins of Gordianus III from Harran (Pl. XXXII, 3, 4).[54] This figure has been explained by G. Macdonald as the sign *Aquarius*, which seems to be pictured above the head of the Tyche on some coins of Severus Alexander struck at Edessa.[55] Actually other astronomical signs, such as Aries and Sagittarius, occur on Mesopotamian coins, but the major difference between these signs and the figure on the

---

[51] Bellinger, *Eighth and Ninth Dura Hoards*, 2ff.; *cf.* T. Dohrn, *Die Tyche von Antiochia*, Berlin 1960, 56.

[52] All variants are listed in Bellinger, *Eighth and Ninth Dura Hoards*, 16ff.; *cf. The Excavations at Dura-Europos, Final Report* VI, *The Coins*, Nos. 1431-1470 and the commentary p. 142.

[53] On the Gad-Tyche see F. Cumont, art. *Gad*, PW VII, 433-435; R. Dussaud, *La Pénétration des Arabes en Syrie avant l'Islam*, Paris 1955, 111ff.; J. Starcky, Deux inscriptions palmyréniennes, *MUSJ* 1962, 136; The conical cap worn by the priests of Atargatis at Hierapolis is decorated with an eight-pointed star and with a sixteen-pointed star, *cf.* R. A. Stucky, Prêtres syriens II, Hiérapolis, *Syria* 53, 1976, 128 and Pl. V, 1-3; the sixteen-pointed star, in fact a kind of doubling of the eight-pointed one, may indicate Atargatis-Venus as morning and evening star.

[54] Hill, *BMC, Arabia* xciiif. and Pl. XIII, 1, 2; *cf.* Babelon, Numismatique d'Édesse, 284: "un petit génie sur un autel".

[55] G. Macdonald, *Cat. of the Hunterian Collection* III, 303 note: *cf.* Hill, *BMC*, xciii and nos. 115-121; Bellinger, *The Eighth and Ninth Dura Hoards*, p. 24, nos. 46, 47, 48.

pedestal is that, being represented on a pedestal, it seems to be a real statue or monument. G. F. Hill considered that it may represent the "Marsyas" of the Forum, but at the same time he uttered severe doubts on this identification. A. B. Cook considered it to be Azizos, one of the Dioscuri, who, according to Julian Apostata (150 C-D; 154 B), were worshipped at Edessa.[56] H. Seyrig draws attention to an "intaille" in a private collection at Aleppo, which represents the same figure to the left of an archaic statue of Apollo-Nebo from Hierapolis. To its right a nude Heracles is represented with his club and the lion skin. The reverse side of this intaille bears the busts of Sol and Luna. (Pl. XXXIV, 3).[57] If the figure on the pedestal as represented on coins and this statue on the intaille are identical, as they seem to be, its identity should be sought in the context of the cult at Hierapolis where, besides Hadad and Atargatis, other gods were worshipped. Moreover, Edessa shared this figure on a pedestal with Harran, so that the conclusion is obvious that both cities possessed this cult in common. Its identification as Aquarius, however, is false, as both are very different ("les deux images sont fort différentes"—H. Seyrig), and the same is the case with Azizos. The cult of Hadad and Atargatis is attested at Edessa in various ways, and the solution for this enigmatic figure should be sought there. It has a kind of stick in its left hand and an uncertain object on its right shoulder. The identification of this last object as a skin by G. F. Hill, et al. ("the figure seems to hold a skin") is based on the assumption that it should be *Aquarius*.

Other coins of Gordianus III, on which the emperor is pictured with an arrow in his left hand, have been dealt with at length by Helga Gesche.[58] It turns out that the arrow, as a traditional sign of royal authority in the monarchian iconography of the Near East, is used to indicate the sovereign position of the Roman emperor

---

[56] A. B. Cook, *Zeus*, III, 429f.; *cf.* Drijvers, The Cult of Azizos and Monimos at Edessa, *Ex Orbe Religionum*, Festschrift G. Widengren, Vol. I, Leiden 1972, 355-371.

[57] H. Seyrig, Sur une idole hiérapolitaine, *Syria* 26, 1949, 19f., n. 1, Pl. I, 4 = *AS* IV, 22f., n. 1 and Pl. I, 4.

[58] Helga Gesche, Kaiser Gordian mit dem Pfeil in Edessa, *Jahrb. f. Num.* 19, 1969, 47-77 and Plate 3-5.

over the local toparch Abgar, who offers a small statue of Victory to Gordianus. These coins offer another example of how autochthonous and traditional symbols are used in Roman imperial coinage in the Near East. The representation on Roman imperial coins struck at Edessa of the temple with pediment and of the figure on the pedestal bear witness to the same phenomenon. They are therefore one of our sources for the study of traditional pagan religion at Edessa.

Literary Sources

Syriac literature contains many pieces of information on pagan cults and practices which are mostly scattered in writings of various kinds: chronicles; theological treatises; hymns and homilies; bible commentaries, etc. This information has partly a learned character, consisting of erudite remarks on religions of foreign peoples and former times, and partly its aim is merely apologetic since pagan religion is described as an evil superstition inspired by Satan. This approach does not warrant an objective description of pagan religion as such in order to use this information as a reliable source. Moreover, it is often traditional to a high degree, not dealing with the author's own time and situation but used only for literary reasons in order to contrast the true belief with what is supposed to be devilish superstition. Nearly every instance, therefore, requires a thorough literary and traditional-historical investigation in order to trace its origin and the reliability of its contents.

Some texts explicitly deal with pagan religion at Edessa, or at least pretend to do so. The first is the so-called *Doctrina Addai,* a legendary tale about the Apostle Addai sent to Edessa after Christ's death and resurrection to preach the gospel and cure King Abgar's disease. It contains the famous but apocryphal correspondence of Jesus and King Abgar of Edessa which is for the first time mentioned by Eusebius of Caesarea in his *Ecclesiastical History.* The present form of the *Doctrina Addai* dates from the end of the fourth century or the beginning of the fifth and is clearly meant to defend orthodox belief at Edessa against all kinds of heretics pretending that orthodoxy goes back to Edessa's first apostle sent by Jesus himself. In fact Addai's preaching at Edessa represents the orthodox views

3

of Ephrem Syrus' times, also of the end of the fourth century.[59] In a sermon delivered before the whole population of Edessa, its king and nobles included, Addai refers to pagan beliefs actually adhered to by the city's inhabitants:

> "For I saw in this city that it abounded greatly in paganism, which is against God. Who is this Nebo, an idol made which ye worship, and Bel, which ye honour? Behold there are those among you who adore Bath Nikkal, as the inhabitants of Harran, your neighbours, and Tar'atha, as the people of Mabbug, and the eagle as the Arabians, also the sun and the moon, as the rest of the inhabitants of Harran, who are as yourselves. Be ye not led away captive by the rays of the luminaries and the bright star; for every one who worships creatures is cursed before God." [60]

Further on Addai mentions a great altar in the center of the city, at which people made offerings to the demons. Addai performed several miraculous healings and then:

> Shavida and Abednebo, chiefs of the priests of this city, with Piroz and Danqu, their companions, when they saw the signs which he did, ran and threw down the altars upon which they sacrificed before Nebo and Bel, their gods, except the great altar, which was in the midst of the city, etc. ....[61]

The king, his nobles, and the greater part of the city's population, are converted to the new belief and behave in such an examplary way "that even the priests of the temple of Nebo and Bel divided with them the honour at all times." [62] The question raised by these texts is, do they give a more or less reliable picture of religious life at Edessa in pagan times, or are they purely fictitious? It is curious

---

[59] cf. W. Bauer, *Rechtgläubigkeit und Ketzerei im ältesten Christentum*, *BHTh* 10, Tübingen 1934, 6ff.; Drijvers, Edessa und das jüdische Christentum, *VigChr.* 24, 1970, 4-33; Drijvers, Rechtgläubigkeit und Ketzerei im ältesten syrischen Christentum, *OrChr. Anal.* 197, Roma 1974, 291-310.

[60] *The Doctrine of Addai, the Apostle*, ed. G. Phillips, London 1876, 23f. (transl.), 24 L. 15ff. (text); cf. C. Winckworth, On Heathen Deities in the Doctrine of Addai, *JThS* 25, 1924, 402f.; cf. *Talmud Babli, Aboda Zara* 11b.

[61] *The Doctrine of Addai*, 32 (transl.), 34 (text).

[62] *The Doctrine of Addai*, 48 (transl.), 39 (text).

that "the great altar" is left untouched. Is this an indication that at the end of the fourth century there was indeed a great altar standing in the middle of the city? We may remember that, most likely about the same time, the Temple of Venus (i.e., Atargatis) was also still standing.[63] However that may be, and even if "by the time the two gods were mentioned by the *Doctrine* their reality must have been elusive" so that "the reference to the cults of Nebo and Bel is an erudite remark by the editor of the *Doctrine*," [64] the question is, do they reliable preserve tradition from pagan times on, or are they sheer fantasy? This problem cannot be solved by literary means alone; we need external evidence of another kind to come to reliable conclusions on the cult of the gods mentioned. In dealing with the various deities we will attack this problem again.

The *Acta* of the Martyr Sharbel date from the same time as the *Doctrina Addai* and are literarily closely related to it. Sharbel was the pagan highpriest of Edessa, who was converted to Christianity by the preaching of Bishop Barsamya. This conversion took place on the occasion of a great feast on the eight of Nisan on the third day of the week. The whole population gathered near the great altar in the center of the city opposite the archives-building. All the gods, Nebo and Bel and their companions, were brought there; they were decorated and were put on a seat of honour.[65] The details afforded by this interesting text regarding the function of the great altar and the date of a feast in the beginning of the month of Nisan will later on again engage our attention.

The *Apology of Ps.-Melito*, written as an original Syriac work in the beginning of the third century, perhaps at Hierapolis-Mabbug, offers interesting details on religion in Syria in general and at Hierapolis and Edessa in particular from an euhemeristic point of

---

[63] *cf.* Éthérie, Journal de voyage, SC 21, Paris 1948, 19, 7.

[64] So J. Teixidor, *The Pagan God*. Popular Religion in the Greco-Roman Near East, Princeton 1977, 151, 152, n. 31.

[65] The Acts of Sharbel in: W. Cureton, *Ancient Syriac Documents relative to the earliest Establishment of Christianity in Edessa*, London 1864, Repr. A'dam 1967, 41-72; *cf.* I. Ortiz de Urbina, *Patrologia Syriaca*, ed. alt., Roma 1965, 193; Segal, *Edessa*, 82ff.; Duval, *Histoire d'Édesse*, 129ff.

view.[66] Although the information included in this apology is sometimes confusing, a closer analysis of this material will show that
its base is solid and becomes quite understandable after comparison
with other evidence. Much of its contents is taken over by Syriac
authors of later times, as for instance, Theodor bar Koni (end of
8th cent.) and Ishodad of Merw (9th cent.).[67]

Ephrem Syrus' polemical works, especially his *Hymni contra
Haereses*, contain many references to magical and astrological
practices at Edessa; after having fled for the Sassanians from
Nisibis, he spent the last eight years of his life at Edessa, until his
death in 373. The *Hymni contra Haereses* were written at Edessa
and reflect the religious situation there; what Ephrem wrote about
Mani, Marcion and Bardaiṣan is fairly reliable, and the same may
be assumed concerning the other information he offers.[68] It would
appear that in his days paganism—or at least pagan practice—is
still alive. The same impression is created by five homilies belonging
to a whole collection usually ascribed to a certain Isaac of Antioch,
who, however, was probably a native of Amida i.e. modern Diarbekir.
It is difficult, if not impossible, to distinguish his works from those
of two other Isaacs, both natives of Edessa; proper assignment to
the different Isaacs already formed a complicated problem in the
seventh century, when it was discussed by Jacob of Edessa in a
letter addressed to Johannan the Stylite.[69] Two homilies describing

---

[66] *cf.* Ortiz de Urbina, *Patrologia Syriaca*, ed. alt. Roma 1965, 41; the
text in: W. Cureton, *Spicilegium Syriacum*, London 1855, 41-51 (transl.),
22-37 (text); *cf.* Baumstark, *Geschichte der syrischen Literatur*, 27.

[67] Especially the passages on the cult of Nebo, *cf.* Theodore bar Khonai,
Buch der Scholien I, ed. A. Scher, *CSCO* 65, 1910, 369, 11.16-21; Ishodad of
Merw, ed. C. van den Eynde, *CSCO* 126, *Script. Syr.* 67, 1950, 6, 11.21ff.

[68] Ephrem Syrus, *Hymni contra Haereses*, ed. E. Beck, *CSCO* 169 (textus),
170 (versio), Louvain 1957; the hymns 1, 4, 5, 6, 8, 9 and 13 deal mainly
with magic and astrology; for Ephrem's information on Marcion see B. Aland,
Marcion. Versuch einer neuen Interpretation, *ZThK* 70, 1973, 420-447;
Ephrem on Bardaiṣan and Mani see Drijvers, *Bardaiṣan of Edessa*, *Studia
Semitica Neerlandica* 6, Assen 1966, 127ff.; *idem*, Mani und Bardaiṣan. Ein
Beitrag zur Vorgeschichte des Manichäismus, *Mélanges H.-Ch. Puech*, Paris
1974, 459-469; E. Beck, Ephräms Rede gegen eine philosophische Schrift
des Bardaiṣan, *OrChr.* 60, 1976, 24-68.

[69] Jacob's letter to Johannan the Stylite in: BM. Add. 12172, fol. 123;
cf. P. Martin, *Gramm. Syr.*, 69; Th. J. Lamy, *S. Ephraemi Syri Hymni et
Sermones* IV, Mechliniae 1902, 362; P. Bedjan, *Homiliae S. Isaaci Syri*

the conquest of Beth Ḥur by Arab tribes, and three other homilies combatting magians, soothsayers and sorcerers, and describing the end of the world and the Last Judgement, should in all likelihood be attributed to Isaac of Antioch, who was virtually a native of Amida and died before 461.[70] Beth Ḥur was situated near Amida-Diarbekir and was founded by Harran. Isaac attributes its conquest and destruction to the pagan beliefs and practices of its inhabitants and describes these at length. It may thus be assumed that paganism at Beth Ḥur represents a local variant of a general pattern in Northern Mesopotamia during that period. In particular the homilies against the magians and sorcerers have much in common with Ephrem's laments about the situation at Edessa, and indeed enhances their value as a source for the study of pagan practice at that time because a literary link between Isaac's homilies and Ephrem's works does not exist. Jacob of Saruǧ (451-521) is the author of a homily on *The Fall of the Idols*. This poetic homily tends to suggest that paganism virtually came to its end by the birth of the Saviour, and thus Jacob lists a whole range of idols and the places where they were worshipped. He displays a rather general knowledge on far-away countries, but his information about cities and areas nearer to Saruǧ is fairly detailed and precise. Since Saruǧ-Batnae is situated west of Edessa along the road to Antioch his knowledge of this area in particular may be correct.[71]

Antiocheni, I, Par. 1903, iv-vi; cf. Baumstark, *Geschichte der syrischen Literatur*, 63-66.

[70] *ed.* G. Bickell, *S. Isaaci Antiocheni doctoris syrorum opera omnia* I, Gissae 1873, Homiliae XI and XII (Beth Ḥur); II, Gissae 1877, Homiliae XXXV and XXXVI (against magians etc.); Th. J. Lamy, *Sancti Ephraemi Syri Hymni et Sermones* II, Mechliniae 1886, 393-426 (against magians and on the End of the World and the Last Judgment); *cf.* A. Klugkist, Pagane Bräuche in den Homilien des Isaak von Antiocheia gegen die Wahrsager, *Orient. Chr. Anal.* 197, Roma 1974, 353ff.; *cf.* Baumstark, *Geschichte*, 65, n. 4.

[71] *cf.* P. Martin, Discours de Jacques de Saroug sur la chute des idoles, *ZDMG* 29, 1875, 107-147; P. S. Landersdorfer, Die Götterliste des Mar Jacob von Sarug in seiner Homilie über den Fall der Götzenbilder. Ein religionsgeschichtliches Dokument aus der Zeit des untergehenden Heidentums, *Programm des Kgl. Gymnasiums im Benediktinerkloster Ettal für das Schuljahr 1913/14*, München 1914; B. Vandenhoff, Die Götterliste des Mar Jacob von Sarug in seiner Homilie über den Fall der Götzenbilder, *OrChr.* 5, 1915, 234-262, corrected Landersdorfer on many points.

The passage in question reads:

51. He (i.e., Satan) put Apollo as idol in Antioch and others with
      him,
    In Edessa he set Nebo and Bel together with many others,
    He led astray Harran by Sin, Ba'alšamên and Bar Nemrê
    By my Lord with his Dogs and the goddesses Tar'atha and
      Gadlat.[72]

These are the most important Syriac texts containing some information regarding pagan religion at Edessa and Northern Mesopotamia in general. Since Edessa did not, like Hierapolis, have its
Lucianus to describe its pantheon and cult, in Greek literature we
are left only with some remarks of the Emperor Julian in his famous
oration on King Helios issued in December 362 at Antioch [73] on
the cult of Azizos and Monimos at Edessa.

    In Syriac literature after 500 A.D. we find all kinds of information
concerning other religions, which partly may go back to earlier
sources, e.g., the works of Theodorus of Mopsuestia.[74] Insofar as
this information can elucidate other evidence it will be adduced in
its due place; otherwise it will be left out. Traditions on Zarathustra
and the Magians in Syriac literature form a special case, since they
often are adduced as strong evidence for Iranian influence on
traditional Syrian religion, a form of Irano-Semitic syncretism.[75]

---

[72] Landersdorfer, Die Götterliste, 19f. 11.51-54; 22-26; cf. Vandenhoff,
Die Götterliste. 236ff.

[73] *Julian* 150 C-D; 154 B = *Oeuvres complètes* II, 2. ed. C. Lacombrade,
Paris 1964, 128-138; cf. Drijvers, The Cult of Azizos and Monimos; J. Starcky,
Relief dedié au dieu Mun'im, *Semitica* 22, 1972, 57-65; J. Henninger, Zum
Problem der Venussterngottheit bei den Semiten, *Anthropos* 71, 1976, 135ff.

[74] A corpus of these texts will be published with translation and commentary by the present author in the *Göttinger Orientforschungen*; especially
Acts of Martyrs, Chronicles and exegetical treatises contain all kinds of
information regarding pagan religions. For Theodorus of Mopsuestia see:
J. Quasten, *Patrology* III, 1963, 401ff., esp. 413., where his treatise *Adversus
magiam* is discussed.

[75] cf. P. de Menasce, Autour d'un texte syriaque inédit sur la religion des
Mages, *BSOS* 9, 1937-39, 587-601, a text from Joḥannân bar Penkayê,
Ketâbâ deres mellê, cf. T. Jansma, Project d'édition du "Ketâbâ deres melle"
de Joḥannân Bar Penkayê, *L'Orient Syrien* 7, 1963, 87-106; J. Bidez -
F. Cumont, *Les mages hellenisés*, II, Paris 1938, 113ff., a text from the
Gannât Bussamê, the Nestorian Commentary on the liturgical pericopes for

On the one hand, Syriac literature shows a good knowledge of Zarathustra's doctrine and its adherents, as well as about other foreign religions.[76] On the other hand, from the fifth century A.D. on, traditions based on Zarathustra and the Magians play a certain role in the exegetical literature and in particular of the Nestorian church, where the first chapter of the Gospel of St. Matthew is explained. It is in the hostile relations between Christianity and the Mazdaean State Church in the Sassanian Empire that the background and origin of this special tradition based on Zarathustra and the Magians should be sought. These traditions offer a strong anti-Iranian trend and try, on the other hand, to prove that Zarathustra already knew about the coming of the Saviour. They are a good example of religious imperialism and hostility in a special situation in Eastern Syria and Iran and should not be used as scientific arguments for an over-all pattern of Irano-Semitic syncretism which might have existed in Parthian times.[77] In any case, these traditions do not belong to our sources for the study of pagan religion at Edessa during the first centuries A.D.

---

the whole ecclesiastical year, cf. G. J. Reinink, Die Textüberlieferung der Gannat Bussame, Le Muséon 90, 1977, 103ff. on this work.

I. E. Rahmani, Studia Syriaca IV. Documenta de antiquis haeresibus, primo edidit etc., In Seminario Scharfensi de monti Libano 1909, 1-2; cf. H. S. Nyberg, Questions de Cosmogonie et de Cosmologie mazdéennes, JA 214, 1929, 238-241; cf. G. Widengren, Iranisch-semitische Kulturbegegnung in parthischer Zeit, Köln 1960, 62ff.: Die Geburtsstätten des Erlöserkönigs; U. Monneret de Villard, Le Leggende orientali sui Magi Evangelici, Roma 1952, 3ff.

[76] cf. J. Teixidor, Reflexiones sobre el Zoroastro siriaco, OCP 28, 1962, 181-185; Theodore bar Khonai, Buch der Scholien, ed. A. Scher, CSCO 65, 1910, 295, LL. 16-26; cf. H. Pognon, Inscriptions mandaites des coupes de Khouabir, Paris 1899, 111ff. (text) and 162ff. (translation); R. C. Zaehner, Zurvan. A Zoroastrian Dilemma, Oxford 1955, 419ff.

[77] cf. Drijvers, Mithra at Hatra? Some Remarks on the Problem of the Irano-Mesopotamian Syncretism, Acta Iranica 17, 1978, 151-186; the present author is preparing an article on Syriac traditions regarding Zarathustra and the Magi mainly from exegetical sources.

CHAPTER THREE

THE CULT OF NEBO AND BEL

Nebo and Bel were the main gods of Edessa according to the *Doctrina Addai*, the *Acts of Sharbel*, and *Jacob of Sarug's Homily on the Fall of the Idols*.[1] In fact two ways are open to examine whether the reference to the cult of Nebo and Bel is only an "erudite remark" made by some Christian authors on two traditional Meso-potamian deities which might, for instance, go back to Jes. 46, 1, or whether it actually refers to the most important cults of Edessa in pagan times. One way consists of an analysis of all passages on pagan cults in the *Doctrina Addai*, the *Acts of Sharbel* and the *Homily on the Fall of the Idols*. The other one is to confront the literary evidence with all other testimonies to the existence of these cults in the same area and period. A combination of both ways and their respective results may seem fairly conclusive.

Besides Nebo and Bel the *Doctrina Addai* mentions the cult of Bath-Nikkal at Harran, of Atargatis (Tarʿatha) at Mabbug (i.e., Hierapolis), of the Eagle which is worshipped by the Arabs, of Sun and Moon which are venerated by the inhabitants of Harran, and of Stars, Planets and especially of the Bright Star, i.e., Venus, the Morning and Evening Star. This information does not come from Biblical tradition, as might be the case with Nebo and Bel, but is very precise regarding names of deities and places of wor-ship. Sin, the Moon god, Ningal or Nikkal, his female partner, and Bath-Nikkal (i.e., daughter of Nikkal), a local form of Ištar-Venus actually were the most outstanding deities at Harran according to local cuneiform texts and other Akkadian traditions.[2] Without

---

[1] *The Doctrine of Addai*, ed. G. Phillips, 23 (transl.), 24, 11.15f.; Acts of Sharbel; W. Cureton, *Ancient Syriac Documents*, 41; Jacob of Sarug, Homily on the Fall of the Idols, Landersdorfer, Die Götterliste, 13 (transl.), 19, 1.52 (text); Moses of Chorene, *Historia Armeniae*, II, 27; cf. D. Chwolsohn, *Die Ssabier und der Ssabismus*, Petersburg 1856, II, 161f.; I, 450.

[2] cf. E. Dhorme, *Les religions de Babylonie et d'Assyrie*, Paris 1945, 54-60; 68ff., 83ff.; Haussig, *Wörterbuch der Mythologie* I, 1965, 102 s.v. Mondgott; 111 s.v. Ningal.

any doubt Atargatis was the goddess par excellence at Mabbug-Hierapolis. Lucianus devoted a special treatise to her temple and cult at that city, which is situated half-way between Aleppo and Edessa.[3] The mention of the Eagle as a special deity of the Arabs has for a long time not been understood. E. Kirsten in *RAC* s.v. Edessa wrote: "Die Bedeutung des Adlers im Kult von Edessa ist ebenfalls unsicher."[4] F. Cumont inclined to link its cult with the so-called "Aigle funéraire," which takes a central position in his conception of after-life in Roman paganism. F. C. Burkitt proposed to change the text of the *Doctrina Addai* on this point and to read *dšr'* = Dusares, instead of *nšr'* = Eagle.[5] Dusares, the main god of the Arab Nabataeans, would be worshipped at Edessa, if this emendation of the text is accepted. In fact the reading *nšr'* = Eagle is excellent and therefore to be preserved because in the desert-city of Hatra near ancient Assur the cult of *Mar^en Nšr'* = Our Lord the Eagle is attested. Hatra was mainly inhabited by Arab desert dwellers who settled there and brought their cults with them. The Eagle represents the god of heaven, who is distinct from the heavenly bodies which may represent him.[6] Therefore in the Hatrene pantheon there is a clear distinction between *Mar^en Nšr'* = Our Lord the Eagle, and *Mar^en* = Our Lord. The latter title always means Šamaš, the Sun god of Hatra in his function of member of the triad which was worshipped in the main temple of that city. The triad consists of *Mar^en* = Our Lord, *Mart^en* = Our Lady and *Bar-Mar^en* = the Son of Our Lords (i.e., of *Mar^en* and *Mart^en*). Mar^en and Bar-Marên were by far the most important

---

[3] *cf.* G. Goossens, *Hiérapolis de Syrie*. Essai de monographie historique, Louvain 1943, 127ff.; R. A. Oden, *Studies in Lucian's De Syria Dea, Harvard Semitic Monographs* 15, 1977; the text of *De Syria Dea* quoted is that of the Loeb edition Vol. IV, 1925, 338-411. With R. A. Oden, *Studies*, 14ff. the present author is of the opinion that Lucian of Samosata and not an unknown Pseudo-Lucian is the author of *De Syria Dea*. H. W. Attridge - R. A. Oden, *The Syrian Goddess (De Dea Syria) Attributed to Lucian*, Texts and Transl. 9, Missoula 1976 gave a text based on the Loeb and Teubner edition of Lucian and a new English translation.

[4] E. Kirsten, *RAC* IV, sp. 563.

[5] F. C. Burkitt, Appendix to Mr. C. Winckworth's Note, *JThS* 25, 1924, 403.

[6] *cf.* H. Seyrig, Le culte du soleil en Syrie à l'époque romaine, *Syria* 48, 1971, 371f.

divinities of Hatra; in comparison with them Mart^en, most likely
a Moon goddess, is only a shadowy figure, probably "invented" in
order to complete the triad, which is an artificial theological
conception.[7]

The information yielded by the *Doctrina Addai* regarding pagan
cults at other places therefore turns out to be very precise, both in
regard to the deities as well as to the sites at which they were
worshipped. Moreover, the *Doctrina Addai* mentions only those
cities and people with which Edessa and its population actually
were in touch: Hierapolis, Harran and the Arab tribes in the
desert. Harran was very close to Edessa, and half-way between
Edessa and Harran the two cities shared the cult of Sin Mar^elahê
at Sumatar Harabesi, where an Edessean functionary entitled
šlyṭ' d'rb = Ruler of Arab, was in charge of the Arab tribes in that
area.[8] Ties between Hierapolis and Edessa seem to be very close:
in the partly legendary biography of Bardaiṣan of Edessa, the
Aramaic philosopher is said to be educated at Hierapolis. Even if
this part of the biography does not refer to historical facts, the
connection between Edessa and Hierapolis might not be sheer
fantasy. Moreover the cult of Atargatis, the Dea Syria, is attested
at Edessa by other evidence. Besides that the whole passage in the
Doctrina Addai shows a kind of systematic structure. It opens by
mentioning Nebo and Bel as the main gods of Edessa; after them
two female deities, Bath-Nikkal and Atargatis are listed, who
have much in common. The list of deified heavenly bodies like
Sun, Moon, Planets and Stars is headed by the Eagle as god of
heaven, ending with the Venus star, whose cult under different
names is widespread in this area.[9]

---

[7] Drijvers, *ANRW* II, 8, 828ff.; *idem*, Mithra at Hatra?, *cf.* Milik, *Dédicaces faites par des dieux*, 334ff.

[8] *cf.* Drijvers, *Old-Syriac Inscriptions*, 5, 1.3; 7, 1.2; 9, 1.4; 10, 1.4; 23,
1.2; 24, 1.6; Segal, *Anat. Studies* III, 1953, 106f.

[9] *cf.* in general J. Henninger, Zum Problem der Venussterngottheit bei
den Semiten, *Anthropos* 71, 1976, 129ff.; the Venus star is called al-'Uzza,
Balti or *Kwkbta* = the Star; Venus is identified with her star by Isaac of
Antioch, *Hom.* XI, 97-102; Ephrem Syrus, *Hymni contra Haereses* (ed. Beck)
mentions the cult of the Star; VIII, 10-14; IX, 8; XLI, 4; P. de Lagarde,
Gesammelte Abhandlungen, 1866, 14-17 listed all the names of Venus occurring
in Syriac sources.

Against this background we may assume that the cult of Nebo and Bel at Edessa, as stated by the *Doctrina Addai*, does not originate in Jesaja's polemics with these deities in Jes. 46, 1, or does not go back to a general knowledge of traditional Mesopotamian religion, but actually refers to a factual religious situation at Edessa.

This impression is reinforced by the analysis of other literary sources. The *Acts of Sharbel*, partly linked with the *Doctrina Addai* from a literary point of view, mentions a great feast on the eighth of Nisan, i.e., April, during which all gods are brought together at the big altar in the center of the city. The eighth of Nisan falls just in the period, during which at Babylon the great New Year or *akitu* Festival used to be held. Since Nebo and Bel, strictly speaking, are Babylonian deities this date fits very well. Just as in Babylon processions were held during this period of festivities at Edessa, the reminiscence of these pompous processions of the gods is to be found in the words of the *Acts of Sharbel*, where it says: "The whole population assembled near the big altar in the center of the city, just in front of the record-office, where all deities were gathered, adorned and got a place of honour: Nebo and Bel and their companions.[10]

The last text calling for analysis is the *Homily on the Fall of the Idols* by Jacob of Saruğ. After having mentioned Rome and the cult of Jupiter the author continues as follows:

> He (i.e., Satan) put Apollo as idol in Antioch and others with him,
> In Edessa he set Nebo and Bel together with many others.
> He led astray Harran by Sin, Baʿalšamên and Bar Nemrê
> By my Lord with his Dogs and the goddesses Tarʿatha and Gadlat.

---

[10] On the *akitu* festival see: Dhorme, *Les religions*, 242-244; Thureau-Dangin, *Rituels accadiens*, Paris 1921, 86ff. 127ff.; H. Frankfort, *Kingship and the Gods*, Chicago, 1948, 313-333; J. Henninger, *Les fêtes de printemps chez les Sémites et la pâque israélite*, Paris 1975, 87ff. The Chronicle of Joshua the Stylite mentions the celebration of this spring festival at Edessa in 498 A.D., *cf.* W. Wright, *The Chronicle of Joshua the Stylite*, Cambridge 1882, 20f. (transl.), 24, 1.15ff. (text): Whilst these things were taking place, there came round again the time of that festival at which the heathen tales were sung; and the citizens (of Edessa) took even more pains about it than usual. The Syriac phrase translated by Wright as "the heathen tales were sung" refers to the reciting of the myths and should be translated: "that festival at which the pagan myths used to be recited".

At first sight it becomes clear that there is no literary link between
Jacob of Sarug's homily on one hand and on the other the *Doctrina
Addai* and related texts. Jacob's list of divinities worshipped at
Harran is different from the text in the *Doctrina*, although that does
not mean that it must be false. On the contrary, Jacob knows about
the name of Harran's moon god, which name does not occur in the
Doctrina. The cult of Baʿalšamên was widespread in Syria; it occurs
at Palmyra, at Hatra and—according to Isaac of Antioch—at
Nisibis. The cult is attested in the Hauran and in the whole West
Semitic area so that it is not amazing that Baʿalšamên was also
venerated at Harran.[11] With the enigmatic expression "My Lord
with (or: of) his Dogs" the Mesopotamian god Nergal is meant,
who is represented with three dogs in the religious art of Hatra.[12]
We may assume that the expression "My Lord of his Dogs" is a
rendering of the way the god used to be spoken of by the population
of Harran. Therefore it is logical to think that the puzzling Bar
Nemrê is a phrasing of the same kind.[13]

Further Jacob makes mention of Atargatis and Gadlat. The
goddess Atargatis is well-known; Gadlat is in all likelihood a
combination of Gad and Allat. The Aramaic word *Gad* means
Tyche, so that Gadlat is the name of Allat in her function of Tyche
of Harran.[14] The whole list of deities venerated at Harran presents
the same mixture of different origins already detected in the

---

[11] On Baʿalšamên at Palmyra, see P. Collart - J. Vicari, *Le sanctuaire de
Baalshamin à Palmyre* I, Topographie et Architecture, Rome 1969, 201ff.;
at Palmyra Baʿalšamên is called 'lord of the Gods' *cf.* M. Gawlikowski,
Nouvelles inscriptions du Camp de Dioclétien, *Syria* 47, 1970, 316f. and the
like by Isaac of Antioch describing Baʿalšamên's cult at Nisibis, *Hom.* XI,
76; Nisibis was founded by Harran and when Baʿalšamên's cult came to an
end there, it continued at Nisibis; see further D. Sourdel, *Les cultes du
Hauran à l'époque romaine*, Paris 1952, 19-31; *cf.* Ephrem Syrus, *Carmina
Nisibina* I, ed. E. Beck, *CSCO, Script. Syri* 93, IX, 6 on the cult of Baʿalšamên at Nisibis.

[12] Drijvers, Mithra at Hatra?, 171ff. and the literature cited at n. 88
and 89.

[13] For various interpretations of Bar Nemrê see Vandenhoff, Die Götterliste, 24off.; P. Mouterde, La couronne ("nemara"?) d'Atargatis à Délos,
MUSJ 22, 1939, 111ff.

[14] *cf.* Dussaud, *La pénétration*, 111ff.; Sourdel, *Cultes du Hauran*, 49ff.;
J. Starcky, Deux inscriptions palmyréniennes, *MUSJ* 38, 1962, 136; Gadlat
also occurs with Isaac of Antioch, *Hom.* XI, 167-168.

Doctrina Addai where the gods of Edessa are listed. Besides traditional Mesopotamian deities like Sin and Nergal, gods from the West Semitic area like Ba'alšamên and Atargatis are present as well as a goddess like Allat who is mainly venerated by the Arab tribes in the Syrian and Mesopotamian desert. This is also a reason to believe that Jacob's homily offers a true picture of cults and gods at Harran in pagan times.

The same holds true for Antioch, to which he attributes the cult of Apollo as main god. To him the famous sanctuary in the suburb of Daphne was dedicated by Seleucus I, when he founded the city of Antioch.[15] Temple and cult statue of Apollo at Daphne were destroyed by lightning in 362 A.D. (Amm. Marc. XXII, 12, 2), for which the Christians were blamed.[16]

From Jacob's record the only conclusion we can draw is that he truly pictures the main cults of Antioch and Harran in pagan times, so that there is not any reason to reject his statement on Nebo and Bel as main gods of Edessa. It is noteworthy that Nebo holds the first place and evidently is Edessa's most venerated god. This may go back to the times of Rammannirari III (811-782) and especially to Neo-Babylonian times, when the cult of Nebo was very popular and the god was often named before Bel.[17] This short analysis of the extant literary sources on the cult of Nebo and Bel makes clear that these gods actually hold the first place in Edessa's pantheon in pagan times. The other evidence available can corroborate this preliminary conclusion.

Bel and Nebo belonged to the traditional gods of Palmyra; both had a temple in the eastern quarter of the city, where the oldest settlement was near the wadi; Bel occupied the ancient tell on which

---

[15] *cf.* G. Downey, *A History of Antioch in Syria*, Princeton 1961, 68; C. B. Welles, *Royal Correspondence*, 183; R. A. Hadley, Royal Propaganda of Seleucus I and Lysimachus, *JHS* 94, 1974, 58; Libanius, *Or.* 11.94; *Justinus*, 15.4.

[16] Downey, *Antioch*, 595f.; Libanius, *Or.* 60; *cf.* A. J. Festugière, *Antioche païenne et chrétienne*. Libanius, Chrysostome et les moines de Syrie, Paris 1959, 82; *cf.* Julian the Apostate 361 B-C; *Amm. Marc.* XXII, 13, 1-4; John Chrysostome, *Hom.* 534 D-E.

[17] *cf. Roscher's Lexicon* III, 1, Sp. 45ff.; Dhorme, *Les religions*, 154; F. Pomponio, *Nabû.* Il culto e la figura di un dio del Pantheon babilonese ed assiro, *Stud. Sem.* 51, Roma 1978, 99ff.

a new cella was consecrated in 32 A.D. that replaced an older one. Nebo's sanctuary is situated close to it to the north of the wadi, to which its propylaea are oriented. The names of both gods form a good deal of the theophorous elements in the known Palmyrene proper names and they often occur on the tesserae.[18] It is amazing, however, that no pictorial representation of Nebo has until now been found among the many religious reliefs which the city and the Palmyrene has yielded. Although this may be due to pure accident, it is noteworthy that, e.g., Bel appears on many reliefs together with a whole range of other deities, but never with Nebo. It is generally assumed that the name Bel for the main god of Palmyra is due to a strong cultural influence from Babylon on the desert city. Palmyra originally worshipped Bol as its main ancestral god, as appears from Palmyrene proper names among which the theophorous element—bol—often occurs, and from the divine names Yarhibol and Aglibol. Bol should most likely be considered a contracted form of Ba'al and as such is an indication for a West-Semitic layer in Palmyra's religion.[19] The name Nebo certainly is due to the same Babylonian influence; it is still unknown, if a local deity with an autochthonous name is hidden behind Nebo, as is the case with Bel. In all likelihood, however, the cult of Nebo at Palmyra is a borrowing from Babylon. That can explain why—at least at Palmyra—ties between Bel and Nebo are rather loose, except for some tesserae on which they occur together. Bel is the ancient ba'al of the site, the ancestral god; Nebo's cult comes from Babylon and therefore in a way stands apart in the religious life of Palmyra.[20]

The cult of Bel and Nebo is attested at Assur according to Aramaic graffiti of the third century A.D., in which they are named together

---

[18] cf. Seyrig, Bêl de Palmyre, Syria 48, 1971, 85-114; H. Seyrig - R. Amy - E. Will, Le temple de Bel à Palmyre, 2 Vols., BAH 83, Paris 1975 (actually published in 1977), 227-243 (the article of 1971 augmented with some pages on 'personel et rituel de Bel'); A. Bounni, Nabû Palmyrénien, Orientalia 45, 1976, 46-52; M. Gawlikowski, Le Temple palmyrénien, Warszawa 1973, 21ff.; Milik, Dédicaces faites par des dieux, 162ff. deals with the cult of Nebo at Palmyra; Pomponio Nabû, 228ff. lists all Palmyrene proper names composed with Nebo, and so does Bounni, art. cit., 52.

[19] Seyrig, Bêl de Palmyre, 86f.; Le temple de Bel, 228f.; Milik, Dédicaces faites par des dieux, 36.

[20] Only the tesserae 136 and 137 mention Bel and Nebo together.

with, e.g., Nergal. Nebo even had a temple there.[21] The famous
dipinto from Assur written on a big sherd of a *pithos* represents an
offering to *nny mlk' mrtn brt bl mrlh'* = Nanai the Queen, our Lady,
daughter of Bel, Lord of the Gods, and to *brmryn 'lh'* = the Son of
our Lords, the God.[22] Since at Babylon Nebo is the companion of
Nana, it is very tempting to consider Bar-Marên = the Son of our
Lords as a local denomination of Nebo, and consequently Nanai
and Bar-Marên as a divine couple.[23] The whole question will draw
our attention later on. There are no clear proofs for the cult of
Nebo and Bel at Dura-Europos, although they are represented
through theophorous proper names.[24] In the Temple of the Gaddê,
however, the excavators discovered a gypsum statue (0.33 m. high)
of Apollo Citharoedus, who is identified as Nebo by the Palmyrene
inscription on the plinth: *nbw 'bd zbd' br zb(d)l'* = Nebo; Zabda son
of Zab(di)lah made it.[25] Since Nebo usually is assimilated to Apollo,
e.g., in the Palmyrene tesserae and in Greek renderings of Semitic
proper names containing the element *nbw*, this statue of Nebo is a
clear hint to his cult, which even may be linked with the cult of the
Gaddê.[26] The worship of Bel actually can be concealed behind Zeus
Theos and his temple in the eastern part of the city near the citadel,

---

[21] *cf.* W. Andrae - P. Jensen, *Aramäische Inschriften aus Assur und Hatra
aus der Partherzeit*, MDOG 60, 1920, Inscription no. 14, p. 20, *cf.* 29ff.; *cf.*
F. Cumont, *Fouilles de Doura-Europos (1922-1923)*, Paris 1926, 200; P.
Jensen, *Sitzungsber. Berl. Akad.*, 1919, 1048, 1050.

[22] W. Andrae - H. Lenzen, *Die Partherstadt Assur*, WVDOG 57, Leipzig
1933, 109-111; H. Ingholt, *Parthian Sculptures from Hatra*, 12, n. 7 and
fig. 5; Milik, *Dédicaces faites par des dieux*, 344-352.

[23] On Nana see Haussig, *Wörterbuch der Mythologie* I, 108 *s.v.* Nanäja;
Pomponio, *Nabû*, 41-44; 66f.; *cf.* Cumont, *Fouilles de Doura-Europos*, 199.

[24] Cumont, *Fouilles de Doura-Europos*, 199; Pomponio, *Nabû*, 203f. gives
a list of all proper names compounded with Nebo that occur at Dura-Europos.

[25] *Excavations at Dura-Europos, Prelim. Report 7th and 8th season*, 266,
281 (inscription), Pl. XXXVI, 1; *cf.* R. du Mesnil du Buisson, *Inventaire des
inscriptions palmyréniennes de Doura-Europos*, Paris 1939, no. 34; S. B.
Downey, *The Stone and Plaster Sculpture. Excavations at Dura-Europos Final
Report* III, Part I, Fasc. 2, Los Angeles 1977, 64f. no. 48 and 226; the fact
that the god wears a beard suggests a connection with the statue of Apollo-
Nebo at Hierapolis, *cf.* Lucian, *De Syria Dea*, 35, as Susan Downey rightly
remarks.

[26] *cf.* R. A. Stucky, Figures apolliniennes grecques sur des tessères
palmyréniennes, *Syria* 48, 1971, 135-141; A. Bounni, *Orientalia* 45, 1976, 49.

where it was built in a residential block in the beginning of the
second century A.D. The deity is referred to in the Greek inscriptions as Zeus and Zeus Theos, which appellation tells nothing of the
Semitic god whom it conceals. In the wall painting in the naos of
this temple, however, the god appears in military dress with an
orb in his left hand and a spear in his right one before a war chariot
drawn by four horses. Two flying victories offer him a laurel wreath.
His whole representation as a kosmokrator justifies the tentative
conclusion that this god represents Zeus Olympios as well as
Semitic Bel. Whether we are entitled to see in him also Parthian
Ahura-Mazda is very questionable and depends mainly on the
problem whether the cults of Dura-Europos actually represent an
Irano-Semitic syncretism.[27] In the whole surroundings of Dura-
Europos, however, the cult of Bel and Nebo was known and widespread. In the Syriac Acts of Mar Ma'in we are told that King
Shapur I ordered the saint who had taken refuge with a Christian
in the desert of Dura to be arrested because he wanted him to
make offerings to Zeus the great god, to Nanai the great goddess
of the whole world, and to the mighty gods Bel and Nebo. The
same Acts mention an altar dedicated to Nebo on a mountaintop
near the Euphrates where people used to hold festivities with music
and dances in honour of their god.[28]

In Northern Syria too the gods Nebo and Bel were known. The
village Kafr Nebo, situated northwest of Aleppo in the Djebel
Sem'an, is called after the god Nebo and the local temple may
have been dedicated to him.[29] At Tell Arr, north of Aleppo, the
lower part of a basalt relief was found. It shows the claws of an

---

[27] C. B. Welles, The Gods of Dura-Europos, 60f. expressed his doubt of
any real Iranian influences on religion at Dura.

[28] G. Hoffman, *Auszüge aus syrischen Akten persischer Märtyrer, AKM* 7,
3, 1880 (reprint 1966), 29, 31; *cf.* Cumont, *Fouilles de Doura-Europos*, 200;
J. M. Fiey, Ma'in, général de Sapor II, confesseur et évêque, *Le Muséon* 84,
1971, 449; Pomponio, *Nabû*, 231.

[29] *cf.* V. Chapot, Antiquités de la Syrie du Nord, *BCH* 26, 1902, 180ff.;
IGLS 376; see W. K. Prentice, *Syria: Greek and Latin Inscriptions, Northern
Syria*, Leiden 1907, IIIB, 180ff.; this inscription gave rise to long scholarly
discussions on the meaning of Seimio, *cf.* Milik, *Biblica* 1967, 567-570; *idem,
Dédicaces faites par des dieux*, 411ff.; see also W. Fauth, Art. *Simia, RE,*
Suppl. XIV, 1974, 679-701, esp. 682 and below p. 100.

eagle and on the plinth an inscription dated in the 13th year of
Caracalla, i.e., 224 A.D. The text is a dedication to Δὶ Βηλέῳ θεῷ
'Αδαδθελα = Zeus Beleos god of Adadthela. Adadthela seems to
be the name of an otherwise unknown village. The local Ba'al
(or Hadad considering the name of the village?), in Greek called
Zeus, is assimilated to the Babylonian god Bel, which assimilation
appears from the epithet Beleos.[30] As at Palmyra this local Bel is
represented by an eagle. At the same place another basalt relief
came to light picturing an eagle; under its wings a goddess with a
torch is represented to the right, and a god with a curved snake in
his hand to the left symbolising, respectively, moon and sun. It is
a crudely made analogon to the well-known relief on the lintel of
the northern thalamos of Bel's cella at Palmyra and related sculptures at Palmyra and elsewhere.[31]

A fragmentary bas-relief originating from Killiz, about fifty
kilometers northwest of Aleppo, and now in the Musée du Cin-
quantenaire at Bruxelles, shows a priest offering at an incense altar.
To the left and the right huge bulls are still partly visible. The
accompanying inscription informs us that the priest Gaius together
with his wife and eight children dedicated this relief to [β]ηλῷ θεῷ
= to Bel the god. According to the script this relief can go back
to the first century A.D., but may also be of a later date. The bull
is the animal par excellence of the Syrian god Hadad, and most
likely this or a related deity was assimilated to Babylonian Bel at
Killiz.[32] Although the relief is much mutilated the priestly dress is
still to be seen. Gaius wears a long chiton girded with a belt and a
high Phrygian cap. This seems to have been the normal dress of
Syrian priests at that time since the priests of the Dea Syria at
Hierapolis are dressed more or less the same.[33]

---

[30] Published by H. Seyrig, *AS* III, 33ff.; for the epithet Beleos see the
lists in G. Studemund, *Anecdota Varia Graeca musica metrica grammatica*,
Berlin 1886, 265 and 274: from *Anonymi Laurentiani duodecim deorum
epitheta*, p. 282.
[31] *cf.* H. Seyrig, *Syria* 12, 1933, 253ff., 257; see also the eagle relief from
the Ba'alšamên temple at Palmyra, Collart-Vicari, *Le sanctuaire de Baalshamin à Palmyre* I, 162-164; II, Pl. XCVII; Drijvers, *The Religion of
Palmyra*, Pl. XXXII.
[32] *cf.* F. Cumont, *Études syriennes*, 257ff.; *IGLS* 174.
[33] *cf.* R. A. Stucky, Prêtres syriennes II, Hiérapolis, *Syria* 53, 1976, 127-140.

4

On the road from Aleppo to Killiz the village Azaz is situated near the Turkish border. A certain Aurelius made a dedication there to Zeus Megistos, according to an inscription which has been recorded at the beginning of this century. This Zeus Megistos is most likely another local form of the same god to which the Killiz relief was dedicated.[34]

An altar found at Hebbe near Safita in the area of Rouad (ancient Arados) to the west of Homs also mentions the god Bel: Ἐν ἱερῷ βωμ/ῷ Βήλου ὑπὲρ / σωτηρίας Πύ/ρρου καὶ Κάσ/τορος καὶ Π/οπλίου. On the sacred altar of Bel for the well-being of Pyrrhus, of Castor and of Publius.[35] This again is an example of the already-mentioned phenomenon that the local Baʿal was called Bel and besides that, it is noteworthy that the influence of Babylon and the great cities of the Syrian desert reached as far as the West Semitic area. The cult of Bel is reminiscent of that of Apamea attested by an unpublished inscription from this city, by a bilingual dedication found at Vaison in France and by Dio Cassius 79, 8, 5 and 79, 40, 4.[36] The bilingual inscription is written on both sides of an altar now kept in the Museum of St.-Germain; the Greek text on one side, the Latin on the other one. Greek text:

εἰθυντῆρι τύχης / Βηλῷ / Σέξστος θέτο βῶ/μον / τῶν ἐν ᾿Απαμείᾳ / μνησάμενος / λογίων

Latin text: Belus Fortunae rector mentisque magister ara gaudebit quam dedit et voluit.[37]

---

[34] *IGLS* 175: δι μεγιστ(ω)
αὐρηλιος
βουλευ[της και εὐ?]
νοια γυνη [αυτου..]
.νοι εποιη[σαν]

[35] *IGLS* VII, 4049; cf. J.-P. Rey-Coquais, *Arados et sa pérée aux époques grecque, romaine et byzantine, BAH* 97, Paris 1974, 243.

[36] The unpublished inscription from Apamea was mentioned for the first time by J.-P. Rey-Coquais, *IGLS* VII, p. 78; see W. van Rengen, L'épigraphie grecque et latine de Syrie. Bilan d'un quart de siècle de recherches épigraphiques, *ANRW* II, 8, 1977, 43; J.-P. Rey-Coquais, Inscriptions grecques d'Apamée, *AAAS* 23, 1973, 39-84, no. 11, cf. *BE* 1976, 718; J. Ch. Balty - J. Balty, Apamée de Syrie, archéologie et histoire I. Des origines à la Tétrarchie, *ANRW* II, 8, 1977, 129, n. 184.

[37] *CIL* XII, 1277 = *IGRR* I, 14 = *IG* XIV, 2482 = *Dessau*, 4333 + add. p. clxxxii, where rightly εἰθυντῆρι is read instead of εὐθυντῆρι; cf.

An otherwise unknown Sextus thus dedicated an altar as ex-voto to Bel, Guide of Fortune, when the oracle he had got from this god at Apamea turned out to be fulfilled. Sextus therefore must have spent part of his life at Apamea, where the oracle was given to him, and which later on at the time when he stayed in Gaul was fulfilled. It seems most likely that Sextus was a military functionary. So far the Greek text is fully clear. The Latin text is partly a translation from the Greek; partly it should be read in addition to the Greek version. Bel is not only Guide of Fortune but also Lord of the human mind, i.e., he is thought to be immanent in the human mind, or all thoughts and plans of human beings are subject to Bel's will.[38] This Bel will enjoy the altar "which he gave and wanted" (quam dedit et voluit). These last words are at first sight far from explicit and therefore gave rise to several comments and learned remarks. From a grammatical viewpoint the soundest interpretation is that Belus is the subject of *dedit et voluit,* but at least from a logical viewpoint it is remarkable that Bel would have given this altar himself, as Sextus put it, although we may assume that the god wanted him to give it, if the oracle was fulfilled. To solve this problem of a logical shift of subject, which is grammatically illogical, Kaibel wrote: "Belus oraculis Sexto editis in aede Apameensi fortunam ad mentem ejus ita erexerat ut ille dives factus aram quam poni deus jusserat posset ponere," which actually implies a shift of subject. Dessau remarks: "Videtur Sextus ita auxilio Beli compotem voti se factum esse significare," which means that, according to Dessau, Bel is a kind of metaphysical subject of *dedit* although the real subject is Sextus. R. Turcan gives the following translation: "Belus, guide de la Fortune et maître de l'esprit, sera content de l'autel que (le dedicant) a offert et voulu" so that Sextus is subject of both *dedit* and *voluit.* It seems to me that this last interpretation is incorrect. In fact, Bel will enjoy this altar because he wanted it himself, according to the oracle which he gave to Sextus. In my view the clue to the right interpretation of *quam*

R. Turcan, *Les religions de l'Asie dans la vallée du Rhône, EPRO* 30, Leiden 1972, 115ff., who, however, missed Dessau's addendum.

[38] *cf.* Cumont, *Les religions orientales,* 230, n. 77; Turcan, *Les religions de l'Asie,* 116f.

dedit et voluit lies in the reciprocity of Belus and Sextus as expressed
in the Greek text: Sextus put up an altar because that is spoken of
in the oracle of the god as given to him. So Sextus is the subject of
everything expressed in Greek: he put up an altar because he is
mindful of the oracle given at Apamea. The Latin text has Bel as
subject: Bel will enjoy the altar, which he ordered in his oracle and
which he wanted. Therefore *quam dedit et voluit* has the meaning
"which he (i.e., Bel) foretold (i.e., in his oracle) because he wanted
it." [39] Bel as oracle god at Apamea is referred to by Dio Cassius
79, 8, 5 and 79, 40, 4. In his narrative of the murder of Caracalla on
the eighth of April 217, Dio refers to some lines of Euripides quoted
by Caracalla at a symposium which in a way foretold what was to
befall him. Dio compares this quotation to an oracle given by
"Jupiter called Belus, a god worshipped at Apamea in Syria" in
the form of two lines from Homer, Il. II, 478-479. This oracle was
given to Septimius Severus, when he was still a private citizen.
Later, when he had become emperor, he consulted the oracle of Bel
at Apamea again and at that time the god gave him this response:
"Thy house shall perish utterly in blood" (Eur., *Phoen.* 20, freely
rendered). It seems that the priests of Bel at Apamea very often
made use of Homer's verses in giving their oracles. Dio refers in 79,
40, 4 to an oracle in the form of Il. VIII, 102-103 [40] given to Macrinus
which foretold his being defeated in 218 by the False Antoninus.

The local god of Shaqqa in the Hauran was also assimilated to
Bel according to a Greek inscription found there. It mentions a
feast organised in honour of an emperor (Antoninus?) ἐν ἱερῷ θεοῦ
Βήλου—in the sanctuary of the god Bel.[41]

An inscription, dated in the times of Alexander Severus (11th of
April 228) and originating from Aboukir in Egypt, commemorates

---

[39] For *dare* with the meaning *foretell* see *Harpers' Latin Dictionary*, 604,
s.v. *do*, G.: to announce, to tell and *Liv.* 33, 13: *Saepe dedit sedem notas
mutantibus urbes*, i.e. foretold!

[40] For the use of Homer's verses in oracles see: H. W. Parke - P. E. W.
Warnell, *The Delphic Oracle*, Oxford 1956, *passim*; for the spiritual background: F. Buffière, *Les mythes d'Homère et la pensée grecque*, Paris 1956;
Hans Lewy, *Chaldaean Oracles and Theurgy*. Mysticism Magic and Platonism
in the Later Roman Empire, Le Caire 1956.

[41] Sourdel, *Les cultes du Hauran*, 44; M. Dunand, Nouvelles inscriptions,
RB 1932, 399-416, No. 8b = *SEG* VII, 1007.

the dedication of a relief or statue of "the god of my fathers Heracles Belos the Invincible" to Zeus Helios the Great (God) Sarapis by a certain Marcus Aurelius Maximus, a Syrian from Ascalon.[42] Leaving aside all other questions connected with this inscription it seems clear that the god Heracles from Ascalon got the epithet Bel evidently for being the main god of that city. It is not really an example of assimilation of Heracles to Bel, but rather an indication that the title Bel—Lord as head of a pantheon—could be given to any other godhead. The god Heracles from Ascalon is the Greek appearance of the Semitic god Melqart, the city god of Ascalon.[43] The same phenomenon is attested by Plinius, N.H. V, 19, where he mentions a river god near Ptolemais-Akko called *rivus Pacida sive Belus*. A god Pakidas (Παχειδᾶ) is one of the main deities at Gerasa, the city of the Dekapolis, evidently an appellation of the god Zeus, since he together with Hera forms a couple; Pakidas is a Greek transcription of the Semitic word *pqyd'* = supervisor, governor, which is an excellent title for a cosmokrator who rules over starry constellations and human activities.[44]

We have therefore ample evidence for the spread of Bel and Nebo in the Syrian area, where Northern Syria in particular seems most to favour these gods. In fact we do not deal with the Babylonian cults as such, but we may assume that at least the name Bel replaced the name of a local Ba'al due to a strong influence of the ancient city and culture of Babylon. Most Bels actually are an *interpretatio Babyloniaca* of a local deity. Whether the same is the case with Nebo is dubious. On the one hand it is likely that a local Ba'al and his divine son were interpreted as Bel and Nebo, on the other, it is also possible that the cult of Nebo was widespread especially in northern Syria since Neo-Babylonian times.

---

[42] Seymour de Ricci, Bulletin épigraphique de l'Égypte romaine, *Archiv f. Papyrusf.* 2, 1903, 450, no. 87, for the identification of Sarapis with Helios see: W. Hornbostel, *Sarapis*. Studien zur Überlieferungsgeschichte, den Erscheinungsformen und Wandlungen der Gestalt eines Gottes, 1973, 23.

[43] *cf.* Seyrig, Les grands dieux de Tyr à l'époque grecque et romaine, *Syria* 40, 1963, 19ff. = *AS* VI, 121ff.; R. Dussaud, *Syria* 25, 1946-48, 205-230; Haussig, *Wörterbuch der Mythologie* I, 297f. *s.v. Melqart*.

[44] *cf.* C. B. Welles in: C. H. Kraeling (ed.), *Gerasa*. City of the Decapolis, New Haven 1938, 383f., Inscr. No. 17, where Pakidas forms a couple with Hera.

Certainty cannot be reached, as proofs are completely lacking. From the whole foregoing evidence we are fully entitled to assume that Nebo and Bel were indeed the main gods of Edessa in pagan times. The name Bel may have replaced a local ba'al; the cult of Nebo can be an offspring of the original cult of the god of Borsippa or the disguise of a local *dieu-fils*.

From older Aramaic inscriptions we get the impression that the cult of Bel and Nebo found strong adherence among the Aramaic-speaking population in the whole Near East and Egypt. An ostracon from Elephantine in Egypt dating from the sixth or fifth century B.C. lists the four main deities of the Babylonian pantheon:

> to my brother Haggai your brother
> Yarḥw. The well-being of my brother
> (may) Bel and Nebo, Šamaš and Nergal (foster it ?) [45]

Already in the eighth century B.C. the Aramaic inscriptions from Sfire mention the same four gods as witnesses to the treaty between Matti'el, King of Arpad and Bar-Gayah, King of Katikka.[46] It is noteworthy that Sfire is situated about twenty-five kilometers northeast of Aleppo, and therefore in an area where the cult of Bel and Nebo is attested to by later inscriptions from Roman times.

At Elephantine there used to be a Nebo temple as appears from the so-called Hermopolis letters. This collection of eight Aramaic letters from the fifth century B.C. found at Hermopolis contains private correspondence of soldiers from the garrison at Elephantine staying at Hermopolis and writing letters home, which however never arrived there. Letter I opens with a solemn salutation to the temple of Nebo: *šlm byt nbw* = hail, temple of Nebo. In other letters of this collection the opening sentence starts with a salutation to the temple of Banit or of Beth'el or of the Queen of Heaven. An Aramaic epitaph found in the necropolis at Saqqarah mentions a priest of Nebo called Ša'il: *lš'yl kmr' zy nbw* = to Ša'il the priest of

---

[45] A. Dupont-Sommer, *RHR* 128, 1944, 28ff.; *cf.* J. T. Milik, *Biblica* 48, 1967, 557; *ANET*, 491.

[46] *KAI*, No. 222, LL. 8-12; *cf.* J. A. Fitzmyer, *The Aramaic Inscriptions of Sefîre*, Rome 1967, 33-39 for a detailed commentary of this passage.

Nebo.[47] Moreover there is a considerable number of proper names found at Elephantine, which contain the theophorous element *nbw*, whereas the element *bl* also occurs.[48] We do not, however, have any evidence for a temple of Bel at Elephantine.

An Aramaic funerary inscription from the fifth century B.C. found at ancient Daskyleion in northwestern Anatolia invokes Bel and Nebo in order to protect the tomb. The inscription is carved on one of three funerary stelae with reliefs found reused in a Byzantine tomb. The inscription reads:

1. These are the reliefs of 'Elnap son of 'ŠY.
2. It was he who made (them) for his funerary monument. I adjure thee.
3. By Bel and Nabu, who(ever) passes by this way.
4. Let no one do harm (to my tomb).[49]

According to his name 'Elnap son of 'ŠY could have been an Aramaized Arab from somewhere in the Syrian or Arab desert. The script of the inscription is close to that of the Tema Stele dating from the fifth or fourth century B.C. and coming from the oasis of Tema in Northern Arabia.[50] In all likelihood, therefore, the Daskyleion inscription should be considered another example

---

[47] E. Bresciani - M. Kamil, *Le lettere aramaiche di Hermopoli*, *AAL* 1966, Serie VIII, Vol. XII, Fasc. 5; republished by B. Porten, *Jews of Elephantine and Arameans of Syene*. Aramaic Texts with Translation, Jerusalem 1974, 151-165. Milik, *Biblica* 48, 1967, 556ff.; Grelot, *Documents araméens d'Égypte*, Paris 1972, 150-168; N. Aimé-Giron, *Textes araméens d'Égypte*, 1931, 98-100, No. 99; *cf.* B. Porten, *Archives from Elephantine*. The Life of an ancient Jewish Military Colony, Berkeley-Los Angeles 1968, 165ff.

[48] See the names listed by Porten, *Archives from Elephantine*, 166, n's 52, 53, 54; the element Bel occurs in the proper name Reʿibel, *cf.* Cowley, *Aramaic Papyri of the Fifth Century B.C.*, Oxford 1923, no. 15, 1.39 and in Belibni, in: *idem*, no. 55, 14.

[49] First published by A. Dupont-Sommer, *CRAI* 1966, 44-57; translation by F. M. Cross, An Aramaic Inscription from Daskyleion, *BASOR* 184, Dec. 1966, 7-10; *cf.* M. Delcor, *Le Muséon* 80, 1967, 301-314; E. Lipiński, *Studies in Aramaic Inscriptions and Onomastics* I, Leuven 1975, 150-153 gives a partly different interpretation of this inscription.

[50] *cf.* Cross, *art. cit.* 9, n. 17 and 18; the use of *npš* = funerary monument also indicates a Syrian or Arab origin, *cf.* M. Gawlikowski, *Monuments funéraires de Palmyre*, Warszawa 1970, 22ff.: Monuments *nefeš*; for the Tema stele see *KAI*, 228-230 with commentary.

of the spread of Bel's and Nebo's cult in the Syrian desert, since
'Elnap son of 'ŠY, who died at Daskyleion, invoked the gods of
his native country in this funerary text.

Other Aramaic inscriptions from Persian times, which were
found at Arebsun in Cappadocia also mention the name of Bel.
From the entire content of these inscriptions, however, it becomes
clear that they do not deal with the cult of the Babylonian god
Bel, but offer an example of the assimilation of Ahura-Mazda to
the Semitic deity. Some of the nine texts inscribed on a basalt block
and belonging to very worn reliefs are apparently not written in a
Semitic language but represent Persian words in an Aramaic
transcription. They should therefore be evaluated as an instance
of the spread of Persian Mazdaism into Asia Minor.[51]

However scanty this material may seem, it gives an idea of the
spread of the main Babylonian cults from the fifth century B.C.
on, and even earlier, into the Syrian area where they are attested
among the Aramaic-speaking population living there and abroad
in Egypt and Anatolia. It is difficult to decide whether in all
cases we actually come across the Babylonian cult as such, or just
a form of assimilation of local deities to Babylon's gods. It seems
reasonable, however, to assume that at least at Edessa the cult of
Nebo and Bel belonged to the traditional religion in an area under
strong influence from the great Mesopotamian centers. In this
respect Edessa must be compared to Harran, Assur, Hatra and other
cities, in which traditional Mesopotamian religion continued to exist
into Christian times. Since Nebo consistently is named first, followed
by Bel, he unquestionably seems to be the main god of the city.

This conclusion is confirmed by Edessean proper names so far
known. Some of them are composed with the theophorous element
bl, e.g., BLBN', BLY, BLŠW, ZLBL. Names composed with *nbw*
are more rare, but 'BDNBW occurs as the name of a priest in the
Doctrina Addai, and *brnbs*, a grecised form of Syriac *brnb'*, on a
mosaic.[52]

---

[51] *KAI* 264; *RÉS* 3, 1785 covers 9 different texts; Seyrig, *AS* III, 33 wrongly adduces these texts as other examples of the spread of Babylonian Bel.

[52] BLBN': Drijvers, *Old-Syriac Inscriptions*, 24 1.3; 25 1.2; BLY: 46
LL. 1, 3, 11, 14; BLŠW; P. 1.5, 29; ZLBL: 65 L. 2; *Doctrina Addai*, ed.

Although the Edessean gods just might have their names in common with the Babylonian ones, there are some hints that they also present the same characteristic features and personalities as the Babylonian deities are supposed to have. Since from this period, however, no myths or rituals have been preserved which can be compared to the Babylonian sources, we are mainly dependent on iconographical sources to grasp some idea of the gods' characters, and in the case of Edessa even the iconography of Nebo and Bel is non-existent there. We pass on, therefore, first to a description of what is generally known from Babylonian Bel and Nebo and return after that to the evidence in our area and period. Bel, Lord, is the title par excellence of the Babylonian city god Marduk, who resided there in his temple, Esagil, overlooking all actions of the city and its kings. In the times of King Hammurapi of Babylon (eighteenth century B.C.) the god became the main god of the whole pantheon and as such played the first role in the Babylonian epic of creation. He was given all power over mankind by Anum and Enlil; he overcame the female chaos monster Tiamat, and he created the ordered human world and kosmos. The description of Bel's fight with Tiamat is especially interesting for several reasons. Armed with bow and quiver with a mace and a net "The four winds he stationed that nothing of her might escape" (Tabl. IV, 41). He sent forth the winds he had brought forth.....he raised the floodstorm, his mighty weapon; he mounted the storm-chariot irresistible (and) terrifying. He harnessed (and) yoked to it a team-of-four, the Killer, the Relentless, the Trampler, the Swift (Tabl. IV, 47-52). Bel appears in this context as a cosmic ruler to whom all elements are subject. After having defeated the chaos monster Tiamat "He split her like a shellfish into two parts: Half of her he set up and ceiled it as sky, pulled down the bar and posted guards. He bade them not to allow her waters to escape. He crossed the heavens and surveyed the regions (Tabl. IV, 137-141). This work of creation is followed by the ordering of the world of stars and planets: "He constructed stations for the great gods, Fixing

---

Phillips, 32; BRNBS, 46, 1.11., *cf.* S. Brock, *JThS* 25, 1974, 93-98, who suggested the reading *br ʿbsmyʾ* instead of *brnbs*, although Euting clearly read this last name.

their astral likeness as constellations. He determined the year by designating the zones: He set up three constellations for each of the twelve months. After defining the days of the year (by means) of (heavenly) figures, He founded the station of Nebiru (i.e., the planet Jupiter) to determine their (heavenly) bands, That none might transgress or fall short" (Tabl. V, 1/=7). Hereafter Ea formed mankind according to Bel's plans out of Kingu's blood, since Kingu made Tiamat to rebel against the great gods. First charge of mankind was to serve the gods "That they might be at ease" (Tabl. VI, 8). The great gods very pleased with their deliverance from the chaos then decided to build a shrine for Marduk at Babylon and in two years "they raised high the head of Esagila equaling Apsu" (Tabl. VI, 62) and then the gods "took their seats, they set up festive drink, sat down to a banquet. After they had made merry within it, in Esagila, the splendid, had performed their rites, The norms had been fixed (and) all (their) portents, All the gods apportioned the stations of heaven and earth." (Tabl. VI, 74-79). Then the gods in their Assembly praised Bel for all he has done and proclaimed his fifty names: He whose ways are glorious, whose deeds are likewise.[53]

These extensive quotations give a rather precise idea of Bel's personality. He is the besieger of the chaos, the divine orderer of the human world and the cosmos who rules the universe through stars, and to whom all cosmic phenomena are subject. He is more a formalized conception, a symbol of power and order, than a personal god, with whom beings may have a personal relation. He virtually embodies "law and order" and that aspect implies strong ties with the Babylonian kingdom and the idea of kingship.[54] It therefore is not astonishing that the god Bel and all other gods of Babylon with the king and the priests play the main roles in the ritual of the New Year Festival, which was held from the second to the twelfth day of Nisan, the first month of the year. It was

---

[53] The epic of creation quoted according to J. B. Pritchard, *ANET*, 61ff. translation by E. A. Speiser; cf. A. Heidel, *The Babylonian Genesis*, 1951, H. Frankfort, *Kingship and the Gods*, 313ff.; Dhorme, *Les religions*, 139ff.; Haussig, *Wörterbuch der Mythologie* I, 121ff. s.v. Schöpfung.

[54] H. Frankfort, *Kingship and the Gods*, 231ff.; A. L. Oppenheim, *Ancient Mesopotamia*, 1964, 98ff.

actually the feast of the spring equinox.[55] The whole ritual, which bears close resemblance to the court ceremonial, was intended to consolidate the order in the cosmos by establishing it again. The Epic of Creation was recited and all the gods were assembled in the feast house of *akitu* situated outside the city. Leaving aside the whole elaborate ritual of washings, absolutions, prayers, offerings to the gods, etc., in which the king and the highpriest played a central role, one of the main features of the feast was a solemn procession of all the statues of gods and goddesses through certain streets of the city to an out-of-town sanctuary (*akitu*). "In this characteristic way the cultic relationship between the city and its god was formalized, manifesting itself at cyclical festivals when the pageantry of the temple was displayed for the citizenry.." [56] The common citizens were only onlookers in these public ceremonies, as they are onlookers in royal ceremonies nowadays. We do not know anything about their personal feelings towards the world of the gods and their *faits et gestes*, since these feelings are of no importance in public religious performances, which actually are demonstrations of divine and kingly power and order. The common citizen's life was determined more by socio-economic than by cultic coordinates and the whole socio-economic system of these urban societies was guaranteed by the proper functioning of royal and divine ritual in the sanctuaries, which were moreover important economic elements in the whole urban social system. We should not be misled by all the complicated myths and rituals having to do with the gods, their doings and needs. These texts belong more to the field of literary production than to that of real myth. In a civilization in which the art of writing was esteemed so much, all these stories are the result of the literary creativeness of the priestly caste, which was the most educated and learned in society: the sanctuaries had an essential share in learning in Mesopotamia and most of the myths are typical products of a learned and sophisticated group, used to endless reflection and observation of what was happening in their world.

---

[55] Dhorme, *Les religions*, 242; Henninger, *Les fêtes de printemps*, 87-100; Frankfort, *Kingship and the Gods*, 313-333.
[56] Oppenheim, *Ancient Mesopotamia*, 187.

The same holds true for the elaborate ritual performed at the temples and during public festivities. The ritual is very often an artificial elaboration of a simpler pattern and, as such, another proof of the enormous influence of the priests, who were constantly busy with enhancing their prestige and establishing the impression of their usefulness and importance. Very often we get the impression that, e.g., the whole complicated ritual at the New Year's Festival, in which the highpriest and the king are the main actors, is only meant to enhance their prestige with the common people. A good example of such a ritual is the ceremonial enacted on the morning of the eighth day of the New Year's Festival.[57] Early in the morning the image of the servant god Papsukkal descends into the court-yard of the temple and takes a position in front of the god Anu. Other images of the deities emerge from their temples and take their places too. Then a complicated ceremonial of offering water to the gods for their morning toilette takes place, followed by the serving of meat and other activities. "These *salutationes matutinae* reappear in the court ceremonials of Byzantium and Europe (the *lever du roi*) and hence must likewise have been practiced at the Babylonian court."

The close ties between the gods on one hand and the king on the other also explain that the Achaemenid King Cyrus paid honour to Bel and Nebo, when he entered the city of Babylon in 539 B.C.: I am Cyrus, king of the world, great king, legitimate king, king of Babylon, king of Sumer and Akkad....., whose rule Bel and Nebo love, whom they want as king to please their hearts.[58] So the cult of Bel continued to exist during Achaemenid times and also in the times of the Seleucides. In fact most of the cuneiform texts which inform us on the ritual in the temples and on the myths date from Seleucid times! Antiochus I Soter (281-260 B.C.) restored the Esagil of Marduk-Bel at Babylon and the temple of Nebo, the Ezida, at Borsippa and directed a long prayer to the last-named

---

[57] *cf.* Thureau-Dangin, *Rituels accadiens* 86ff.; 127ff.; Dhorme, *Les religions*, 243; Oppenheim, *Ancient Mesopotamia*, 193; Frankfort, *Kingship and the Gods*, 325f.

[58] *ANET*, 316.

god.[59] Berossos, a priest of Bel at Babylon dedicated his book on Babylonian history and religion to this Seleucid sovereign, who quite evidently had great interest in Babylonian traditions. The fragments of Berossos' *Babyloniaka*, Liber I, dealing with the primeval history, are in complete accordance with the whole course of events as described by the Babylonian epic of creation. The remarkable figure of Oannes, pictured by Berossos as partly a fish and partly a human being, hides the god Ea, who in certain aspects is a kind of culture hero. He teaches all kinds of crafts, among them the art of writing and city building. The god Ea, "surpassing in wisdom, accomplished, resourceful, the all-wise," is superseded by his son Marduk-Bel, in the Babylonian epic of creation, but most likely he originally was the god, who had the foremost place.[60] After the description of the chaos embodied by all kinds of abnormal animals of which the images are on view in Bel's temple at Babylon, Berossos mentions the defeat of this chaos (Θαλάτθ = Tiamat) by Belos, who stormed against it and split it into two parts. From one part he made the heaven, from the other the earth. Even the creation of mankind from the blood of Kingu mixed with earth is recorded by Berossos, as he also tells that Belos fixed the stars, sun, moon and the five planets.[61]

We are safe to assume that Bel's character as a besieger of the chaotic forces in the world, as a bringer of law and order embodied in the fixed course of stars and planets was a permanent aspect of his personality: he is actually the symbolized order in the world, more an idea or divine conception than a clear-cut outlined divine person, to whom personal feelings of joy or grievance may be directed.

Besides Bel, Nebo is the most important god of Babylon, originally the city-god of Borsippa near Babylon, where his temple

[59] F. H. Weissbach, *Die Keilinschriften der Achämeniden, Vorderasiatische Bibliothek* 47, Leipzig 1911, 132ff.; Dhorme, *Les religions*, 154; J. Bidez, Les écoles chaldéennes sous Alexandre et les Séleucides, *AIPh* 3, 1935, *Volume offert à Jean Capart*, 45.

[60] On Oannes see W. G. Lambert, *JCS* 16, 1962, 74; W. Hallo, *JAOS* 83, 1963, 176 n. 79; *cf.* Oppenheim, *Ancient Mesopotamia*, 195, and P. Schnabel, *Berossos und die babylonisch-hellenistische Literatur*, Leipzig 1923, 253; Haussig, *Wörterbuch d. Mythologie*, 117 *s.v. Oannes*.

[61] *cf.* Schnabel, *Berossos*, 255 after Polyhistor quoted by Eusebius, *Chronicon* ed. Karst, 7, 29-9, 2.

Ezida stood. In the ceremonial of the New Year's Festival Nebo's
role is nearly as important as that of Bel. According to Babylonian
theology Nebo is Bel's son, and during the festivities in the month
of Nisan Nebo's image is brought to his father's sanctuary, where
he has his own chapel. Nabu is the divine scribe par excellence and
thus the patron of the scribes, who formed a special group in the
highly bureaucratic Mesopotamian society.[62] Scribal schools were
attached to the palaces and the temples and the scribes played an
important role in the administration of society as executed by the
king, his officials and the priests. As a divine scribe Nebo is the
inventor of script and the holder of the tablets of destiny, of divine
laws valid for everybody. As divine destiny fixes the length of
human life, which in fact is completely dependent on the will of
the gods, Nebo also is a life-giving god, who even can raise the
dead and gives fertility.[63] So Nebo is a kind of organizer of human
life, who carries through what the great gods, and among them his
father Bel, decided in the first place. So he can give oracles, since
divine wisdom is his privilege. One can imagine that Nebo is closer
to humanity—unlike Bel, who is the kosmokrator reigning from
a great distance. Especially in Neo-Babylonian times the cult of
Nebo predominates over that of Bel, as already becomes clear
from the names of the Neo-Babylonian kings, who nearly all are
composed with the name of the divine scribe. But also during the
reign of Sargon of Akkad (721-705) and Esarhaddon (680-669)
Nebo had the most outstanding place among all the gods and was
listed first.

Just as Bel is identified with the planet Jupiter, so Nebo personifies Mercurius; even his name, meaning "shining" or "brilliant,"
seems to denote this planet.[64] Iconographically Nebo is characterized by the stylus, which he often bears in his left hand. On the

---

[62] See Oppenheim, *Ancient Mesopotamia*, 228ff.; on Nebo see now F.
Pomponio, *Nabû. Il culto e la figura di un dio del Pantheon Babilonese ed
assiro. Stud. Sem.* 51, Roma 1978: esp. 177ff. on Nabû as divine scribe.

[63] Dhorme, *Les religions*, 152; Pomponio, *Nabû*, 189ff.

[64] Dhorme, *Les religions*, 151; for *nabû* = to shine see: AHw *s.v. nabû
IV* and *nebû III*; the question of the etymology of Nabû's name is dealt
with by Pomponio, *Nabû*, 5ff.; *cf.* W. Eilers, *Sinn und Herkunft der Planetennamen, SBAW.PPH* 1975, 5, München 1976, 44ff.

kudurru and on seals just the stylus may denote the god as a symbol typical of him.[65] It is noteworthy that the size of this stylus in comparison to the god who uses it, and to the purpose it is meant for, is much too large, so that this useful utensil looks more like a spear or an arrow than like a stylus. This may be due to the importance attached to this characteristic symbol, but it may have given rise to confusion and to an assimilation of the stylus to the arrow of Apollo, usually borne in the left hand too. As has been known for a long time Nebo was assimilated to the Greek gods Apollo and Hermes-Mercurius.[66]

The cult of Nebo at Babylon surely continued to exist during Seleucid times. As already mentioned before, Antiochus I Soter directed a long prayer to Nebo asking for the safety and long life of his dynasty "through your sublime sceptre, which fixes the limits of heaven and earth." The "sublime sceptre" clearly denotes Nebo's stylus, which the god uses to fix the destiny of men.

The foregoing surely does not give a complete survey of everything known about Bel and Nebo in their Babylonian context; it may, however, give an idea of Mesopotamian religious traditions, in which the display of royal and divine power with all ceremonial connected to it warrants and ensures an orderly, protected and lucky human life within the borders set to it. Leaving aside for a moment all literary flounces and furbelows in myths and rituals, we are left with the strong impression that the gods, and among them Nebo and Bel in the first instance, represent an overwhelming transcendental power, which governs and orders the whole cosmos and human life in combined action with the king, the priests and the magistrates. Common people are only onlookers gazing at that which is shown to them and that which is supposed to protect their lives. Although the relationship between Bel and Nebo is not clear in all aspects—Nebo is considered Bel's son, but very often they are adorned with the same stereotype epitheta—it is quite certain that Bel's position is more that of a remote governor of the world,

---

[65] cf. *Roscher's Lexikon*, s.v. *Nebo*; G. Hoffmann, *ZA* 11, 251; Dhorme, *Les religions*, 171; Pomponio, *Nabû*, 207ff.

[66] *Strabo XVI*, 1, 7; Plinius, *N.H.* II, 39; cf. Bidez, Les écoles chaldéennes, 74; Pomponio, *Nabû*, 226f.

whereas Nebo is more the skillful translator and bearer of the will of the gods to mankind. As a divine scribe he is the patron of all kinds of arts and crafts and the prophesier of the future and may therefore be closer to men. Actually he is a teacher and protector of cultural activities, who gives lives and teaches the right path to follow.

Insofar as there is any evidence available the foregoing impression is corroborated by what we know from much later times. The iconography of Bel, extant at Palmyra, pictures the god as a real kosmokrator. The northern thalamos of Bel's temple is very instructive in this aspect. Its ceiling represents Bel as Jupiter, surrounded by the four other planets and sun and moon, each of them occupying sixty degrees of a circle. In a second circle the signs of the Zodiac are pictured. In the four corners of this astrological bas-relief the four winds are represented as eagles with outstretched wings. It is an exact rendering of Bel, as he is described in the Babylonian epic of creation. The lintel of the same northern thalamos bears a relief of an eagle with outstretched wings. To the right the sun god Yarhibol stands. Under the right wing the sun is again represented amidst a number of stars. As the left part of the lintel is heavily damaged nothing has been left there, but we may assume that the moon god Aglibol was depicted there and the moon with an equal number of stars. A curved snake flanked by six globes, which is pictured just below the eagle, surely represents the planetary system: six planets and the snake symbolizing the sun. The whole relief renders the conception of Bel as kosmokrator governing stars, planets, sun and moon.[67] One of the beams, which in Bel's temple at Palmyra were supporting the ceiling of the peristyle, is decorated with a bas-relief of a fight of the gods with a mythical animal, a snake-tailed monster. The whole scene is reminiscent of the fight of Bel with Tiamat as recorded in the Babylonian epic of creation, although it is not an exact rendering of the primeval myth.[68] Berossos' version, however, is another

[67] H. Seyrig, AS I, 102-109 and AS IV, Preface for some corrections; idem, Bêl de Palmyre, Syria 48, 1971, 85-114; P. Brykczyński, Astrologia w Palmyrze, Studia Palmyreńskie VI, 1975, 52ff.; Seyrig-Amy-Will, Le temple de Bel à Palmyre, 45, 83 and Album 53, 56, 57, 58, 59; Pl. 27; fig. 22.

[68] H. Seyrig, AS II, 20-27, Pl. XX, Pl. XXIV, 1; D. Schlumberger, L'Orient hellénisé, Paris 1970, 85, 89; E. Will, Le relief cultuel gréco-romain.

example of the various ways in which this myth could be reported; hence the conclusion is justified that the scene of the beam of Bel's Temple is such a variant of the well-known story of Bel's fight with the chaos monster. The cella of Bel's Temple at Palmyra, which replaced an older building, was consecrated on the sixth of Nisan of 32 A.D., which date again brings us into the Babylonian context of the New Year's Festival celebrated in that month.[69]

It is not only the Palmyrene Bel that has close connections with the Babylonian god; Zeus Theos in his temple at Dura-Europos also is represented as a victorious kosmokrator. The painting on the rear wall of his naos pictures Zeus Theos at the very moment in which he is crowned by two flying victories. As a ruler of the world he holds a globe in his left hand. His head shows a halo and he stands beside his chariot drawn by four horses. Is this not an exact rendering, in a Hellenistic style strongly reminiscent of Palmyrene art, of Babylonian Bel riding his storm-chariot drawn by a team-of-four, "his head turbaned with his fearsome halo?" [70] The painting in the *naos* pictures Bel's victory over chaos; all attributes symbolize this, and the chariot in particular, which makes clear that the victory is won after a fight. Every spectator is reminded of this famous myth which laid the foundations for an ordered human society.

For Nebo nearly all iconographical evidence is lacking in later times. The excavations in his temple at Palmyra have not yielded any relief of the god so that we are completely dependent on the *tesserae* to grasp his personality. These present him in different ways, as Apollo with the lyre, either dressed *à la grecque*, or in an Oriental style, or as an Oriental god with a long tunic and a *kalathos*.[71] At

---

Contribution à l'histoire de l'art de l'empire romain, Paris 1955, 234ff.; Seyrig et al., *Le temple de Bel à Palmyre*, 87, Album 90, Pl. 44; see now R. du Mesnil du Buisson, Le bas-relief du combat de Bêl contre Tiamat dans le temple de Bêl à Palmyre, *AAAS* 26, 1976, 83ff.

[69] *Inventaire des inscriptions de Palmyre* IX, 1; *cf.* Gawlikowski, *Le temple palmyrénien*, 68; a Greek inscription mentions a holocaust offered on "the good day" i.e. the sixth of Nisan, *cf. Inventaire* 6, 13; Seyrig, *AS* I, 126ff.

[70] *cf. Dura-Europos, Prel. Report seventh and eighth season*, 196ff. and Fig. 50; *The Babylonian epic of creation*, IV, 49-60.

[71] *cf.* A. Bounni, Nabû Palmyrénien, *Or.* 45, 1976, 49f.; R. du Mesnil du Buisson, *Les tessères et les monnaies de Palmyre*, Paris 1962, 285ff.; both

Dura-Europos, as we have already seen, the god is also pictured as Apollo.[72] Apollo, who played an important role in the sanctuary at Atargatis, the Dea Syria, at Hierapolis, and whose image is described at length by Macrobius, *Saturn.*, I, 17, 66sqq., is very likely also the Babylonian god Nebo, worshipped as Apollo, giver of oracles.[73] A statue, which fully answers to the description given by Macrobius, turned up in the excavations at Hatra; it is usually called Assurbel, but its appearance at least is in complete accordance with the image of Apollo which stood near the entrance of the sanctuary of Hierapolis.[74]

A remarkable feature of Apollo's image at Hierapolis according to Macrobius' statement is a female figure lying at his feet. The Hatra statue reveals the true identity of this figure: she wears a mural crown and therefore she is a *Tyche*. The same *Tyche* occurs on a bas-relief from Northern Mesopotamia representing Atargatis and Hadad, the gods of Hierapolis, sitting, respectively, to the right and to the left of the *semeion*, Atargatis between her lions, Hadad between his bulls. To the left of this well-known scene Nebo-

---

representations recall the Mesopotamian iconography of Nabû, *cf.* Pomponio, *Nabû*, 215ff., who discusses a seal picturing Nabû.

[72] *cf. Dura-Europos, Prel. Report seventh and eighth season*, 266 and Pl. XXXVI, 1; the statuette is a crude imitation of a familiar Apollo Citharoedus type and not, as stated in *CRAI* 1935, 13ff. and *Revue des Études sémitiques* 100, 1936, 37f., a tablet at which, as god of writing, he points with his finger; G. Goossens, Hiérapolis de Syrie, 115 is wrong on this point ("On peut se le figurer, comme telle statue d'époque hellénistique, trouvée à Doura-Europos, tenant ses attributs, la tablette et le style"); see Downey, *The Stone and Plaster Sculpture*, 64f.

[73] Seyrig, *Syria* 49, 1972, 104-108; Lucian, *De Syria Dea*, 35; J. Pirenne, *Sacra Pagina* I, 291; R. Dussaud, Peut-on identifier l'Apollon barbu de Hiérapolis de Syrie?, *RHR* 126, 1943, 128-149, identified Apollo with El, which is certainly wrong.

[74] *cf.* Seyrig, *Syria* 49, 1972, 107f.; H. Lenzen, *Arch. Anz.* 1955, 339f.; fig. 2-3; R. du Mesnil du Buisson, De Shadrafa, Dieu de Palmyre, à Ba'al Shamîn, dieu de Hatra, aux IIe et IIIe siècles après J.-C., *MUSJ* 38, 1962, 149ff., Pl. I; Milik, *Dédicaces faites par des dieux*, 337ff. reads Iššar-Bel instead of Aššur-Bel and considers it a goddess, which may be true. The only reason for identifying the statue with a god Aššur-Bel are two inscriptions from the same fifth sanctuary where the statue was found, mentioning a god or goddess ʾšrbl as giver of honorific statues, no's 35 and 38, see A. Caquot, *Syria* 30, 1953, 240-243; J. T. Milik, *Dédicaces*, 337ff. and 352f. gave the correct readings.

Apollo is pictured wearing a cuirass; at his feet the lying *Tyche* is visible.[75] The combination of Nebo-Apollo and *Tyche* begs for an explanation, the more so as it occurs several times. At Dura-Europos the image of Nebo-Apollo, identified as Nebo by the Palmyrene inscription and as Apollo by its visual representation with lyre and plectrum, was found in the Temple of the Gaddê or Tychai, i.e., the Tyche of Dura-Europos and the Tyche of Palmyra.[76] The Tyche of Dura-Europos appears as Zeus Olympios crowned by Seleucus I Nicator on a relief found in this temple. The Tyche of Palmyra is a sitting goddess with a nude female figure lying at her feet, which symbolizes the spring Ephqa. She is crowned by a standing female godhead. Both reliefs were dedicated in 158 A.D. by a member of a very distinguished Palmyrene family called Ḥairan son of Maliko son of Naṣor; a later offspring of the same family was in the third century the famous Septimius Odainat, the king of kings. We may surmise that Ḥairan son of Maliko son of Naṣor was the head of the Palmyrene colony at Dura-Europos.[77]

It is noteworthy that in this very temple a relief of Yarhibol, called "the betyl of the spring" (*mṣbʾ dy ʿynʾ*) was also found; this epitheton links the god to the relief of the Gad of Palmyra, on which the spring is symbolized by the lying nude female figure.[78] This whole complex of representations of Zeus, Apollo and Seleucus Nicator on one hand, and the Tyche of Palmyra and the tutelary spirit of its Spring on the other, mainly dedicated by a member of a noble Palmyrene family, becomes still more interesting if we take into consideration that, according to a parchment found at

---

[75] H. Seyrig, Bas-relief des dieux de Hiérapolis, *Syria* 49, 1972, 104-108.

[76] *Dura-Europos, Prel. Report seventh and eighth season*, 266 and Pl. XXXVI, 1; *cf.* for the Tychai; J. M. Rostovtzeff, Progonoi, *JHS* 55, 1935, 56-66; A. Perkins, *The Art of Dura-Europos*, Oxford 1973, 79-83; Downey, *The Stone and Plaster Sculpture*, 14-19.

[77] See *Dura-Europos, Prel. Report seventh and eighth season*, 258ff. and Pl. XXXIII and XXXIV; M. Rostovtzeff, Le Gad de Doura and Seleucus Nicator, *Mélanges R. Dussaud*, Paris 1939. Vol. I, 281ff. M. Gawlikowski, À propos des reliefs du temple des Gaddê à Doura, *Berytus* 18, 1969, 105ff.; Downey, *The Stone and Plaster Sculpture*, 14-19.

[78] *Dura-Europos, Prel. Report seventh and eighth season*, 264f. and Pl. XXXV, 2; R. du Mesnil du Buisson, *Inventaire des inscriptions palmyréniennes de Doura-Europos*, 18, no. 33; Downey, *The Stone and Plaster Sculpture*, 62ff.; 213ff.

Dura (*Dura Perg. 23*), the cult of Zeus, the protector of the founder
of the Seleucid dynasty, and of Apollo, the most favorite god of
the Seleucids, is attested in 180 A.D. together with the cult of the
divine PROGONOI and Seleucus Nicator himself, the founder of
the city of Dura-Europos.[79] The real context of the combination
of Apollo-Nebo and Tyche seems therefore to be the Seleucid royal
cults which were founded in different cities.

It is worth noting in this connection that at Palmyra a relief of
the Tyche of the city with another Tyche standing beside her was
found in the Temple of Nebo. It is strongly reminiscent of the relief
of the Gad of Palmyra found at Dura-Europos. Therefore, at least
some relation between Nebo and the Tyche of the city may have
existed at Palmyra too.[80]

The relation between Nebo-Apollo and the Tyche indicated by
these different finds and their contexts become still more evident,
if we look at the archetype of nearly all representations of Tyche
in the various cities of Syria and Mesopotamia, i.e., the Tyche of
Antioch made by Eutychides of Sicyon for this city.[81] The bronze
statue showed the goddess sitting on a rock (i.e., Mount Silpius)
and supporting herself with her left hand on the rock. A turreted
crown on her head symbolized the city wall. In her right hand she
held a sheaf of wheat. A youth god at her feet represented the river
Orontes. The goddess is at the same time the city's protector and
personification, and is also thought of as the guardian of the king.[82]

The composition of this Tyche of Antioch clearly is taken over
in the images of Nebo-Apollo with a Tyche at his feet: the male
river god at the feet of the female Tyche is replaced by a Tyche
lying at the feet of Nebo-Apollo. This god, at least at Hierapolis,
is considered a giver of oracles according to the description of his

---

[79] cf. M. Rostovtzeff, Progonoi, *JHS* 55, 1935, 56-66.

[80] cf. A. Bounni - N. Saliby, *AAS* 15, 1965, 127ff.; F. Mellinghoff, Ein
Relief aus Palmyra. Untersuchungen zu seiner geschichtlichen Einordnung
und Deutung, in: Altheim-Stiehl, *AAW* V, 2, Berlin 1969, 58-164; Milik,
Dédicaces faites par des dieux, 164ff.; Drijvers, *Religion of Palmyra*, Pl. LI.

[81] cf. T. Dohrn, *Die Tyche von Antiochia*, Berlin 1960, 9ff.; G. Downey,
A History of Antioch, 73 and the literature quoted at n. 88.

[82] Downey, *A History of Antioch*, 74; L. Ross Taylor, *The Divinity of
the Roman Emperor*, 1931, 32.

activities as given by Lucianus, *De Dea Syria*, 35, 36. As contrasted
with most Greek oracles, the foretellings of the god are not given
by a priest or priestess, but only by the god himself by moving his
image in different directions when the highpriest asks him questions.[83] In contradistinction to Greek habits Apollo at Hierapolis
is not a young and naked god, but an aged and bearded one properly dressed. His whole representation has much in common with
the two statues from Kalchu erected there in Nebo's temple by
Adad-nirari III (810-783).[84] All cult and oracle practice connected
to Nebo-Apollo at Hierapolis seems therefore to be a continuation
of Mesopotamian traditions about Nabu, god of wisdom and destiny,
whose special task consisted of fixing the destiny of the king and
the country during the New Year's Festival. Especially in Neo-
Babylonian times his role became more and more important and
therefore at the beginning of the New Year's Festival he arrived
at his chapel Ezida in Esagil, Bel's sanctuary, for the feast of
zagmuku or Feast of Fortunes.[85]

Besides his relation to Nebo and Bel the king also had a special
relationship to certain other deities of the pantheon, most often
to Ishtar, who were determining his power and well-being and
consequently the well-being of his subjects. According to these
conceptions Ishtar's function regarding the king corresponds precisely with what in Greek is called the *Tyche* of the king, in Latin
the *fortuna imperatoris* and in Aramaic *gadda d⁰malka*.[86] The
fortune and prestige of the king consequently depend on various
divine powers, of which Nebo and Bel on one hand, and Ishtar on
the other, are the most important. Nebo fixes his destiny and

---

[83] Lucian, *De Syria Dea*, 35, 36; *cf.* for an example of Nebo's prophetic
capacities H. Seyrig, *AS* III, 34f., who published an inscription from
Hierapolis.

[84] *cf.* Dhorme, *Les religions*, 154f.; *Roscher's Lexicon*, art. *Nebo*, I, 49;
Pomponio, *Nabû*, 69f., 217; C. Gadd, *The Stones of Assyria*, London 1936,
151 adduced convincing arguments that the statues represent servants of
the god.

[85] Dhorme, *Les religions*, 244f.; *cf.* Langdon, *Neubabylonische Königsinschriften*, 234, 29; 126, 54ff.; 130, 12f.; see for the feast of *zagmuku* Frankfort, *Kingship and the Gods*, 313ff.

[86] *cf.* Oppenheim, *Ancient Mesopotamia*, 205; F. Cumont, *Études syriennes*,
263-276; J. Gagé, *Revue Historique* 171-172, 1933, 1-43.

future in a cosmic framework governed and symbolized by Bel;
in this setting Ishtar embodies his Tyche. These Mesopotamian
conceptions regarding the king and his fortune form the background
of the remarkable iconography of Nebo-Apollo, the oracle god at
Hierapolis.

In addition to this Mesopotamian background the cult of the
Seleucids can be adduced in order to elucidate ideas connected
with Nebo-Apollo as expressed in his iconography. Apollo and
Zeus were the gods most favoured by the Seleucids, as is apparent
from the mainly numismatic evidence. As stated by a famous
inscription (CIG 2, 3595, 28sq.) dealing with major contributions
of Antiochus I to a sanctuary near ancient Troas, Apollo is ἀρχηγὸς
τοῦ γένους. The same line of the inscription mentions Nike and Zeus
as gods to whom offerings should be made.[87] Seleucus I founded
the famous sanctuary of Apollo at Daphne, the suburb of Antioch;
and the same king issued all kinds of coins from Susa, Seleucia-on-
the-Tigris, other cities in Mesopotamia and from Antioch, with a
laureate head of Apollo on their obverses. Moreover the coins from
Antioch show a tripod, the importance of which is shown by the
obols which Seleucus minted at Seleucia after 293 B.C. These obols
show on their obverses a tripod-lebes, and on the reverses of some
a bow and quiver. Tripod, bow and quiver are unmistakably symbols of Apollo in his capacity as an oracle.[88] The Apollo portraits
and the symbols of the god on these Seleucid coins commemorate
the Didymaean oracle and its earlier prophecy of Seleucus' kingship, and function in this way as a form of royal propaganda.[89]

---

[87] E. R. Bevan, *The House of Seleucus*, London 1902, I, 121; II, 275; *RE*
Bd. II 3 A, Sp. 1232; *cf.* Downey, *A History of Antioch*, 68 and n. 63;
Bikerman, *Institutions des Séleucides*, Paris 1938, 253; L. Robert, *Études
anatoliennes*, 172ff.; for the inscription see: P. Frisch, *Die Inschriften von
Ilion* (Inschriften griechischer Städte aus Kleinasien 3), Bonn 1975, 84-91,
no. 32.

[88] *cf.* Hadley, Royal Propaganda of Seleucus I and Lysimachus, *JHS*
94, 1974, 57f.; Newell, *Eastern Seleucid Mints*, 119, Nos. 329, 331 and Pl.
XXV, 5, 8; 13, Nos. 99A, B, and Pl. I, 7, 8; 94-96, Nos. 911-922 and Pl. XVI,
9-22, XVII, 1-6; 82, Nos 884, 885, and Pl. XII, 11, 12.

[89] *Diodorus* XIX, 90, 2-4; Appian. *Syr.* 56.56; *cf.* Bikerman, *Institutions*,
250; C. B. Welles, *Royal Correspondence in the Hellenistic Period*, 1934,
ad. 22, 4.

Seleucus attached great importance to Apollo of Didyma, began rebuilding his temple in c. 300, and returned to the sanctuary the bronze statue of Apollo which Darius I had removed in 494.[90] In fact, representations of Apollo outnumber all other pictures on Seleucid mintage and as such give a firm proof of the god's predominant position in cult and worship of the Seleucids. His main attributes are the omphalos, bow and arrow(s) and the tripod and, less often, the lyre. The god is usually represented nude, but he also occurs draped.[91] The combination of all these symbols, especially of the omphalos with arrow(s), unmistakably characterize Apollo as an oracle. All other variants, which occur during the whole history of Seleucid coinage, make it very unlikely that the coins were made after one model, e.g., a statue of Apollo. On the contrary, the carvers felt free in combining the given attributes of the god exactly in order to stress his main character as an oracle. It should be noted that the sanctuary of Apollo at Daphne was dedicated to Apollo Pythius according to the ancient testimonies.[92] The most important aspect of the cult at Daphne, however, was that it actually and essentially was a royal cult propagated by the Seleucid sovereigns. In particular Antiochus III the Great (222-187 B.C.) propagated this royal cult and organized its priesthood.[93] Thus the gods of Daphne were venerated at Susa, at Dura-Europos and elsewhere.[94]

It can be assumed that the great veneration of the Seleucid dynasty for Apollo the oracle contributed significantly to the spread and importance of the cult of Nebo in their realm. He also

[90] Hadley, Royal Propaganda, 58; A. Rehm, *Didyma* Vol. II, *Die Inschriften*, Berlin 1958, No. 480; Pausanias, I, 16, 3; VIII, 46, 3.

[91] *cf.* Newell, *Eastern Seleucid Mints*, and *idem, Western Seleucid Mints*, Indices *s.v.* Apollo; R. H. McDowell, *Stamped and inscribed Objects from Seleucia on the Tigris*, Ann Arbor 1935, 47f.: Impressions of Official Seals representing Apollo; 74, 90: Impressions of Private Seals representing Apollo; 245-249: Catalog of Models.

[92] *cf.* L. Lacroix, Copies de statues sur les monnaies de Séleucides, *BCH* 73, 1949, 171ff.; 173, n. 1, 2, 3; Bikerman, *Institutions des Séleucides*, 252.

[93] Bikerman, *Institutions des Séleucides* 247, 256; Welles, *Royal Correspondence*, 36.

[94] Cumont, *Mém. de la Mission en Perse* 20, 1928, 85; *idem, CRAI* 1931, 279 = *SEG* VII, 17; *Dura-Europos. Prel. Report of third Season*, 63: Ἀρτέμιδι καὶ Ἀπόλλωνι ἀρχηγοῖς; *cf. Prel. Report of sixth Season*, 407f.

is in first instance an oracle god. It may even be that the stylus he
is represented with as a god of wisdom is a kind of analogon with
Apollo's arrow. In any case it may be more than coincidental that
Antiochus I Soter was deified as Antiochos Apollon Soter, introduced
the coins with a representation of Apollo sitting on the omphalos
with an arrow and showed a special reverence for Nebo and his
temple at Borsippa, and even addressed a long prayer to this
deity.[95] It is not amazing that a Greek considered the Mesopotamian
oracle god Nebo with his stylus to be Apollo, and an Oriental saw
some resemblance between Apollo with his traditional arrow and
Nebo with his stylus. In fact the identity of a god does not only
depend on the way he or she is represented, but also on the way he
or she is looked at! [96] The same holds true for the remarkable
"mixed" iconography of Nebo-Apollo at Hierapolis: an Oriental
bearded godhead accompanied by a Hellenistic Tyche. A Greek
is reminded of Apollo and the Tyche, e.g., of the Seleucid king; an
Oriental interprets this sculpture in the traditional Mesopotamian
pattern of Nebo, who fixes human destinies and the fortune of the
king. In Seleucid times the traditional New Year's Festival was
still held at Babylon where the Seleucid kings were the real suc-
cessors of an indigenous dynasty.

This whole religious pattern may even provide us with an explanation of the enigmatic figure on coins of Gordianus III (Pl.
XXXII, 3, 4; XXXIV, 1, 2). It may represent a local image of
Apollo-Nebo, the god *par excellence* of Edessa, with an arrow in his
left hand and a bow or quiver on his right shoulder. Among the
many variants of Apollo and his attributes on coins this one is
surely possible.[97] The combination with the Tyche or *Gad* of Edessa
points in the same direction, and so does the altar which is pictured
between the Tyche and the statue on the pedestal. This altar may

---

[95] L. Lacroix, Copies de statues, 170f.; Bikerman, *Institutions*, 245; *OGIS*
245, *cf. BCH* 1902, 188.

[96] See H. Gesche, Gordian mit dem Pfeil, 50, n. 25: "Es ist nicht ausge-
schlossen, dass die Seleuciden ihrerseits mit Hinblick auf Vorstellungen der
unterworfenen Völker den Apollo-Typ mit Pfeil bevorzugten".

[97] I had the opportunity to discuss this problem with Professor Lily Kahil
at Princeton, who also was of the opinion that the figure on the pedestal
might represent Apollo.

actually be the one which is mentioned in the *Doctrina Addai* and the *Acts of Sharbel* as standing in the center of the city, where Nebo, Bel and the other gods were brought at the great feast on the eighth of Nisan. The coins of Gordianus III thus would represent a local religious phenomenon; the statue of Nebo and the great altar in the middle of the city, like other coins of the same emperor also picture local deities, e.g., Apollo Smintheus.[98] The local character is also accentuated by the altar, which is missing on the coins of Harran which show the same deity on his pedestal. If this tentative interpretation of the statue on Gordianus' coins holds true, the identity of the god with the figure on an "intaille" found at Aleppo, as stated by H. Seyrig, is less likely. In fact, on closer investigation, the figure on the "intaille" seems to hold something in his uplifted right arm and does not bear an object on his right shoulder; moreover, the gesture of the left arm is different from that of the god on the pedestal. We therefore consider the whole scene on the reverse of these coins of Gordianus III as a representation of Nebo, the Gad of Edessa, and the central altar in this city, in a certain sense comparable with Apollo and the Tyche of Antioch.[99]

Summarizing our tentative conclusions we can state that Nebo and Bel were indeed the traditional gods of Edessa, most likely belonging to the oldest religious stratum. The very name Bel may be due to Babylonian influence and disguise an indigenous Baʿal; the cult of Nebo surely is imported from the Mesopotamian metropolis, from where it already spread in Assyrian times when, e.g., King Sin-šar-iškun (-612 B.C.) built a temple for Nebo and Tashmetum his spouse at Assur.[100] This coupling of Bel and Nebo, father and son, kosmokrator and symbol of divine wisdom, the one governing the starry heaven and ordering the kosmos, creator of life on earth, the other bringer of destiny and teacher of rational skills, embodies a special religious view on the world. The gods warrant the order in the kosmos and society and make their plans,

---

[98] L. Lacroix, *Les réproductions de statues sur les monnaies grecques*. La statuaire archaique et classique, *Bibl. de Liège*, Fasc. 116, Liège 1949, 77f.

[99] The Tyche of Edessa like those of other cities is modelled on the Tyche of Antioch, *cf.* Dohrn, *Die Tyche von Antiochia*, 56.

[100] Dhorme, *Les religions*, 156; Pomponio, *Nabû*, 67ff.

fixed destinies, known to mankind mainly by giving oracles. Sharing this divine wisdom actually means human life and the god Nebo thus is a life-giving god, making human life in a given social order possible. Bel in his function of kosmokrator is head of the pantheon too, and thus consistently called *Marᵉlahê* = Lord of the Gods in Syriac literature, when it deals with pagan religion. Jacob of Edessa (end of seventh century A.D.) records a Chaldaean kosmology in his *Hexaemeron*. According to the Chaldaeans there was first chaos and then the spirit hovering over the waters created the seven planets as the start of ordering the kosmos, "and it made Bel first and after him Marud as lords of the gods (*Marᵉlahê*)." [101] Marud may echo the name Nimrod and therefore indicate Nebo. As planet Bel is considered to be Jupiter, whereas Nebo is Mercurius-Hermes.[102] The same title Lord of the gods is given to Bel in other Syriac exegetical works.[103] Very instructive is Ishodad of Merw's commentary on Acts XIV, 12, the visit of Paul and Barnaba to Lystra: "This, They called Barnaba Lord of the Gods, and Paul Hermes. He calls Zeus, the son of Kronos Lord of the Gods......, but they called Hermes one of the gods who was more rational and skillful and intelligent than all of the Gods; and they called him Hermes Trismegistos, that is to say, who knows three things, what is past and what is present, and what will happen; and because of this they called Paul Hermes." [104]

From the related commentary in the *Gannat Bussamê* it appears that Zeus and Hermes are similar to Bel and Nebo. Paul and Barnaba are described as two planets (stars) coming down from

---

[101] Chabot, *CSCO* 70, col. b, L. 7-71, col. a, L. 6; Vaschalde, 56, 13-28; *cf.* A. Guillaumont, Genèse 1, 1-2 selon les commentateurs syriaques, *In Principio*. Interprétations des premiers versets de la Genèse, Paris 1973, 128. Bel is also called Marᵉlahê on a tessera from Assur, see *MDOG* 60, 1920, 21, no. 15; Andrae-Lenzen, *Die Partherstadt Assur*, 108-111; Milik, *Dédicaces faites par des dieux*, 344ff.

[102] Nimrod = Henoch = Hermes Trismegistos = Nebo/Apollo, *cf.* *Thesaurus Syriacus*, *s.v.* *nbw* (col. 2268).

[103] *e.g.* G. Hoffmann, *Opuscula Nestoriana*, Kiel 1880, 116, 6 in a commentary on Dan. from the so-called *Dirasṭarsinos.*

[104] Ishodad of Merw commentary on Acts XIV, 12, ed. M. D. Gibson, *The Commentaries of Ishoʿdad of Merv* Vol. IV, *Horae Sem.* X, Cambridge 1913, 24f.

heaven; Barnaba is called *mwštry* = Jupiter = Bel and Paul *ʿwṭrd* = Mercurius = Nebo, "the giver of speech." [105] When Ephrem Syrus at the end of the fourth century speaks of Nebo as the planet Mercurius he calls him *kwkbʾ mlylʾ* = the speaking (or: rational) star.[106] Moreover, the Syriac tradition knows Nebo as the inventor of the art of writing, or in an euhemeristic way, as the first schoolmaster.[107]

One tomb inscription from Kirk Mağara, an ancient cemetery at Edessa, mentions *Marʿlahê* = Lord of the Gods. It dates from the second or third century A.D. and according to the text the owner of the tomb wishes that "whoever will remove my bones—may he have no latter-end, and may he be accursed to *Marʿlahê.*" [108] It is usually assumed that *Marʿlahê* is identical with the god of Sumatar Harabesi, Sin the moon god of Harran, who also is called *Marʿlahê*, but that is in no way certain. *Marʿlahê* at Edessa in this particular inscription itself may denote, e.g., Bel, who as maintainer of cosmic order also will punish offences against the dead.[109]

The foregoing exposition has tried to lay down part of the religious pattern at pagan Edessa in which Nebo played the first role. Since this godhead also is linked with the cult of Atargatis and Hadad at Mabbug-Hierapolis, where he had a special place and function, and since the cult of Atargatis and Hadad is attested at Edessa too, it seems appropriate now to discuss the place and character of the Dea Syria in Edessa's religion.

---

[105] According to the manuscript of the Gannat Bussamê in the John Rylands Library, fol. 213ro; *cf.* G. J. Reinink, Die Textüberlieferung der GB, *Le Muséon* 90, 1977, 103ff.; see further *Thesaurus Syriacus*, ed. R. Payne Smith *s.v. mwštry* and *ʿwṭrd*; W. Eilers, *Sinn und Herkunft der Planetennamen*, 51ff., 84ff.

[106] Ephrem Syrus, *Hymni contra Haereses* IX, 1.

[107] Theodore bar Khonai, *Book of Scholia*, ed. A. Scher, *CSCO* 65, Louvain 1910, 369, 16-21; Ishodad of Merw, ed. C. van den Eynde, *CSCO* 126, Louvain 1950, 6, 21ff.

[108] Drijvers, *Old-Syriac Inscriptions*, no. 35.

[109] *cf. e.g.* Die Daskyleion inscription quoted above p. 55, and A. Parrot, *Malédictions et Violations de Tombes*, Paris 1939, 17ff.

CHAPTER FOUR

THE CULT OF ATARGATIS

Edessa

The worship of Atargatis at Edessa is explicitly connected to
Hierapolis-Mabbug by the *Doctrina Addai*: "Behold there are those
among you who adore .... Tarʿatha as the people of Mabbug
....," and all evidence from Edessa actually confirms this relation
to the great cultic center of the *Dea Syria*.[1] The relation even seems
to be so strong that Strabo XVI, 1, 27 identifies Mabbug, Hierapolis
and Edessa:

.... ἡ Βαμβύκη, ἣν καὶ ᾿Εδεσσαν καὶ ῾Ιεραν πόλιν καλοῦσιν,
ἐν ᾗ τιμῶσι τὴν Συρίαν θεὸν τὴν ᾿Αταργάτιν.

although as authoritative a scholar as W. von Baudissin denied
the cult of Atargatis to Edessa on the very ground of this text.[2]
The worship of Atargatis is, however, so well attested at Edessa
that there can be no doubt that the statement of the *Doctrina
Addai* rests on firm ground.

The so-called *Book of the Laws of Countries*—actually a dialogue
on the influence of Fate on human life originating from the school
of the Aramaic philosopher Bardaiṣan of Edessa (154-222 A.D.)—
records a law given by King Abgar against the practice of castration
which could be part of the service in worship of the goddess: "In

---

[1] For the cult of Atargatis at Hierapolis in general see: H. Stocks, Studien
zur Lukians 'De Syria Dea', *Berytus* 4, 1937, 1-40; C. Clemen, *Lukians
Schrift über die syrische Göttin*, AO 37, 3-4, Leipzig 1938; G. Goossens,
Hiérapolis de Syrie. Essai de monographie historique, Louvain 1943. 33ff.;
art. Atargatis, *RAC* I, 854-860. R. A. Oden, *Studies in Lucian's De Syria
Dea*, Harvard Semitic Monographs 15, 1977; bibliography in H. D. Betz,
Lukian von Samosata und das Neue Testament, *TU* 76, Berlin 1961, 218-251
and in Oden, *o.c.* 163ff.; a comprehensive monograph on Atargatis is still
wanting; useful is P.-L. van Berg, *Corpus Cultus Deae Syriae (CCDS)* 2 Vols,
EPRO 28, Leiden 1972 that deals with the Greek and Latin sources.
[2] See P.-L. van Berg, *CCDS* 1, no. 83, p. 52f.: Strabon fait ici une confusion....; cf. *Roscher's Lexicon* IV, 1637; Von Baudissin, *Studien zur semitischen Religionsgeschichte* II, Leipzig 1878, 159, 166; H. Stocks, Studien
zu Lukians "De Syria Dea", *Berytus* 4, 1937, 6, n. 15.

Syria and Edessa there was the custom of self-emasculation in honour of Tar'atha (*ltr't*), but when King Abgar had come to the faith, he ordered that every man who emasculated himself should have his hand chopped off. And from that day to this no one emasculates himself in the territory of Edessa." [3] This example of royal legislation is adduced in the context of "barbarian laws" (νόμιμα βαρβάρικα) in order to prove that human liberty, which expresses itself in ethical commandments, is actually stronger than the power of Fate residing in stars and planets. The statement of this treatise, that Abgar's law was the result of his conversion to the Christian belief, is almost certainly due to a (later?) revision of Bardaiṣan's dialogue on Fate which may have been caused by the legendary tale in the *Doctrina Addai* on King Abgar becoming a Christian.[4] The effect of Abgar's measure is somewhat exaggerated for still in the fifth century A.D., Rabbula Bishop of Edessa forbade self-emasculation in his canons for the clergy.[5] The same kind of laceration is also attested among the Marcionites, but there it must be considered an expression of gnostic hate for the body and for procreation. The practice of self-emasculation is attested in the cult of the *Dea Syria* at Hierapolis according to the description given of it by Lucianus, *De Syria Dea* 20 and 51. His story about Kombabos and Stratonike, of which the first castrated himself for fear of falling in love with Stratonike the queen, echoes on the

---

[3] Drijvers, *The Book of the Laws of Countries*. Dialogue on Fate of Bardaiṣan of Edessa, Assen 1965, 58, 20-24 (text), 59 (translation); *Patrologia Syriaca* II, 607; *cf.* Drijvers, *Bardaiṣan of Edessa*, 76ff., esp. 92; *cf.* G. Sanders, art. Gallos in *RAC* 8, 1026ff. Sanders mistakenly speaks of King Abgar IX and his conversion.

[4] *cf.* Drijvers, Edessa und das jüdische Christentum, *VigChr* 24, 1970, 4ff.; *idem*, Rechtgläubigkeit und Ketzerei im ältesten syrischen Christentum, *Symposium Syriacum 1972*, Orient. Chr. Anal. 197, 1974, 291ff.

[5] Castration was held in high esteem among the monks and often practised, *cf. Constitutiones apostol.*, VIII, III, 490 (ed. F. X. Funk, Paderborn 1905); Severus of Antioch, *Selected Letters*, ed. E. W. Brooks, 2 Vols, London 1902-03, I, 461f.; *cf.* A. Vööbus, *History of Asceticism in the Syrian Orient* II, CSCO Subs. 17, Louvain 1960, 257f.; Rabbula of Edessa, *Canon LV*, ed. A. Vööbus, *Syriac and Arabic Documents regarding Legislation relative to Syrian Monasticism*, PETSE 11, Stockholm 1960, 49; G. M. Sanders, art. Gallos, *RAC* 8, 1026ff. gives many examples of emasculation among christians, especially in Phrygia and Syria, the homelands of the cults of Atargatis and Cybele.

one hand the Anatolian myth of Cybele and Attis, but on the
other hand reminds very much of Huwawa/Humbaba, the name
of the monster who guards the cedar forest in the Gilgamesh epic.[6]
Stratonike actually is not the cause of Kombabos' misfortune,
because Lucianus knows a variant of the story, told by the people
of Hierapolis, according to which Hera originated the self-emasculation (ch. 21 and 26).[7] Taking into consideration the whole background of Near Eastern mythology and religious conceptions,
which is transparent in Lucianus' satyrical story, it is very likely
that the practice of emasculation and the function of eunuchs are
connected with Syrian and Mesopotamian goddesses of fertility
and have nothing to do with Anatolian or Hittite myths.[8]

In this connection Bardaiṣan's legendary biography should be
mentioned mainly because it tells of Bardaiṣan's education by a
pagan priest at Hierapolis-Mabbug, who taught him the pagan
doctrine when he was still young. Later on the boy went to Edessa
and there Bardaiṣan happened to hear Bishop Hystaspes preaching,
which appealed to him. He was initiated into the mysteries of the
Christians, became a deacon and wrote against the heretics. Finally, however, he was won over again by the pagans.[9] However
legendary and apocryphal this biography may be, with all stereo-
types of anti-heretical writings, it is noteworthy that it connects
pagan doctrine at Edessa, and of Bardaiṣan in particular, with
Hierapolis and not with Harran, another famous center of paganism

---

[6] Goossens, *Hiérapolis de Syrie*, 36f. connects Kombabos with the Anatolian goddess Kubaba(t), who is related to Cybele, *cf.* Haussig, *Wörterbuch der
Mythologie* I, 183f., *s.v.* Kubaba; E. Laroche, Koubaba, déesse anatolienne,
et le problème des origines de Cybèle, *Éléments orientaux dans la religion
grecque ancienne*, Colloque de Strasbourg 1958, Paris 1960, 113-128; for
Huwawa see *Wörterbuch der Mythologie* I, 70 *s.v.* Gilgameš und Huwawa and
80 *s.v.* Huwawa; Huwawa is probably of Hurrian origin; see also A. Dupont-
Sommer - L. Robert, *La déesse de Hiérapolis Castabala (Cilicie)*, Paris 1964, 7ff.
[7] See Oden, *Studies*, 37f. for a commentary on these chapters, which he
rightly connects with the Gilgamesh epic.
[8] H. A. Strong - J. Garstang, *The Syrian Goddess*, London 1913, wrongly
sought the origin of Atargatis in Hittite religion.
[9] *cf.* Drijvers, *Bardaiṣan of Edessa*, 188ff.; this legendary biography is
handed down by Michael Syrus, *Chronique de Michel le Syrien* I, ed. J. B.
Chabot, Paris 1900, 109-111 and by Agapius of Mabbug, *Kitâb al-ʿUnwân*,
PO VII, 518-521.

in Late Antiquity and in Muslim times.[10] Moreover, some fragments of Bardaiṣan's hymns, which are preserved in Ephrem Syrus' *Hymns contra Haereses*, might betray certain conceptions in his doctrine which clearly fit into the pattern of the *Dea Syria* and ideas connected to her. *Hymn* LV, 1 contains an exhortation of Ephrem to pray for the Bardesanites, as they aver insane things; they say that:

> Something streamed down from that Father of Life
> And the Mother became pregnant with the mystery of the fish
>   and bore him;
> And he was called Son of Life.[11]

The idea of a divine couple, Father and Mother of Life, is supposed to hold a central place in Bardaiṣan's doctrine in its more mythological form. The whole strophe contains on the one hand the concept of a divine triad—Father, Mother and Son—which is represented as ἰχθύς = fish; on the other hand the life-giving aspect of the Mother, represented in the shape of a fish, reminds very much of the *Dea Syria* at Hierapolis who also has fish as her sacred animals, and which symbolize her character as a goddess of fertility.[12] Atargatis, therefore, had a pond with sacred fish in every sanctuary dedicated to her—at Hierapolis, Ascalon, Delos and elsewhere.[13] At Edessa too there was a pond with sacred fish situated north of the citadel which still exists at modern Urfa (Pl. II, III).[14] Today the carp is sacred to Ibrahim and the pond is called

---

[10] It was the city of the Sabians, a pagan group, which actually adhered to traditional local religious traditions in a philosophical and astrological disguise; *cf.* in general Chwolsohn, *Die Ssabier und der Ssabismus*, 2 Vols, 1856; J. B. Segal, *Edessa and Harran*. An inaugural Lecture, London 1963.

[11] *cf.* Drijvers, *Bardaiṣan of Edessa*, 144; S. P. Brock in a review of this work *JSS* 1970, 115 proposed the translation: "in a mystery with a fish"; the Syriac *w'm' br'z nwn' bṭnt* should, however, be translated: and the Mother became pregnant with (or: through) the mystery of the fish, since *br'z nwn'* is a status constructus; the fish Jesus is a mystery Himself.

[12] *cf.* Goossens, *Hiérapolis de Syrie*, 62-64; F. Dölger, *IXTHUS* I, 1910, 90f.; Lucian, *De Syria Dea*, 45-47.

[13] Lucian, *De Syria Dea*, 46; *cf.* Cumont, *Études syriennes*, 35ff.; Stocks, *Studien*, 6; Goossens, *Hiérapolis de Syrie*, 62; for Ascalon see *Diod. Sic.* II, 4; for Delos, Ph. Bruneau, *Recherches sur les cultes de Délos à l'époque hellénistique et à l'époque impériale*, Paris 1970, 467ff.

[14] Segal, *Edessa*, 54, Pl. 10b; Kirsten, art. Edessa, *RAC* IV, 562.

after this patriarch, but this is clearly a shift from traditional motives into another religious context linked with a change of religion. The carp-pond existed there in the fifth century A.D., when it was shown to a Gallian nun called Egeria or Etheria, who made a long journey in the Near East in order to see all kinds of holy places. On her journey she also went to Edessa, where she stayed for three days. The royal palace of King Abgar, situated just north of the citadel, was shown to her by the local bishop who diligently quoted the apocryphal letter of Jesus to the king: Item perintravimus in interior parte palatii; et ibi erant *fontes piscibus pleni*, quales ego adhuc nunquam vidi, id est tantae magnitudinis vel tam perlustres au tam boni saporis. Nam ipsa civitas aliam aquam penitus non habet nunc nisi eam, quae de palatio exit, quae est ac si fluvius ingens argenteus (*Itinerarium Aetheriae* 19, 7).[15] We may assume that these *fontes piscibus pleni* were the original ponds with the sacred fish of Atargatis, which partly were situated within the palace area. Up to the present a whole system of ponds and canals still exists at Urfa just north of the citadel. The temple of Atargatis probably once stood in this quarter of the city.

The very existence of a sanctuary of Atargatis at Edessa, or even a sanctuary of Atargatis and Hadad as at Hierapolis, becomes even more likely through a relief representing the divine pair which was found at Urfa and now is on view in the local museum (Pl. XXII). It was considered an ordinary funerary stele and therefore was practically unnoticed. It is made from limestone and measures 56 cms long, 39 cm high, 16 cm thick; its relief is between 3 and 4 cm. Although the surface is rather worn and damaged, the similarity to two other known reliefs of Hadad and Atargatis—one from Dura-Europos and one from Northern Mesopotamia—is striking.[16] It represents the goddess to the right of the *semeion*, and the god to the left of it. Both of them wear a high *kalathos* and a long

---

[15] Quoted after Éthérie, *Journal de voyage*, éd. H. Pétré, *SC* 21; Paris 1948; n. 53 on p. 277 of Drijvers, Die Götter Edessas, *Festschrift F.-K. Dörner*, *EPRO* 66, Leiden 1978, should accordingly be corrected.
[16] See *Dura-Europos, Prel. Report of third Season*, 1932, 100f.; A. Perkins, *The Art of Dura-Europos*, 94-96 and Pl. 38; Downey, *The Stone and Plaster Sculpture*, 9-11; H. Seyrig, Bas-relief des dieux de Hiérapolis, *Syria* 49, 1972, 104-108 and Pl. I; Drijvers, Die Götter Edessa, 276f.

dress which leaves feet and the lower part of the legs visible. The head and the upper part of the body is represented *en face*, but the lower part of the body is turned towards the *semeion*. The deities appear to grasp the *semeion* with one hand—Atargatis with her right hand, Hadad with his left one—or to be connected to it otherwise. The *semeion* itself still shows some traces of a decorative linear pattern comparable to the decoration of the *semeion* on the relief from Northern Mesopotamia. Its upper part has a conical shape. Just where the deities grasp the *semeion* two sticks—one at each side of the *semeion*—rise from it like branches from a tree. At the end of the left stick a square blade is discernible; the right stick was probably adorned with the same blade or with another symbol. It is even possible that the two sticks do not belong to the *semeion*, but actually are held by the two deities. It should be noted that the characteristic animals of Hadad and Atargatis, i.e., his bulls and her lions, are missing on this relief, but that on the other hand its whole arrangement reminds very much of the traditional representation of the gods of Hierapolis as known from reliefs and coins. Our relief shows besides a clear resemblance to certain Syrian cylinder seals from the second millenium B.C., which H. Seyrig already adduced in order to prove that at Hierapolis no triad was venerated, but only two gods, Hadad and Atargatis, together with a divine symbol, the *semeion*, which stood in between the gods according to Lucian, *De Dea Syria*, 33.[17] Moreover, the relation between the divine standard as pictured on the Syrian seals and the *semeion* at Hierapolis makes it very likely that the cult at Hierapolis is a traditional autochthonous Syrian one and was not imported there from elsewhere. An imprint of a seal from Kultepe is of special interest in this connection. It pictures, a.o., a woman sitting to the left of a *semeion* who raises her right hand towards it in a gesture of adoration. The dress of the sitting woman, in all likelihood a goddess, is identical with the dress of Atargatis on our relief, except for the high *kalathos*.[18] Another seal from the collection of the American University at Beyrouth (no. 6212) shows

---

[17] Seyrig, Les dieux de Hiérapolis, *Syria* 37, 1960, 233-252 = *AS* VI, 79-98.
[18] B. Hrozny, *Inscriptions cunéiformes de Kultépé* I, Prague 1952, Pl. LXX; Seyrig, *art. cit.*, 234, no. 1 and Fig. 1.

an analogous scene: a sitting goddess with, a.o., the *semeion* in
front of her.[19] A Syrian seal offered for sale at Beyrouth represents
the well-known Syrian god of the thunder-storm standing with his
right foot on a lying bull and keeping in his right hand a mace or a
sword or a sceptre. In front of him the *semeion* is pictured.[20] These
seals and other ones discussed by Seyrig, although they do not
offer exact parallels to our relief, provide us with enough evidence
to assume that the combination of a goddess, i.e., Atargatis, and
a god of heaven and thunder-storm like Hadad, with a divine
standard or *semeion* is an autochthonous Syrian religious element.
The real interest of our relief is, in particular, that it furnishes a
kind of missing link between the well-known reliefs of Hadad and
Atargatis with the *semeion* between them with each of them accompanied by his or her characteristic animals (bulls and lions)
and moreover represented in full frontality, and the typical Syrian
representations as found on the seals on which human beings and
deities in most cases are not represented in frontal position but
are most of the time turned to the left or the right. The scenes on
the seals therefore are a kind of narrative art, whereas a cult-relief
is static and hieratic, intended to be an object of worship. The
absence of bulls and lions and the only partly frontal representation
connect our relief with the seals from this area. The scene, as such,
leads us to the reliefs of Hadad and Atargatis. All these considerations simply exclude the possibility of identifying the sitting persons
to the left and the right of the *semeion* as ordinary human beings.
The high *kalathos* also is no common dress, but the special head-
covering of deities so that this feature also makes the identification
to Hadad and Atargatis more than plausible. Since the relief is not
inscribed its exact date is difficult to determine, but the strong
Syrian influence on it makes an early date more likely than a
dating into the first or second century A.D. It seems safe to assume
that it should be dated in the first or second century B.C., although
Syrian art from that period is rather rare and therefore does not
provide us with analogous scenes.

[19] Seyrig, *art. cit.*, 236, no. 15 and Pl. IX; *cf.* E. Porada, *JNES* 16,
1957, Pl. XXX, 2.
[20] Seyrig, *art. cit.*, 234, no. 4 and Pl. IX.

These preliminary considerations of the Edessene relief supposedly of Hadad and Atargatis leave us with some questions,
which may be dealt with in more detail after a comprehensive
survey of all remaining evidence of the cult of (Hadad and) Atargatis at Edessa. Moreover, it seems appropriate to list all evidence
of the worship of the *Dea Syria* in Syria and Mesopotamia together
with its different forms in order to assign its proper place to this
particular relief because it shows some special features which are
not portrayed elsewhere. The most striking are the special shape
of the *semeion*, the absence of bulls and lions, and the non-frontal
position of the deities. In addition to the inscriptions an iconographical inventory of Atargatis' cult is of special interest, in the
first place for reasons of comparison to our relief, and in the second
place since such a list has not been set up till now. P.-L. van Berg
gave an inventory of all literary sources dealing with the cult of
Atargatis except for Lucian, *De Syria Dea*, which R. A. Oden quite
recently studied in more detail.[21] The same P.-L. van Berg very
properly observed that inscriptions and archaeological remains of
Atargatis' cult "n'ont encore fait l'objet d'aucun classement systé-
matique. Sans doute est-ce l'approche des monuments figurés qui
est la plus malaisée: ..."[22] Since Syria is the homeland of this
cult, from where it spread into the whole *imperium*, it seems justified
to restrict our inventory to that area. Lucian's *De Syria Dea* and
the inscriptions, reliefs and coins from Syria with representations
of Atargatis and Hadad are, in fact, our only sources for the knowledge of the cult of the Syrian mother-goddess and her partner.
The Edessene material is part of them and should therefore be
adduced as completely as possible before turning over to the rest
of the Syrian area.

Besides the literary sources mentioned before and the enigmatic
relief, proper names composed with the whole name of the Syrian
goddess or with only part of it (which occur in the Old-Syriac
inscriptions from the first three centuries A.D.) give additional

---

[21] R. A. Oden, *Studies in Lucian's De Syria Dea, Harvard Semitic Monographs* 15, 1977.
[22] P.-L. van Berg, *CCDS* 1, 2, Étude critique des sources mythographiques
grecques et latines, note préliminaire.

proof of the cult of the goddess. Her name, which in Aramaic as
in Greek is spelled in different ways—ʿtrʿth, ʿtrʿʿ, ʾtrʿth, ʾtrʿʿ, trʿt—
actually is a composite name of ʿAštart, and ʿAnat. That the divine
name ʾAšerah is also one of the composing elements originating
the shift of *ayin* to *aleph*, as is stated by R. A. Oden,[23] is very
dubious. Among the proper names of the Old-Syriac inscriptions
there occur ʿbdʿtʾ = servant of ʿʿ, brʿʿ = son of ʿʿ, mʿʿ = ʿʿ is
mother, mtrʿʿ = maidservant of trʿʿ (or: trʿʿ is mother), and
šlmʿʿ = salvation of ʿʿ.[24] That names composed with Hadad do
not occur is another indication of the dominant position of Atargatis
in comparison to her partner.

In addition to all clear references to Atargatis' cult at Edessa
there is evidence of a more dubious character. A relief in the Urfa
Museum portrays a Triton with a fish (a dolphin?) on her left arm
(Pl. XXI). In view of the evident relations of Atargatis to the sea
and water as symbols of fertility, which found expression in the
story about the flood in Lucian, *De Syria Dea*, 12 and 13, and
rites connected with water in ch. 45-48, and in the usual ponds
with fish in her sanctuaries, it surely is possible that this Triton
relief has something to do with the cult of Atargatis. There are
parallels to it in the Nabataean temple of Hadad and Atargatis
at Khirbet Tannur.[25]

Since Atargatis often functions as the Tyche of a city it is worth
considering if the Tyche which is portrayed on the Edessene coins
may represent the local Atargatis, the goddess of the springs and
ponds. The coinage of Caracalla portrays on the reverse the bust
of the City-goddess wearing a turreted crown and veil, and so
does the coinage of Macrinus and other emperors. But coins struck

---

[23] Oden, *Studies*, 6off.

[24] cf. Segal, *BSOAS* 1954, 28f.; Drijvers, *Old-Syriac Inscriptions*, Index
of proper names.

[25] cf. N. Glueck, *Deities and Dolphins*, London 1966, 346f.; Ch. Picard,
Une Atargatis méconnue à Leptis Magna, *RA*, Sér. 6, Tom. 37, 1951, 231-233;
Ch. Picard, Sur l'Atargatis-Derkétô des Thermes d'Aphrodisias en Carie,
Hommages J. Bidez et F. Cumont, Collection Latomus II, 257-264; cf. J.
Starcky, Le temple nabatéen de Khirbet Tannur. A propos d'un livre récent,
RB 75, 1968, 228ff., who drew attention to the fact that the goddess of
Khirbet Tannur shows aspects of Atargatis of Hierapolis and of Derketo of
Ascalon, both goddesses being local variants of the Dea Syria.

under the reigns of Elagabalus, Severus Alexander, and Julia Mamaea depict the Tyche seated on a rock and below the half-figure of a river-god swimming. Sometimes the goddess holds in her right hand fruits, or a branch, or ears of corn, or an uncertain object, and very often a flaming altar is depicted in front of her (Pl. XXXIII, 4; XXXIV, 1, 2, 4).[26] Thisr epresentation is clearly inspired by the Tyche of Antioch, but may depict at the same time the Edessene Atargatis as goddess of the life-giving springs and protectress of the city. The altar in front of her reminds us of the great altar in the center of the city as recorded by the *Doctrina Addai*. If this relation is correct, this altar was not linked to a special cult of a certain pagan god, but embodied the solidarity with the luck and prosperity of Edessa symbolized by its Tyche. This may be the reason why it was not destroyed according to the *Doctrina Addai*, whereas all other altars and statues were supposed to have disappeared immediately after the sudden conversion of King Abgar and his city. Atargatis in her function as Tyche will reclaim our attention after a survey of all evidence of her cult and various manifestations in the Syrian area. Since the Dea Syria herself appears to be an all-embracing great goddess who combines all different aspects connected with female deities in the Syrian area, it is to be expected that this survey will bring to light a whole range of varieties in the iconography and epitheta of the Dea Syria, which even appear at Hierapolis, the center of her cult.[27]

Hierapolis

Since very little is left of the ancient sanctuary of Atargatis and Hadad in the modern city of Mabbug, our only sources for the study of the *Dea Syria* are Lucian's treatise, local coinage and some lucky finds of sculpture coming from Membig and its surroundings.[28]

---

[26] See Hill, *BMC*, Arabia, 97ff. no's 39-46 (Caracalla), Pl. XIV, 11; 47-51 (Macrinus), Pl. XIV, 13, 14; no's 52-54 (Diadumenian), Pl. XIV, 15; no. 55 (Elagabalus) Tyche holds branch; 58 (Elagabalus), Tyche holds fruits; 61 (Elagabalus) Tyche holds fruits; in field behind her, cornucopiae; 67 (Elagabalus) Tyche hold branch; before her, altar flaming; the coinage of Severus Alexander and Julia Mamaea repeats these types sometimes with minor variants.

[27] *cf.* Cook, *Zeus* I, 1914, 584, n. 2 lists the varieties; H. Seyrig, Sur une idole hiérapolitaine, *Syria* 26, 1949, 24ff. = *AS* IV, 27ff. discusses them.

Local coinage is known from two periods. The first is the period between about 332-312 B.C., when the reigning priests of Hierapolis struck silver coins with Aramaic legends. The second covers the period between Trajan and Philippus Arabs, when the local mint produced imperial coins. The silver coins of the local priests from the fourth century B.C. have been studied by S. Ronzevalle and H. Seyrig and we therefore will rely mainly on their results.[29] Fourteen different types are known, which all contribute to the study of the gods venerated at Hierapolis. The first shows a standing bearded person in a long Persian dress with uplifted hands on the obverse. The reverse bears a picture of a standing priest wearing a high tiara, with outstretched right hand and his left hand extending to an altar in front of him. An Aramaic inscription beginning on the reverse and continuing on the obverse reads: ʿbdhdd priest of Manbog, who resembles Hadaran his Lord (?).[30] *Hdrn* which probably means "The splendid one" is an epithet of Hadad also attested elsewhere.[31] The second coin shows on the obverse a bust of Atargatis turned to the left wearing a cylindrical tiara. The goddess is identified as such by the legend *ʿtrʿth*. The reverse shows a bearded person in a chariot and the legend ʿbdhdd. The third one pictures Atargatis *en face* wearing a cylindrical tiara, her

---

[28] *cf.* F. Cumont, *Études syriennes*, 35ff. for a description of the remains of ancient Hierapolis; D. Hogarth, *BSA* 14, 1907, 187; Goossens, *Hiérapolis de Syrie*, 13ff.: La disparition de la ville ancienne.

[29] S. Ronzevalle, Les monnaies de la dynastie de ʿAbd-Hadad et les cultes de Hiérapolis-Bambycé, *MUSJ* 23, 1940, 3-82; H. Seyrig, Le monnayage de Hiérapolis de Syrie à l'époque d'Alexandre, *RNum* VIe Série, 13, 1971, 11-21 and Pl. I, II; R. A. Oden, *Studies* missed Seyrig's important article.

[30] See Seyrig, Le monnayage, 16f.; A. Caquot contributed a note on the Aramaic inscription and read ʿbdhdd kmr mnbg zy ydmh bhdrn bʿih. I have serious doubts about the translation 'who resembles Hadaran' of the phrase zy ydmh bhdrn; one expects something like 'who is the servant of', but I am not able for the moment to give a better interpretation. The verb dmh-to resemble is always constructed with the preposition *l*. Have we here to do with a different verb?

[31] Hadarân occurs in the *Apology of Pseudo-Melito*, ed. W. Cureton, *Spicilegium Syriacum*, p. 25 (text), 45 (transl.); J. Bidez - F. Cumont, *Les mages hellénisés* II, Paris 1938, 94; *IGLS* VI, 2908; 2928; *cf.* J. T. Milik, *Biblica* 48, 1967, 573, n. 4 for the meaning of the name Hadarân; the name also occurs at Delos, cf. Ph. Bruneau, *Recherches sur les cultes de Délos*, 471 for the etymology of Manbog/Mabbug see Oden, *Studies*, 30ff.

face flanked by two long plaits; the accompanying legend reads
ʿtrʿth and on one copy *trʿth*. The reverse pictures *ʿbdhdd* performing
his priestly functions in an Ionic distylos temple. The fourth coin
portrays a female head with thick hair wearing a necklace and
accompanied by the legend *hdd wʿth*—Hadad and Ateh. The reverse
pictures the bearded god in his chariot and the legend *ʿbyty*. The
fifth one represents a bust of Atargatis turned to the left; her hair
combed to the top of her head, from which a long tress hangs down;
the legend reads *trʿth*. The reverse shows the bearded god Hadad
in his chariot wearing a tiara and the legend *ʾb*. The sixth coin
shows a female head *en face* with long ear-drops and the legend
ʿth; the reverse pictures Zeus aetophoros turned to the left and the
inscription: *hdd mnbg*—Hadad of Manbog. The seventh coin shows
as phinx turned to the right and on the reverse side a lion is pictured
turned to the right, but his head *en face*, accompanied by the legend
ʿth. The eighth dates from the time of Alexander the Great; it
shows a lion with open mouth and in front of it a flower with a
bird sitting on it. Above this scene the legend *ʾlksndr*—Alexander,
is to be read. The reverse pictures a horse-rider with lance and the
same legend. Coin number nine shows a sitting Zeus turned left
and the legend *ʿtrʿth*. The reverse bears the representation of a
horse-rider hunting a lion and the legend *ʾlksndr*. The tenth coin
shows a bust of Atargatis turned right; she has straight hair, wears
a necklace and an ear-drop. The legend *ʿth* identifies this female
head. The reverse portrays a lion attacking a bull and the legend
ʾlksndr. The eleventh one has a sitting Zeus in front of an incense-
altar; he holds ears of corn in his right hand. The legend *ʾlksndr*
accompanies this scene. The reverse shows Atargatis riding on her
lion, turned left; she wears a veil and her left hand is uplifted. The
twelfth coin portrays Atargatis sitting between two sphinxes, a
branch in her right hand. To the right of this representation the
legend *ʿtrʿth* leaves no doubt regarding the identity of the sitting
goddess. The reverse shows a lion attacking a deer, and the legend
ʾlksndr. The thirteenth one represents a throned Atargatis turned
to the right; she wears a long dress and a tiara, around which a
diadem is pictured. With her left hand she brings a cup to her mouth,
while her left hand is outstretched towards an incense-altar in front

of her. The legend ʿtrʿth also is to be read. The reverse shows a
lying lion with open mouth and the legend ʾlksndr. The last coin of
this series shows a head of Atargatis turned left; the goddess wears
a tiara. The reverse side shows a sitting Atargatis turned to the left;
she wears a long dress with a belt, holds in her right hand a cup,
and leans with her left hand on a sceptre. The legend SE dates this
coin in the time of Seleucus (I Nicator).[32]

Some conclusions can already be drawn from this very varied
series of coins. The name of the goddess occurs in three different
forms: ʿth (nos. 4, 6, 7, 10, 11), ʿtrʿth (nos. 2, 3, 9, 12, 13) and trʿth
(nos. 3, 5). It seems certain that the original name of the Dea Syria
at Hierapolis is just ʿth—Ateh, and that the element ʿtr derived from
ʿštr has the meaning of goddess, so that the full name ʿtrʿth means
"the goddess ʿAteh," Ateh being the goddess par excellence. The
name ʿth originates from ʿanat and should be considered the Ara-
macized form with assimilation of the n and the female ending—h
(or -ʾ).[33] That ʿAteh is the goddess' original name is also attested
by the theophorous proper names formed with that element which
are much more numerous than proper names formed with the fuller
form ʿtrʿth.[34] The iconography of the goddess from Hierapolis shows
an even greater variety at the end of the fourth century B.C. when
her temple was rebuilt by Stratonike. On her head she wears a
turreted tiara (nos. 2, 3, 14) or no headdress at all (nos. 10—en
profil, 4, 6—en face); no. 5 shows a clear resemblance to an ivory

---

[32] I follow Seyrig's numbering, Le monnayage, 17ff., who superseded
Ronzevalle, Les monnaies de la dynastie de ʿAbd-Hadad, 5ff., who listed
only 11 coins.

[33] I follow the etymology as given by Ronzevalle, Les monnaies, 28ff.,
and Seyrig, Le monnayage, 13 contra Oden, Studies, 60ff.; I will return to
this subject elsewhere.

[34] cf. above p. 84 and n. 23; and the Palmyrene names ʾtʿmn - ʿAthe is
with us, ʾtʿqb - ʿAthe has protected; brʾtʾ and brʿtʾ - Son of Athe; (brʿth,
brʾty brʿ, brʿy, brtʾ also occur); ʿtʾm - ʿAthe is (my) mother; ʿthzbd - ʿAthe
has given; (hypocoristicon: ʿtzʾ) (variant: ʿtzbd); ʿthn - ʿAthe is gracious;
ʿtyk - ʿAthe is here; ʿtyʿqb - ʿAthe has protected; ʿtnwr - ʿAthe is light;
ʿtnwry - ʿAthe is my light; ʿtntn - ʿAthe has given; ʿtšʾ - ʿAthe is (my)
stronghold; etc. cf. J. K. Stark, Personal Names in Palmyrene Inscriptions,
Oxford 1971, Lexicon and the review by R. Degen, BiOr 29, 1972, 210-216
with useful comments, criticism and additions. Proper names with ʿAthe
also occur in Hatrene onomastics and at Dura-Europos. In fact proper
names compounded with ʿAthe are the most frequent of all at Palmyra.

pyxis from Rash Shamra.[35] When the goddess is fully represented
she sits on a lion (no. 11), between two sphinxes (no. 12) or on a
throne (nos. 13, 14) and besides these different positions there is
a variety in the objects she holds: she has a branch in her left hand
(no. 12), a cup in her right hand with the left one outstretched
(no. 13), or a cup in her right hand while the left one leans on a
sceptre (no. 14). Although the lion represents the goddess in different ways (nos. 7, 8; the scenes on 10 and 12 are derived from
coins of Tarsus, and 13 from Amathontes) there is only one representation of Atargatis riding a lion (no. 11).[36] The enthroned
goddess, however, is *not* accompanied by lions (nos. 13 and 14),
but only once by sphinxes, which type seems to be borrowed from
Cilician coins. Here we have another *Vorstufe* of the enthroned
Atargatis as portrayed on the Edessene relief without her traditional
lions and another indication of the relatively early date of this
relief.

It is clear that, already in the fourth century B.C., Atargatis
had surpassed her male companion Hadad. He is represented as
the Baal of Tarsus (nos. 9, 11) and as Zeus aetophoros (no. 6),
and perhaps as a bearded person wearing a high dentate tiara
riding in his chariot (nos. 2, 4, 5)—unless we suppose that the
bearded person in the chariot represents the high priest of Hierapolis, whose name is to be read on the same reverse sides. Hadad,
is never accompanied by the bulls as on later reliefs, and that
again links these coins with the Edessene relief.

The imperial coinage of Hierapolis shows the same variety in
representations of Atargatis or the divine couple with the *semeion*.
A small bronze coin dating from the time of Antoninus Pius shows
on its obverse the Tyche of Hierapolis with a turreted headdress
and a veil, and on its reverse a standing bull turned to the right
with a crescent above it. It can be assumed that the Tyche with
veil represents Atargatis and the bull Hadad in his function of
Atargatis' partner, this partnership indicated by the crescent.[37] A
bronze coin struck under Commodus shows on the reverse a lion

---

[35] Ronzevalle, Les monnaies, 23, Fig. 2; Seyrig, Le monnayage, 14, Fig. 1.
[36] *cf.* Seyrig, Le monnayage, 20f.
[37] *BMC, Galatia*, Pl. XVII, 8.

walking to the right.[38] Under Caracalla several silver coins represent
an eagle with a wreath in beak and beneath it a lion walking to the
right; sometimes the lion is accompanied by a star. This lion clearly
is Atargatis' animal; whether the eagle as the bird of heaven
represents Hadad on these coins is dubious.[39] Bronze coins of
Caracalla show Atargatis enthroned between two lions. She wears
a turreted headdress, chiton and peplos, holds in her right hand a
tympanum and in her left two ears of corn. Variants of this coin
struck under Caracalla, Severus Alexander and Julia Mamaea
represent the goddess in the same position, but holding a tympanum
in her left hand with the right resting on the throne.[40] Other bronze
coins of Caracalla and Philip sen. and jun., and a silver tetradrachme
of Julia Domna, portray the Dea Syria riding on a lion to the right,
wearing turreted headdress, chiton and peplos, a scepter in her
right hand and occasionally a tympanum in her left.[41]

A famous bronze coin of Severus Alexander at Vienna represents
Hadad and Atargatis accompanied, respectively, by bulls and
lions and sitting next to the *semeion*, which is put in a small shrine.
The *semeion* has four rings on it. Below this main device a lion is
depicted walking to the right.[42] A provincial tetradrachm very
similar to this Severus bronze has been lost and is only preserved
in a drawing by J. Pellerin. It also shows Hadad and Atargatis
sitting next to the shrine with the *semeion*, but there are some
differences according to Pellerin's drawing. Hadad is accompanied
by only one bull sitting to his right and Atargatis by one lion sitting
to her left. Both hold a sceptre in their right hands. The *semeion*
has only three rings and below the main scene there is an eagle

---

[38] *BMC, Galatia*, Pl. XVII, 11.

[39] *BMC, Galatia*, Pl. XVII, 12, 13 and Bellinger, *Syrian Tetradrachms*,
94-105, Pl. VIII, 2-15.

[40] *BMC, Galatia*, Pl. XVII, 14, 17; *Dura-Europos, Final Report* VI,
A. R. Bellinger, *The Coins*, no. 1798.

[41] *BMC, Galatia*, Pl. XVII, 15; *Dura-Europos, The Coins*, no's 1796, 1797,
1799-1802.

[42] Seyrig, Bas-relief des dieux de Hiérapolis, *Syria* 49, 1972, 105, Fig. 4;
F. Imhoof-Blumer, *Griechische Münzen*, 1890, 235, no. 772; H. A. Strong -
J. Garstang, *The Syrian Goddess*, 1913, Frontispiece and 70, Fig. 7; related
types published by F. Imhoof-Blumer, no. 773 (Pl. XIV, 7) and 775 (Julia
Mamaea).

with outstretched wings, its head turned right.[43] The main variants of Atargatis' representation are therefore a) Atargatis enthroned between two lions with various objects in her hands, among which the tympanum occurs, which surely is a borrowing from the iconography of Cybele; b) Atargatis riding on a lion with a sceptre and occasionally a tympanum, which type also occurs in the extant iconography of Cybele; and c) Atargatis and Hadad accompanied respectively by one or two lion(s) and bull(s) sitting next to the *semeion*, which is put in a shrine. A comparison of the coinage of the fourth century B.C. with the imperial coinage makes clear that the share of the lion in her various representations becomes larger and that she never is portrayed on the Hierapolis coins as an enthroned goddess without her animal(s). The whole development of this varied iconography and the traditions which influenced it ought to be studied in more detail. On the other hand, it is clear that the cult and iconography of Cybele exercised a certain influence on what was going on at Hierapolis.[44]

A restricted number of sculptures and reliefs from Hierapolis, and places nearby, confirm the impression of a varied iconographical rendering of the Dea Syria.

A small basalt stele from Hierapolis, now in the Louvre, pictures the Dea Syria enthroned between two lions. It clearly was a dedication to her temple because a fragmentary inscription below the relief reads ὑπὲρ σ[ωτηρίας ...] = on behalf of the well-being of.[45] This stele is most likely to be dated in the second century A.D.

A bronze breast with a small slit, originally belonging to the collection Froehner and originating from Northern Syria, functioned as the lid of an offertory-box used by the priests of the Lady Atargatis to collect money. The typical shape of this lid links it with a whole series of terracotta figurines from Hierapolis and

---

[43] J. Pellerin, *Mélanges de divers médailles* I, 17, 189, no. 12; A. R. Bellinger, *Syrian Tetradrachms*, 42, Fig. 2.

[44] *cf.* Drijvers, De matre inter leones sedente. Iconography and Character of the Arab goddess Allât, *Hommages à M. J. Vermaseren*, Vol. I, EPRO 68, Leiden 1978, 351 and n. 72; *cf.* R. Turcan, Cybèle et la déesse syrienne: à propos d'un relief du Musée de Vienne (Isère), *REA* 53, 1961, 45-54; M. Hörig, *Dea Syria*. Studien zur religiösen Tradition der Fruchtbarkeitsgöttin in Vorderasien, *AOAT* 208, 1979, 237ff.

[45] Goossens, *Hiérapolis de Syrie*, 116, n. 5; IGLS 231.

Northern Syria which picture the Syrian goddess nude and pressing her breasts.[46] This breast symbolizes her function as a fertility goddess which is also expressed by the ears of corn she sometimes holds. These terracotta figurines often picture the goddess with long plaits, an "archaic" Syrian representation found on the coins from Hierapolis discussed before, and also on the famous gold plaquette from Karak Nouh.[47] Others picture her with a high kalathos which forms another link with the Hierapolis iconography.

A life-size basalt statue of Atargatis at Aleppo shows the goddess sitting on a throne with her right hand raised in benediction, wearing a veil, and holding in her left hand a sceptre that is supported on her left knee. The lions are absent.[48] The combination of the raised hand and the sceptre unites protection and divine power; the sceptre in the right hand and this hand raised as a symbol of protection may alternate with each other in the iconography of Atargatis. Full stress is laid on her protective power in a curious scene on an altar found at Arime, half-way between Suruǧ (Batnae) and Mabbug; it pictures in a niche a hand with a thunderbolt and to the right of it an open right hand between two lions. The two hands symbolize Hadad and Atargatis, a short-form of their life-giving and protective powers.[49]

A rather worn bas-relief from Northern Mesopotamia now in the Museum at Beyrouth represents the three idols of Hierapolis: Hadad between his bulls, Atargatis between her lions; and the *semeion* between them. Atargatis' throne is decorated with fish, Hadad's throne with "calices floraux," and on top of these thrones respectively are pictured doves and eagles with outstretched wings. The *semeion* is adorned with a much-damaged bust, a plaque of

---

[46] cf. P. Perdrizet, A propos d'Atargatis I. Le sein d'Atargatis, *Syria* 12, 1931, 267ff., Pl. LIII; the inscription was published by F. Cumont, *Aréthuse* 1930, 41, Pl. VIII.

[47] Seyrig, Le monnayage, 18, no. 3; Ronzevalle, Les monnaies, 25f.; *idem*, Jupiter Héliopolitain. Nova et Vetera, *MUSJ* 21, 1937, 106-116, Pl. XXXII-XXXV; 144-156, Pl. XLIII-XLVIII; the gold plaquette from Karak Nouh: Ronzevalle, Les monnaies, 20; *idem, MUSJ* 12, 1927, 173ff. Pl. XXII, 5; *idem*, Jupiter Héliopolitain, 107, Pl. XXXIII, 1.

[48] First published by Ronzevalle, Jupiter Héliopolitain, 106ff. Pl. XXXIV; for the cult of Atargatis near Aleppo see Xenophon, *Anab.* I, 4, 9.

[49] Seyrig, Représentations de la main divine, *Syria* 20, 1939, 189f., Fig. 9 = *AS* III, 21f.

pentagonal shape, five medallions, and most likely with a dove on top; on each side four ribbons hang down from a horizontal pole which is fixed to the shaft of the *semeion* just above the damaged bust. To the left of this scene the bas-relief represents Apollo-Nebo of Hierapolis in such a way that one is reminded of a well-known statue from Hatra.[50] Several features of this relief connect it to the coinage of Hierapolis: the "calices floraux" remind of the flower in front of the lion as represented on the eighth coin of the fourth century B.C. series; the eagles on Hadad's throne make it more plausible that the eagle with the lion between its legs on various types of imperial coinage struck at Hierapolis actually represents Hadad.

At the same time this relief shows a *semeion* which greatly resembles the divine standard as described by Lucian, *De Syria Dea*, 31; it is, however, noteworthy that it is considerably different from the *semeia* that are pictured on the coins.

In this context the Syriac Apology of *Pseudo-Melito* and its records on the cult at Hierapolis should be mentioned and discussed.[51] This Apology contains a long euhemeristic section on pagan cults which doubtless is a translation from a Greek original. This text, however, has preserved some interesting information on the gods of Hierapolis: "The Syrians worship 'Aty from Hadib, who sent the daughter of BLT a physician; and she (i.e., the daughter of BLT) cured Simi, the daughter of Hadad, king of

---

[50] Seyrig, Bas-relief des dieux de Hiérapolis, *Syria* 49, 1972, 104ff., Pl. I; for the statue from Hatra see H. Lenzen, *AA* 1955, 339f. Fig. 2-3; R. Ghirshman, *Parthes et Sassanides*, Paris 1962, p. 1; F. Safar - M. A. Mustafa, *Hatra*. The City of the sun God, Baghdad 1974, 236ff. (in Arabic); J. M. Rosenfield, *The Dynastic Arts of the Kushans*, Los Angeles 1967, Fig. 140; R. du Mesnil du Buisson, De Shadrafa, dieu de Palmyre, à Ba'al Shamîm, dieu de Hatra, aux IIe et IIIe siècles après J.-C., *MUSJ* 38, 1962, 149ff., Pl. I; Macrob. *Saturn* I, 17, 66ff.; *cf.* Seyrig, *Syria* 26, 1947, 19f. = *AS* IV, 21f.; for the various *semeia* see S. B. Downey, A Preliminary Corpus of the Standards of Hatra, *Sumer* 26, 1970, 195-225; W. Fauth, *PW*, *Suppl.* XIV, 1974, 679-701, art. Simia.

[51] On Pseudo-Melito from Sardis see I. Ortiz de Urbina, *Patrologia Syriaca*, sec. ed. Roma 1965, 41; Oden, *Studies*, 127ff.; the Syriac text is a translation of a Greek original dating from the third century A.D.; W. Cureton, *Spicilegium Syriacum*, London 1855, 22-35 published the Syriac text, 41-51 an English translation.

Syria." The *Apology* then relates a long story on Nebo at Mabbug,
who actually is a statue of Orpheus the Thracian magian, and
Hadaran, who is supposed to be a statue of Zaradušt (= Zarathustra). Both magians practice their art near a well at Mabbug in
which an unclean demon lived. They ordered Simi, daughter of
Hadad, to bring water from the sea and to pour it into this well in
order to slay this demon.[52] The name ῾Aty is a Syriac transcription
of the Greek ῎Aθη, which again renders the original name of the
Dea Syria, namely, ῾Ateh. The original name of Apollo of Hierapolis,
namely, Nebo, is also preserved by Pseudo-Melito and likewise a
title of Hadad, namely, Hadaran which already occurs on one of
the coins from the fourth century B.C.[53] The Apology knows about
the magic (foretelling?) qualities of Nebo and Hadad and their
relation to an ancient flood tradition linked with Hierapolis. The
unclean demon personifies the flood, and Hierapolis was long
considered the site of a χάσμα which was worshipped as a sacred
spring. This link with the deluge story is attested by Lucian, *De
Syria Dea*, 12-13, and substantiated by the Aramaic name of
Hierapolis—Manbu/ig which derives from a Semitic root *nbg* or
nb῾, which means "to break forth"; their derivates *nbg'* and *mbb῾*
have the meaning of "spring." [54] In a characteristically euhemeristic
way *Pseudo-Melito* personifies the *semeion* as Simi, daughter of
Hadad, but he has exact information about the role of the *semeion*
in the water rite at Hierapolis which is recorded in detail by Lucian,
De Syria Dea, 13, 33, 47-48. This ritual has a twofold meaning:
allaying the dangerous flood and preserving the life-giving spring;
and so it is explained by Lucian, 13: συμφορῆς τε καὶ εὐεργεσίης

---

[52] Cureton, *Spicilegium Syriacum*, 44, 11.26ff.; Seyrig, Les dieux de
Hiérapolis, *Syria* 37, 1960, 243ff. = *AS* VI, 89ff. offers a commentary on
this passage; *cf.* Milik, *Dédicaces*, 409; Oden, *Studies*, 109ff. on the *semeion*;
by Hadib most probably Aleppo is meant, *cf.* Oden, *Studies*, 131, who drew
attention to the fact that Hadib may be a transliteration of Greek χαλέπ
misread as χαδέπ one of the commonest Greek textual errors.

[53] *cf.* Seyrig, Le monnayage, no. 1 and 14, n. 4; J. Marcadé, *Au Musée
de Délos*. Étude sur la sculpture hellénistique en ronde bosse découverte
dans l'île, Paris 1969, 381; *IGLS* 2908, 2928.

[54] *cf.* Oden, *Studies*, 30ff. esp. 32; *cf. Thesaurus Syriacus*, ed. R. Payne
Smith, *s.v. nbg* and *nb῾*.

μνῆμα ἔμμεναι. It should be considered a typical example of imitative magic and has nothing to do with rain magic or the like.[55]

We may take for certain now that a deity Simia or Semia, or the like, never existed but that all these different forms in Greek inscriptions are intended to transcribe the Aramaic *smy'*, of which Lucian gives the Greek homophone with the same meaning *semeion*.[56] It is interesting that Pseudo-Melito links this *semeion* to Hadad in particular (Simi, daughter of Hadad) and not to both deities equally, as could be expected from the iconography. Simi, daughter of Hadad, actually is an euhemeristic phrasing of "the semeion of Hadad," whereas the *semeion* as described by Lucian, 33, seems to be a schematization and symbol of Atargatis.[57] If the *semeion* is in fact a symbolical schematization of a certain deity's representation, it is worth considering whether the *semeion* on the Edessene stele may represent Hadad with both arms raised, exactly in the same manner as the god is portrayed on the first coin of the fourth century B.C. series. It is even possible that a certain historical development is indicated by these different literary traditions and iconographical renderings in this way, that the oldest tradition linked the flood and its destructive and life-giving power to Hadad alone and his *semeion*, and that Atargatis gradually became more

---

[55] So Stocks, Studien, 23-28; C. Clemen, *Lukians Schrift über die syrische Göttin*, 52.

[56] A fairly complete survey of all the evidence concerning Simia and related forms was given by W. Fauth, art. Simia, *PW, Suppl.* XIV, 1974, 679-701, who, however, comes to no firm conclusion about its meaning and etymology; *cf.* also Milik, *Dédicaces*, 408-411, who tried to prove the existence of a deity 'name' (*šm'* = name), but is not convincing; see already Milik, *Biblica* 48, 1967, 567-570; Fauth, art. Simia, 685f. and the literature quoted there; the most plausible solution of this complex problem is to assume that Aramaic *smy'* (from a root *sym/swm* = to put, to set up) means (divine) standard or 'symbol' and can symbolize as such various divinities; male and female. That is why the Aramaic word was variously rendered in Greek, matters being even further complicated by its homophony with Greek *semeion* = standard. There is, therefore, no reason to assume that Aramaic *smy'* is a borrowing from the Greek, but rather the other way round. The Syriac *symy* in the Apology of Pseudo-Melito can only be understood if it is considered a 'translation' into Syriac from the Greek *semia* or the like. *cf.* also Oden, *Studies*, 115 for a sensible discussion of this problem, to which I hope to return in another context.

[57] Oden, *Studies*, 148f.

important as representative of the life-giving power of the water. Hence the *semeion* became Atargatis' symbol according to its description by Lucian. The text of Pseudo-Melito and the Edessene relief, on the contrary, may preserve an older and more original tradition. In this context the remarkable polarity between Hadad and Atargatis in the fulfilling of the water rite deserves to be mentioned; it is recorded by Lucian, *De Syria Dea*, 47: if Hadad should come near the pond all fish will die, and that is why Atargatis keeps him at a safe distance! Hadad is only left with his destructive power as giver of the flood, whereas Atargatis represents divine life, symbolized by the fish. But originally Hadad and Nebo allayed the flood by sending Hadad's *semeion*! That Atargatis gets a more and more predominant position in relation to Hadad is also expressed by her different names. The oldest phase of her nomenclature is plain *'Ateh*, a name preserved by some coins from the fourth century B.C. by Pseudo-Melito and by a whole series of proper names which, generally speaking, were very traditional. In a later phase the goddess is called *'tr'th* = Atargatis, which name can be paraphrased as *'Ateh* the goddess *par excellence*; she always is accompanied by her lion(s). The various sources for the study of her cult at Edessa and at Hierapolis preserve testimonies of both phases. Lucian's treatise pictures the situation in the middle of the second century A.D. Combined with other sources, however, it offers a glimpse of a long development under various influences which we can grasp in the fourth century B.C. but which had started much earlier. The other testimonies will confirm this view.

Harran

The cult of Atargatis in this city is attested by Jacob of Saruǧ's *Homily on the Fall of the Idols*, ll.53-54:

> He (i.e., Satan) led astray Harran by Sin, Ba'alšamên and Bar-Nemrê
>
> By my Lord with his Dogs and the goddesses Tar'atha and Gadlat.[58]

---

[58] *cf.* Ch. II, n. 69; Landesdörfer, Die Götterliste, 13, ll.53f.; Ms. O (Ms. Syriac Oxford 135) reads *wtr'ṭ' wgd' 'lht'* and Atargatis and Gad the goddesses; Ms. L² (BM 14624) *wltr'ṭ' gdlt 'lht'* = and Atargatis Gadlat of the goddesses.

Although some textual variants in this homily might suggest that Tar'ata is conceived as Gad-Tyche or that Gadlat is an epithet of the Dea Syria, the best reading considers them different goddesses, and such an interpretation is supported by the 11th homily of Isaac of Antioch on the conquest of Beth Ḥur, XI, 167-168: "The demon that is called Gadlat wove his (i.e., Satan) wrath on his servants." [59] The most plausible explanation of the name Gadlat is to consider it a composite of Gad and Allat, the Arab goddess widely worshipped by the desert people in Syria and Mesopotamia, so that it means: Allat is Gad. Gad is the Aramaic equivalent of Greek Tyche and a whole range of deities can fulfill the function of Gad of a certain city, village, a garden or a spring. At Palmyra, e.g., 'Ateh as Gad occurs on a tessera, where she is called *gd'ť dy bl* = Gad'ateh of Bel. It remains to be seen, if 'Ateh as Gad actually is the consort of Bel.[60] In the pantheon of Palmyra a great number of female deities occur according to the inscriptions and the tesserae, so that J. Teixidor assumed that the same goddess was invoked under different names, and therefore he identified Allat, Aštarte-Ishtar, Beltak, Belti, Gad of YDY'BL as fundamentally the same deity.[61] At Harran, however, Atargatis and Allat clearly are different deities. The complex problem of the many different female deities at Palmyra, their relations to each other, to various groups of the population and to Bel, the traditional theos patroios, will require our attention later on.

The cult of Atargatis linked Harran to Hierapolis and this relation is indicated by the same Homily on the Fall of the Idols; 11.59-62:

> Mabbug made he (i.e., Satan) a city of the priests of the goddess(es)
> And called it with his name in order that it would err forever (going after its idols),

---

[59] There is a wordplay here between Gadlat (Syriac *gdlt*) and the verb *gdl* = to twist, to weave; cf. M. Lidzbarski, *Ephemeris für semitische Epigraphik* I, Giessen 1902, 260.

[60] *RTP* 680; cf. J. Starcky, Deux inscriptions palmyréniennes, *MUSJ* 38, 1962, 130f.; 'Athe as Gad is an exact equivalent of Atargatis, who functions as Gad/Tyche of Palmyra; see further H. Seyrig, La parèdre de Bêl à Palmyre, *Syria* 37, 1960, 68-74 = *AS* VI, 72-79.

[61] J. Teixidor, *The Pagan God*, 116, n. 44; see already, Gawlikowski, *Le temple palmyrénien*, 52, n. 159.

A sister of Harran, which is also devoted to the offerings;
And in their error both of them love the springs.[62]

Hierapolis and Harran are considered by Jacob of Saruğ as the
centers of paganism in his time and that is why he gives so much
attention to both of them and their connections.[63] The Tyche of
Harran is attested in two different representations on the coins:
as a city-goddess with turreted crown and veil, seated on a rock
with the river-god below her feet; or as a turreted and veiled bust,
sometimes crowned by a crescent, which also may portray the local
Atargatis.[64] This is even more likely since the cult of Atargatis is
attested by literary texts in the same cities in Northern Mesopotamia which show the Tyche on their coins: Edessa and Harran,
but also Nisibis,[65] and Resh Aina.[66]

By-passing the other literary attestations of Atargatis' cult in
Northern Mesopotamia and Syria,[67] and restricting ourselves to
epigraphical and archaeological evidence, there is clear proof of
the worship of the Dea Syria at Niḥa in the Beqa. A Niḥa limestone
stele bears two inscriptions:

Sex(tus) Allius Iullus
vet(eranus) monumen-
tum Ochmaeae
virgini vati
Deae Syr(iae) Nihat(enae)
fecit

---

[62] Landersdorfer, Die Götterliste, 13, 11.59-62; 51-53.

[63] Isaac of Antioch also connects the paganism of Beth Ḥur and Nisibis
with Harran in his homilies on the conquest of Beth Ḥur; both share the
cult of Atargatis and of Baʿalšamên, Lord of the gods (*ryšʾ dʾlhʾ*).

[64] See Hill, *BMC, Arabia*, Pl. XII, 7, 13, 21, 24; Pl. XIII, 1sqq.

[65] See Hill, *BMC, Arabia*, Pl. XVII, 10-12, 14; Moses of Khorene, *History
of Armenia* 37 = *FHG* 5, 326.

[66] *cf.* Aelianus, *Hist. an.* 12, 30; P.-L. van Berg, *CCDS* I, 2, 114ff.: Héra-
Atargatis à Ressaina; *BMC, Arabia*, Pl. XVIII, 5; cf. K. O. Castelus, Coinage
of Rhesaena in Mesopotamia, *NNM* 108, 1946, 26ff., Pl. IV.; T. Dohrn,
Die Tyche von Antiochia, 56f.

[67] Béséchana, Isid., *Man. Parth.* I, 5; Aleppo, Xenophon, *Anab.* I, 4, 9;
Babylon, *Diodorus II*, 9 (after Ktesias), *cf.* E. Will, Aspects du culte et de
la légende de la grande mère dans le monde grec, *Éléments orientaux dans la
religion grecque ancienne*, Paris 1960, 102; *cf.* also E. Will, *Le relief cultuel
gréco-romain*, Paris 1955, 125f.; M. Hörig, Dea Syria, *passim*.

A Greek inscription has been written just below it:

'Οχμαια παρθένος
θεᾶς 'Αταργάτεις
ἔζη ἔτη ἑκατον.[68]

Another inscription from the same place records that the virgin Hochmaeae kept her promise to the god Hadaran not to eat bread for twenty years: *Hocmae|a virgo | dei || Ha|dara|nis | quia | annis | (viginti) pan|em | non || edi|dit | iussu | ipsius || dei | v(otum) l(ibens) a (nimo) s(olvit).*

It has been written to the left and the right of a heavily damaged relief of an enthroned god between two bulls, quite apparently the god Hadaran, which covers one of the sides of an altar. One of the other sides shows a veiled bust of the virgin Hochmaea with the inscription: *Deo Hadrani | Hochmaea v(otum) s(olvit).*[69] An altar from Deir al-Aḥmar in the Beqa also mentions the god Hadaran:

[Deo Ha]daran[i]
Haiaeus pro [salute sua et]
[fili]orum suor[um].[70]

A base or lintel from Niḥa records a dedication by the *pagus Augustus*, a corporation of Roman citizens in the *civitas* of Niḥa:

Dea Suria Nihathe(na)
pro Aug(usto), Pagus
Augustus fecit
et dedica[vi]t.[71]

The *pagus Augustus* seemingly dedicated a statue of the Dea Syria which now has been lost. This *dossier* of inscriptions deals with the cult of a local form of Atargatis at Niḥa, where she was coupled with the god Hadaran, quite apparently another name of Hadad. Hadaran had a small temple at Niḥa; another larger temple at the same place may be the sanctuary of the Dea Syria.[72] The

---

[68] *IGLS* 2929; Pl. XLVIII; *cf.* Milik, *Dédicaces*, 374.

[69] *IGLS* 2928, Pl. XLVII.

[70] *IGLS* 2908.

[71] *IGLS* 2936.

[72] *cf. IGLS* 2928: Krencker-Zschietzschmann, *Römische Tempel in Syrien*, 1938, 105ff.; G. Taylor, *The Roman Temples of Lebanon*, Beyrouth 1967, 34ff. offers recent photographs of these temples.

virgin Hochmaea functioned as a prophetess of the local Atargatis
and also was a virgin of Hadaran; this indicated a common sanctuary of both deities or at least tied relations between them. The
function of the virgin, who lived for a hundred years, is perhaps
alluded to in her name which is related to the Semitic root *hkm*
= to be wise. The prophecying qualities of our goddess also are
recorded by Diodorus Siculus in a long story about a slave Eunus
at Henna on Sicily originating from Apamea in Syria, who instigated
the slave revolt in 136 B.C. The Dea Syria appeared to him in a
vision and promised him that he would become a king.[73] It is noteworthy that the function of oracle-giving and foretelling at Hierapolis was exercised by Nebo-Apollo and not by Atargatis herself.
This may be an indication of the fact that Nebo, the Babylonian
oracle-god *par excellence*, took over some functions from Atargatis
when he arrived at Hierapolis and was venerated at the local
sanctuary.

Salamiyeh

A small bas relief from Salamiyeh, half-way between Palmyra
and Apamea on the Orontes, might represent the goddess Atargatis
enthroned with a lance or sceptre in her right hand and a lion sitting
to her left.[74] Since this area is especially dedicated to the cult of
the Arab goddess Allat, it is, however, quite possible that this
fragmentary relief actually represents Allat, whose iconography
has much in common with that of the Dea Syria.[75]

Kafr Nebo

Since the lion is the animal typical of Atargatis, there are several
reasons to consider its mention in a much-discussed Greek dedication from Kafr Nebo in Northern Syria as an indication of the Dea

---

[73] *cf.* P.-L. van Berg, *CCDS*, 100f.: Photius, *Bibliotheca no. 244* = *Diodorus, F. lib.* 34/35, 2, 5-7 = *Posidonius, F.* 108a, 5-7; a parallel story in
Florus, *Epitome de Tito Livio* 2, 7 = Tit. Livius, *Hist. Romana* LVI, no. 82.

[74] Seyrig, *Syria* 14, 1933, 17, n. 3; the bas-relief is in the National Museum
at Damascus; its size: h. 32, b. 32; Seyrig considers it a representation of
Atargatis.

[75] Drijvers, De matre inter leones sedente. Iconography and character
of the Arab goddess Allât, *Hommages M. J. Vermaseren*, 340ff.

Syria. The inscription in question is a dedication of an olive-press
with accessories to:

Σειμιω και Συμβετυλω και Λεοντι θεοις πατρωοις

which was built on the income from their temple (ἐκ των των θεων
προσοδων).[76] The most plausible explanation of this enigmatic
dedication is that the Greek renders and describes a cultic relief
or other representation in the local temple which portrays a divine
standard (Σειμιον) and a lion (Λεων) flanking a baetyl belonging to
or connected with both of them (Συμβετυλον). The Greek Σειμιον
is therefore another transcription of the Aramaic *smy'* which is
rendered in different ways.[77] If this standard really represents
Hadad in a symbolical manner, as may be the case in the Apology
of Pseudo-Melito and in a Latin inscription from the temple at
Deir el-Qal'a near Beyrouth, then we may assume that the gods of
Hierapolis or a local variant of them are pictured in the temple at
Kafr Nebo as a standard and a lion at both sides of a baetyl.[78] The
baetyl is reminiscent of the *semeion* on the Edessa stele discussed
before, which has kept the shape of that typical Semitic idol.

Hatra

The cult of the goddess of Hierapolis apparently spread as far
as the famous desert-city of Hatra near ancient Assur in Northern
Mesopotamia.[79] The worship of the Dea Syria is attested in three

---

[76] *IGLS* 376, 383; cf. Milik, *Dédicaces*, 411; *idem, Biblica* 48, 1967, 568f.;
W. Fauth, art. Simia, 682; Milik's reading Σειμω instead of Σειμιω, one of
his main arguments for the existence of a deity 'Name', is to be rejected;
cf. Fauth, Simia, 685ff.

[77] Fauth, 689 interpreted the Lion as Atargatis, Symbetylos as Hadad
and Seimios as the young god (Hermes, Nebo) starting from R. Dussaud,
Syria 21, 1940, 367ff. Pl. LVI, 4. This interpretation brings these deities
close to the triad of Heliopolis-Baalbek; see Y. Hajjar, *La triade d'Héliopolis-
Baalbek*, I, *EPRO* 59, Leiden 1977, 155; cf. also H. Seyrig, *Syria* 40, 1963,
17-19 = *AS* VI, 119-121 and *idem*, Un ex-voto au dieu Bétyle, *Mémorial
Jean de Menasce*, Louvain 1974, 87ff.

[78] The inscription from Deir el-Qal'a: *CIL* III, 159; P. Perdrizet, *RA*
1898, 2, 39; R. Dussaud, *REA* 42, 1940, 132: *I.O.M. B(almarcodis) et Iunonis
fil(iae) Iovis Sim(a)e*.

[79] See Drijvers, *ANRW* II, 8, 1977, 803-837; with bibliography; F. Safar -
M. A. Mustafa, *Hatra. The City of the Sun God*, Baghdad 1974 (in Arabic)
with good photographs. The majority of the inscriptions were first published

inscriptions and two reliefs. Inscription no. 5, originating from a
small temple outside the central sanctuary, records a priest of
Atargatis (*kmr᾽ d᾽tr῾t᾽*) who had a statue of his wife erected.[80]
Inscription no. 29 is an invocation of the triad of Hatra, Mar[e]n,
Mart[e]n and Bar-Marên followed by ŠḤRW, Ba῾alšamên (*b῾šmyn*)
and Atargatis (᾽*tr῾t᾽*) which comes from the temple no. 4.[81] Inscription no. 30 is written on the socle of the statue of a young lady
who died when she was eighteen years old. The triad of Hatra,
Ba῾alšamên and Atargatis are invoked in order to punish her
murderer.[82] The context in which Atargatis occurs, i.e., together
with Ba῾alšamên and ŠḤRW, suggests that the goddess arrived
at Hatra with some tribes from a more Western area where Ba῾al-
šamên and ŠḤRW were at home.[83] One of the minor temples at
Hatra outside the central area may have been dedicated to her,
just as Ba῾alšamên had a temple of his own, but unhappily
enough we do not know which it was.

On the well-known Nergal relief from Hatra, Atargatis is pictured
to the left of the underworld deity sitting between two lions, with
fish at her feet and a sacred standard in her left hand. She is crowned
by an eagle with outstretched wings. Being represented on this
relief she may be Nergal's companion at Hatra as is the case on

---

by F. Safar in Sumer and re-edited by A. Caquot in Syria, see the list in
ANRW II, 8.

[80] See A. Caquot, *Syria* 29, 1952, 92f.; B. Aggoula, Remarques sur les
inscriptions hatréennes, *Berytus* 18, 1969, 87 offers some minor corrections
of Safar's and Caquot's reading; Milik, *Dédicaces*, 166; the inscription is
written on the socle of the statue in question:

> ṣlmt᾽ dy smy brt ῾g᾽br
> ᾽šntty br slwq dy ᾽yqym lh ῾g᾽
> b῾lh br ᾽b᾽ kmr᾽ d᾽tr῾t᾽
> ᾽b᾽ glp br ῾g᾽ zrq᾽

[81] A. Caquot, *Syria* 30, 1953, 235f.; Milik, *Dédicaces*, 166 and 359 offers
a special interpretation of this inscription.

[82] A. Caquot, *Syria* 30, 1953, 235f.; Milik, *Dédicaces*, 381.

[83] On Ba῾alshamên see in general Haussig, *Wörterbuch der Mythologie* I,
273, s.v. Baal-Samēn; 429f. s.v. Ba῾alšamīn; P. Collart - J. Vicari, *Le sanctuaire de Baalshamin à Palmyre* I, 201ff.; on ŠḤRW, whose name means
'dawn', 'twilight', see: G. Ryckmans, *Les religions arabes préislamiques*,
Louvain 1951, 42; Haussig, *Wörterbuch der Mythologie* I, 525f., s.v. Šaḥar
and 306f., s.v. Šaḥr und Šalim; H. Gese - M. Höfner - K. Rudolph, *Die
Religionen Altsyriens, Altarabiens und der Mandäer*, Stuttgart 1970, 253, 271.

some Palmyrene tesserae.[84] A small statuette from Hatra, now in the Museum of Istanbul, should be compared to Atargatis on the Nergal-relief. Here, too, Atargatis is represented seated between lions and dressed like the goddess on the Nergal slab with a high girdle. In her right hand she holds a short staff or a spindle, in her left hand a leaf. The goddess on the Nergal relief holds the leaf in her right hand.[85] The Istanbul statuette also shows the characteristic fish on the base panel of her throne. The deity Hadad seems to be absent at Hatra; instead of him Nergal perhaps functions as Atargatis' partner.[86] Something similar may be the case at Palmyra, which sheds another light on some of the major qualities of the Dea Syria.

Palmyra

According to two honorific bilingual inscriptions—Greek and Palmyrene—one originating from Baʿalšamên's temple and dated to 132 A.D.,[87] and the other from the sanctuary of Allat and dating from 144 A.D., there was a temple of Atargatis at Palmyra, which probably belonged to one of the four tribes that formed the body of the citizens.[88] The four sanctuaries listed in the inscription from 132 are the temple of Baʿalšamên, that of Ares-Arṣu, the so-called sacred wood—perhaps the sanctuary of Aglibol and Malakbel—and the temple of Atargatis (ἱερόν 'Αταργάτειος). In each of them was

---

[84] For a detailed discussion of this relief see Drijvers, Mithra at Hatra?, 171ff.; *RTP*, no's 233-236; H. Seyrig, Héraclès-Nergal, *Syria* 24, 1945, 79f. = *AS* IV, 18f.

[85] H. Ingholt, *Parthian Sculptures from Hatra*. Orient and Hellas in Art and Religion, *Memoirs of the Conn. Acad. of Art and Sciences* 12, New Haven 1954, 33 and Pl. VI, 1.

[86] *cf.* Drijvers, Mithra at Hatra? 173; it is noteworthy that the Hatrene Nergal has much in common with the healing god Shadrafa, *cf.* Drijvers, *art. cit.*, 176, *cf.* A. Caquot, Chadrapha. A propos de quelques articles récents, *Syria* 29, 1952, 74-88; does this healing aspect form part of the background of the story in the *Apology of Pseudo-Melito*?

[87] *cf.* C. Dunant, Nouvelle inscription caravanière de Palmyre, *MH* 13, 1956, 216-223; *idem, Le sanctuaire de Baalshamin à Palmyre* III. *Les inscriptions*, Rome 1971, 56ff., no. 45.

[88] The inscription from the sanctuary of Allât is still unpublished; it is another honorific inscription for Soados son of Bôliadès, in whose honor the inscription from Baʿalshamên's temple was also made; *cf.* Gawlikowski, *Le temple palmyrénien*, 51.

put a statue of So'adu son of Bolyad'a, a famous caravan leader, in order to honor him because of his meritorious exploits. In the inscription from 144 A.D. the temple of Allat heads the list instead of Ba'alšamên's sanctuary. This remarkable shift might be explained within the context of the close connections between the two sanctuaries, but it also makes clear that the temple of Allat and the temple of Atargatis are not identical, although Allat often is represented with all the distinctive iconographical traits of Atargatis.[89] The number of female deities mentioned in the Palmyrene inscriptions, represented on the reliefs and portrayed on the tesserae, is indeed rather high, but that does not always mean that the same deity was invoked under different names, as J. Teixidor suggests.[90] The solution for this confusing problem should rather be sought in a more "sociological" and less "theological" direction, namely, that all these goddesses, although they make the impression of being all the same, were worshipped by different groups of the population.

The existence of a temple of Atargatis also appears from the third inscription that records her name. It is a dedication, dating from 140 A.D., of a statue to a certain Ahofali, who performed pious works (*mḥrmn*) for Malakbel, Gad Taimi and Atargatis (*'tr't h*).[91] The Aramaic word *mḥrmn* is not completely clear, but most likely refers to some constructions offered to a temple.

The religious iconography of Palmyra provides us with some examples which may shed some light on the goddess' personality. She occurs on one of the beams of Bel's temple which used to support the ceiling of the *peristylium*. It portrays a fight against a chaos monster with various deities participating in this primeval struggle: Shadrafa, Atargatis dressed like Artemis with a bow, but

---

[89] Drijvers, De matre inter leones sedente, *passim*.

[90] J. Teixidor, *The Pagan God*, 116, n. 44; *cf.* Gawlikowski, *Le temple palmyrénien*, 52, n. 159; Seyrig, La parèdre de Bêl à Palmyre, *AS* VI, 72ff.; R. du Mesnil du Buisson, *Les tessères et les monnaies de Palmyre*, Paris 1962, 359ff.: La Grande déesse, épouse de Bêl et protectrice de la ville, peut apparaître sous divers noms . . . . I am preparing an article on the goddesses of Palmyra, which will appear in the near future.

[91] *CIS* II, 3927; *cf.* Gawlikowski, *Le temple palmyrénien*, 51 for a discussion of *mḥrmn*, deriving from *ḥrm* = to devote (aphel); a substantive *ḥrm* = a devoted thing; *cf. DISO*, 96, *s.v. ḥrm*.

recognizable as the Dea Syria by a fish; Ichthys son of Atargatis-
Derketo, Arṣu, Heracles and an unidentifiable goddess, of whom
the lower part of a long robe is only visible.[92] This context characterizes Atargatis as a warrior-goddess and a tutelary deity of well-
ordered human society which is saved from a threatening chaos.
At Hatra Nergal exercised this special function, often identified
with Heracles, who moreover has much in common with Shadrafa.
This may be the reason that Nergal and Atargatis occur together
at the Nergal relief from Hatra, and that Atargatis fights side by
side with Shadrafa on this Palmyrene piece.[93]

Atargatis' militant and protecting qualities are the main ground
for her functioning as a Tyche and as such she is represented on a
famous stele found during the excavations of Nebo's temple at
Palmyra and most likely originating from that sanctuary.[94] It
shows the goddess enthroned and a dog sitting to her right. Beside
her stands another Tyche with mural crown and olive branch,
perhaps the *Gad Taimi*.[95] The right foot of the enthroned goddess
rests on a swimming figure symbolizing the spring Ephqa, a local
adaptation of the Antiochene Orontes figure. The sitting dog connects the goddess with Nergal, her partner at Hatra, where he is
portrayed with (three) dogs, symbolized by a dog, and even is
called dog. The dog apparently indicates Nergal's guardian function
and may have the same meaning in relation to Atargatis as Tyche
of Palmyra.[96]

---

[92] Seyrig-Amy-Will, *Le temple de Bel*, 87; Album 90, Pl. 44; *cf. AS* II,
24f.; Drijvers, *The Religion of Palmyra*, Pl. IV, 2; the goddess next to
Heracles represented on Pl. XIV is more or less identical with the goddess
next to Heracles on the beam from the temple of Bêl and consequently is
not Atargatis.

[93] *cf.* Drijvers, Mithra at Hatra?, 173-177.

[94] It should be dated about 100 A.D.; see A. Bounni - N. Saliby, *AAS* 15,
1965, 127ff.; F. Mellinghoff in: F. Altheim - R. Stiehl, *AAW* V, 2, 1969,
58-164; Milik, *Dédicaces*, 164ff.; Drijvers, *The Religion of Palmyra*, Pl. LI.

[95] For the *Gad Taimi* see: *CIS* II 3927; *RTP* 135, 273, 274, 275, 277, 279;
cf. J. Starcky, Deux inscriptions palmyréniennes, 137, n. 1; Gawlikowski,
Le temple palmyrénien, 52; The *Gad Taimi* is usually associated with the
god Malakbêl.

[96] Nergal is called dog in Hatrene inscriptions, represented as a dog or
together with three dogs and, moreover called dḥšptʾ = chief of the guard(s),
cf. Drijvers, Mithra at Hatra?, 171f. for all references.

The Palmyrene colony at Dura-Europos also had its own tutelary spirit, the *gd' dy tdmwr* = Tyche of Palmyra, which had the Tyche of Dura as counterpart. She is to be seen together with the Durene Tyche on the mural in the temple of the Palmyrene gods, in which Julius Terentius, the Roman tribune, makes his offering to three Palmyrene deities.[97] A relief coming from the temple of the Gadde or Tychai shows Atargatis as Tyche of Palmyra with mural crown and lion, accompanied by a Victory with palm-garland, and a priest. This last relief in particular shows a certain resemblance to the one from the Nebo temple.[98]

Although only one *tessera* (no. 201) mentions the name of Atargatis (*'tr'th*) and pictures her as a star above a *bukranion*, which should symbolize Hadad, the goddess is most likely attested on other tesserae too. The goddess sitting between two animals (lions?) (nos. 234, 236), or standing with a lance or sceptre (nos. 233, 235) who accompanies Nergal characterized by the double ax and a lion, is certainly Atargatis.[99] Other items are less clear, but the enthroned goddess with a large fish in front of her (no. 432) probably is Atargatis, all the more so since the reverse shows a lion attacking a deer, both animals being typical of our goddess.[100] Tessera no. 389 shows a sitting Atargatis or Allat with a lion, as may be the case with no. 207 showing a goddess flanked by two lions. No. 430, picturing a sitting goddess with a long sceptre and

---

[97] See F. Cumont, *Fouilles de Doura-Europos*, 89ff., Pl. XLIX-LI; Seyrig, *AS* I, 31f.; Pl. XLIII; A. Perkins, *The Art of Dura-Europos*, 42ff., Fig. 12; Drijvers, *The religion of Palmyra*, Pl. XIX; Downey, *The Stone and Plaster Sculpture*, Pl. XLVII.

[98] *Dura-Europos, Prel. Report of seventh and eighth seasons*, 260-262, Pl. XXXIV; Gawlikowski, A propos des relief du temple des gaddê à Doura, *Berytus* 18, 1969, 105-111; Perkins, *The Art of Dura-Europos*, 79ff., Pl. 32; the inscription: du Mesnil, *Inventaire des inscriptions palmyréniennes*, no's 31-32; Ingholt, *Berytus* 3, 1936, 114-115, Pl. XXIII; Milik, *Dédicaces*, 290; Drijvers, *The Religion of Palmyra*, Pl. XX; Downey, *The Stone and Plaster Sculpture*, 17-19, Pl. III, 5.

[99] *cf. RTP*, 233-236; the editors, however, do not identify the goddess; nor the god with double axe and lion; tessera 394 may also represent Nergal and Atargatis, although the editors suggest Shadrafa (with question mark!).

[100] *cf.* Drijvers, A New Sanctuary at Palmyra, *Archeology* 31, 1978, 60f., where an orthostat representing a standing lion with a gazelle has been published. This stood near the entrance of Allat's sanctuary at Palmyra.

on the reverse a dolphin, should, however, be considered a representation of Atargatis if we may assume a certain relation between the
frontside and backside of the tessera. Whether the various Tychai
(nos. 344, 378, 415) and other female deities (nos. 507, 510) may
refer to the Dea Syria is still more dubious. A medallion in the
British Museum, clearly pictures Atargatis, turned to the right,
the sceptre in her right hand, the lion beside her.[101]

The coinage of Palmyra is a rather neglected branch of numismatic studies, but, insofar as it is now known, some of the small
local bronze coins show the bust of the Tyche, and on the reverse
side, a lion walking to the right; and one coin even portrays Atargatis riding on a lion. The combination of the Tyche with the lion
makes it fairly certain that she renders Atargatis.[102]

The mainly iconographical evidence from Palmyra regarding the
Dea Syria stresses her protective character which finds its strongest
and fullest expression in her functioning as Tyche of the city. It is
utterly unknown in which period she made her entrance into the
religious life of Palmyra, but considering that her temple was
one of the four sanctuaries, it must be quite early for her to have
developed into the guardian goddess *par excellence*.

Dura-Europos

Several pieces of sculpture, terracottas and inscriptions bear
witness to the cult of Atargatis at Dura-Europos, where she had
a temple of her own near the temple of Artemis.[103] The oldest dated

---

[101] First published by M. Rostovtzeff, Hadad and Atargatis at Palmyra,
AJA 1933, 58-63, no. 1; according to Rostovtzeff, the goddess is pictured
sitting between two lions, which is incorrect; cf. Seyrig, *AS* I, 87, n. 1 for a
severe criticism of Rostovtzeff's views; see R. du Mesnil, *Les tessères et les
monnaies*, 371, Fig. 205; Drijvers, *De matre inter leones sedente*, 345 and
n. 39.

[102] For the coins of Palmyra see R. du Mesnil, *Les tessères et les monnaies*,
752, where the relevant coins are listed; the subject is in need of a fresh
treatment, cf. A. Krzuzanowska, Trésor de monnaies palmyréniennes trouvé
à Alexandrie, *Actes du 8ème congrès international de numismatique N.Y.-
Washington 1973*, Paris-Bâle 1976, 327-332, Pl. 40.

[103] *Dura-Europos, Prel. Report of third season*, 1929-1930, 9-11; 18-24;
35-36; *cf.* C. Bradford Welles, The Gods of Dura-Europos, *Festschrift F. Altheim*, Berlin 1970, 56ff.; Downey, *The Stone and Plaster Sculpture*, 172-180,
188.

inscription from this temple goes back to 31/32 A.D. It yielded the much-discussed and well-known relief of Hadad and Atargatis sitting enthroned between bulls and lions each at a side of the *semeion*.[104] Atargatis' predominant position in relation to her consort is stressed by her being represented considerably larger. An inscription incised upon the front of a limestone altar found in the temple records a dedication to 'Αταραγάτιδι made by a certain Gemellus *legatus Augusti*.[105] Fragments of a red dipinto upon plaster dated into 235 A.D. records a painting (ζωγρᾰ[φημα]) of 'Αδων[ιδι] and 'Ατραγάτη, and small fragments of colored plaster have indeed been found which could belong to a fresco of both deities.[106] It is not self-evident that the fragmentary 'Αδων[ιδι] actually means Adonis, as C. Bradford Welles assumes. It may have the meaning "lord" and denote Hadad. An inscription on a stone tablet discovered in the same temple and dating from 92/93 A.D. mentions the construction of a οἶκον καὶ το ἐν αὐτῷ ταμιεῖον πρὸς εὐκοσμίαν,[107] τοῦ ἱεροῦ τῆς 'Αταργάτειος ... whereas a certain Ammonius son of Apollophanes had (two?) φάλλους set up in the year 34/35 A.D., and a religious society and its president had something built 'Αγαθῇ Τύχῃ in the year 35/36 according to an inscription on a slab of gypsum.[108] In the court of the temple there was a great altar facing the temple entrance; a Greek inscription on its east side mentions Abbas son of Abbas, who had the altar built in 69/70 A.D.[109] It is of interest that one of the two Hatrene inscriptions

---

[104] *Dura-Europos, Prel. Report of third season*, 100-139, Pl. XIV; Perkins, *The Art of Dura-Europos*, 94-96, Pl. 38; Downey, *The Stone and Plaster Sculpture*, 9-11, Pl. I, 2; for other standards used in the cult of Atargatis see Downey, *o.c.* 178-180.

[105] *Dura-Europos, Prel. Report of third season*, 43ff., D. 145.

[106] *Dura-Europos, Prel. Report of third season*, 46ff., D. 146; *cf.* Welles, The Gods of Dura-Europos, 57.

[107] *Dura-Europos, Prel. Report of third season*, 61ff., D. 159.

[108] R. N. Frye - J. F. Gilliam - H. Ingholt - C. B. Welles, Inscriptions from Dura-Europos, *YCS* 14, 1955, 127-213, no. 1 and 2; the φάλλοι constitute another link with the cult at Hierapolis, *cf.* Lucian, *De Syria Dea*, 28, 29; Drijvers, Spätantike Parallelen zur altchristlichen Heiligenverehrung unter besonderer Berücksichtigung des syrischen Stylitenkultes, *Aspekte früh-christlicher Heiligenverehrung*, Oikonomia 6, Erlangen 1977, 54ff.

[109] Inscriptions from Dura-Europos, *YCS* 14, 1955, no. 4.

found at Dura-Europos comes from the temple of Atargatis.[110]

The Priests' House at Dura yielded a stone mold containing in its center a medallion with the bust of a deity—according to the *kestos* most likely Atargatis. Preliminary Report IV of the Dura-excavations mentions in this context "a small head of Atargatis wearing kestos and necklace with disk-shaped pendant which was found recently at Dura. It is of glass frit covered with a silvery glaze." [111] A fragment of a terracotta relief seems to be made from the same mold as the one once in the possession of Sarre, which frequently has been described. It represents Atargatis standing in or before an *aedicula* in the attitude of blessing, with raised right hand.[112] In the debris of the Christian chapel, where this terracotta came to light, another terracotta has also been found in room 5 close to the door of the chapel. It portrays probably the same Atargatis with her right hand raised in a gesture of blessing or protection.[113]

The temple of Adonis provided the excavators with the upper part of a limestone relief showing the head of a goddess flanked by doves in high relief. She wears a mural crown in the form of a stone wall with three towers. Since the doves are sacred to Atargatis, who can function as Tyche, this first-century relief may picture the Dea Syria in one form or another.[114] It is, however, not self-

---

[110] First published by R. du Mesnil du Buisson, Un bilingue araméen-grec de l'époque Parthe à Doura-Europos, *Syria* 19, 1938, 147-152; *cf.* A. Caquot Inscriptions et graffites hatréens de Doura-Europos, *Syria* 30, 1953, 244-246; J. Naveh, Remarks on Two East Aramaic Inscriptions, *BASOR* 216, 1974, 9f. gave an improved reading and translation; the Greek text: *YCS* 14, 1955, no. 3; Welles, The Gods of Dura-Europos, 57 should accordingly be corrected.

[111] *Dura-Europos, Prel. Report of fourth season,* 236ff., Pl. X, 1 and 237, n. 42 which refers to *Prel. Report of third season,* 107, n. 31, where more instances are adduced; for the κεστός see Goossens, Hiérapolis, 117, n. 6; Campbell Bonner, κεστὸς ἱμάς and the Saltire of Aphrodite, *AJPh.* 70, 1949, 1-6 (cf. Ilias XIV, 214-215); *cf.* Downey, *The Stone and Plaster Sculpture*, 173.

[112] *Dura-Europos, Prel. Report of fourth season,* 13, 242f., Pl. VIII, 3; *cf.* Cumont, *Fouilles de Doura-Europos,* 266, Fig. 58; Downey, *The Stone and Plaster Sculpture*, 173, however, utters doubts on this identification.

[113] *Dura-Europos, Prel. Report of fifth season,* 253, Pl. XX, 2.

[114] *Dura-Europos, Prel. Report of seventh and eighth season,* 163-165, Pl. XXXI, 1; the reference 164, n. 2 to *Report* V, 210, Pl. XIX, 3 is incorrect; it should be Report IV, 210, Pl. XIX, 3; *cf.* A. Perkins, *The Art of Dura-Europos,* 103f., Pl. 44; Downey, *The Stone and Plaster Sculpture*, 47f.

evident that this fragmentary relief portrays the goddess from
Hierapolis, since she—at least in her sanctuary there—does not
have any relations to a youthful lover like Adonis. Since the iconography of Atargatis is not exclusive to her but was taken over by
other goddesses, this relief might represent Aštarte-Belti-Uzza'-
Aphrodite, Queen of Heaven or Venus star, who was supposed to
have a love affair with Tammuz according to a whole range of
passages in Syriac literature.[115] If we assume a kind of connection
between this relief and the temple of Adonis, then it most likely
pictures, e.g., the Lady of Byblos (*b'lt gbl*) or her more Eastern
manifestation Aštarte-al-Uzza', the Venus star (*kwkbt'* in Syriac),
who is not the same as the Dea Syria from Hierapolis.[116] The last
goddess is never conceived as Venus star, and temple prostitution
was not practiced at her sanctuary, as is reported about Aštarte-al-
Uzza'-Aphrodite. For the time being, therefore, it seems best to
interpret this relief as a representation of the goddess of love.

That the traditional iconography of Atargatis is not exclusive to
her also appears from a relief of the goddess Azzanathkona found
in the *salle aux gradins* of her temple situated in the northern part
of the city. It functioned perhaps as the original cult-relief and may

---

[115] *cf.* Isaac of Antioch, ed. G. Bickell, II, 210, 125-126; Ephrem, *Hymni
contra Haereses* (ed. E. Beck), 41, 4; on al-Uzza see J. Wellhausen, *Reste
arabischen Heidentums*, third ed., Berlin 1961, 34-45; T. Fahd, *Le panthéon
de l'Arabie centrale à la veille de l'hégire*, Paris 1968, 163-182; Haussig,
Wörterbuch der Mythologie I, 475f.; Ephrem Syrus, *Hymni contra Haereses*
VIII, 10-14; where *kwkbt'* = Venus and *shr'* = the moon is a cloak for
Atargatis; the same distinction is made in the *Doctrina Addai* between
Atargatis and the Bright Star (= Venus); on Belti and Tammuz v. Išo'dad
of Merv, *Livre des Sessions* III, ed. C. van den Eynde, *CSCO* 229-230, Louvain
1962-63, commentary on Judges 2, 13; *Apology of Pseudo-Melito*, ed. Cureton,
Spicilegium Syriacum 44, LL. 12ff.: The people of Phoenicia worshipped
Belti, queen of Cyprus, because she fell in love with Tammuz, son of Kuthar,
king of the Phoenicians, and left her own kingdom, and came and dwelt
in Gebal (= Byblos), a fortress of the Phoenicians, etc.; *cf.* Theodore bar
Koni, *Liber Scholiorum*, ed. A. Scher, I, 204, 22-205, 14; I, 312, 1-313, 20
(ad Ezechiël 8, 14); G. Hoffmann, *Opuscula Nestoriana*, Kiel 1880, 105, 8-11;
Ms. Syr. Vat. 573, fol. 145b-146a (anonymous scholia). These and other
traditions regarding Adonis-Tammuz will be published in a corpus containing
Syriac sources for the study of pagan religions.

[116] *cf.* in general B. Soyez, *Byblos et la fête des Adonies*, EPRO 60, Leiden
1977, which should be supplemented with the eastern sources.

date back to 33 A.D., when one of the rooms of the sanctuary was
built. The relief makes the impression of a little *naiskos* with two
Corinthian columns framing the sides. The main scene of the relief
is the crowning of "Artemis, the goddess called Azzanathkona,"
who sits between two lions in a stiff hieratical way. Her right hand
is raised in a gesture of blessing and she holds an indistinct object
in her left hand. Above the rather small goddess and the much
larger male person who crowns her, a man leading a bull is pictured,
which may be an offering-scene, although the bull is Hadad's
animal.[117] The unexplained element "kona" in the goddess' name
may be the Semitic root *qn'* = create, so that the name Azzanathkona means "the power of Anath the creator"; the goddess Anath,
who is the same as 'Ateh, is therefore conceived as a powerful
creative deity.[118] This recalls the role of Artemis-Atargatis on the
beam of Bel's temple at Palmyra, which pictures the fight against
the chaos monster—actually an act of creation—and of Atargatis
at Hierapolis, where she transforms the destructive flood into life-
giving water. The crowning scene of the Dura relief, which usually
indicates a kind of victory, is in conformity with the interpretation
given here. The Dura material regarding the worship of Atargatis
therefore corroborates and adds nuances to the results thus far
obtained. The remaining evidence will bring still more shades into
this picture.

Damascus

The cult of Hadad and Atargatis at Damascus, explicitly recorded
by Iustinus, *Epitoma*, 36, 2, 1-3 and the *Etymologicon Magnum*
247, 20-22 *s.v.* Damaskos,[119] must go back to the time of the reign
of the Aramaeans as several of their kings were called Barhadad.[120]

---

[117] *Dura-Europos, Prel. Report of fifth season*, 142ff., 171-176, Pl. XIV,
XXIV; Inscription no. 453 dated 161 A.D.; Welles, The Gods of Dura-Europos, 58; Perkins, *The Art of Dura-Europos*, 91ff., Pl. 37; Downey, *The Stone
and Plaster Sculpture*, 11-14, 185-187.

[118] For *qn'* = to create, see G. Levi della Vida, *RSO* 21, 1945-46, 247f.;
RTP, 181, where the divine name 'LQNR' is discussed (= El creator of the
earth).

[119] *cf.* P.-L. van Berg, *CCDS*, no's 64, 65 and Vol. II, 111ff.

[120] *cf.* I. Kings 15, 18-20; II Kings 13, 3, 24; II Kings 6, 24; 8, 7ff.; *KAI*
201, 1; 202 A, 4 and the commentary. E. Lipiński, *Studies in Aramaic In-*

Hadad occurs on coins of Damascus struck under Antiochus XII,[121] and Atargatis is portrayed on coins of Demetrius III as a standing goddess with outstretched arms, wearing a long veil and with a flower in her left hand. An ear of corn rises up from behind her shoulders, and she wears a halo.[122] This picture of a still and hieratic statue of the goddess surely is an echo of the original *xoanon*, of which the *Etymologicon Magnum* speaks. The same text attributes the erection of the *xoanon* to the activities of Damas and Dionysos, who are also credited with the erection of the phalloi in the sanctuary at Hierapolis (Lucian, *De Syria Dea*, 16). Dionysos' building activities are reminiscent of the role of Bar-Marên, the *dieu-fils* of the Hatrene triad, who, e.g., is said to have built the temple for his father Šamš and has special ties with sculptors and architects, but is also represented as Dionysos-Bacchus.[123] He represents human culture and specific cultural occupations like building and sculpting, but also making wine. The Nabataean Dusares, who is pictured as Dionysos too, is more or less a god of the same category, and Damascus was once an important Nabataean city.[124] This may provide us with sufficient explanation for Dionysos being mentioned in the context of the cult of the Dea Syria at Damascus.

A basalt plaque with the portraits of a nude Heracles leaning on his club and a female person wearing a long veil and dress with her right hand on her breast originates from the region of Damascus. R. Mouterde, who published it, assumed that it is a funerary monument, which, however, seems very unlikely. The female person is in his view Alkestis rescued by Heracles from the under-

---

scriptions and Onomastics, Leuven 1975, 15ff.; A. Malamat, The Aramaeans, *Peoples of the Old Testament Period*, ed. D. J. Wiseman, Oxford 1973, 134ff.

[121] *cf.* Dussaud, *Syria* 3, 1922, 221, Fig. 1; L. Lacroix, Copies de statues sur les monnaies des Séleucides, *BCH* 73, 1949, 161, n. 2; the coins were assembled and classified by E. T. Newell, *Late Seleucid Mints in Ake-Ptolemais and Damascus*, NNM 84, 1939, 78ff., Pl. XIV, XV; 86f., Pl. XV.

[122] Dussaud, *Syria* 3, 1922, 222, Fig. 2; *cf.* Lacroix, *art. cit.*, Pl. III, 8; R. Fleischer, *Artemis von Ephesos*, 263ff., Pl. 111, 112, 113a.

[123] *cf.* Drijvers, *ANRW* II, 8, 829ff.; Hatrene inscription 107 mentions Bar-Marên's building activities, *cf.* Milik, *Dédicaces*, 377ff.

[124] On Dusares see Haussig, *Wörterbuch der Mythologie* I, 433f. *s.v.* Dusares; J. Starcky, *Pétra et la Nabatène*, *SDB* VII, 986ff.; on the Nabataeans at Damascus see F. E. Peters, The Nabateans in the Hawran, *JAOS* 97, 263ff.; *cf.* T. Fahd, Le panthéon, 71ff.

world.[125] The possibility is worth considering that the female person might be a goddess, e.g., Atargatis or a related figure, but firm results cannot be reached in this case.

The Hauran

If we may believe the *Book of the Maccabees* there once was an *Atargateion* at Qarnaim, and this is, in fact, the earliest mention of a sanctuary of Atargatis in the Hauran.[126] A dedicatory inscription on an altar from Djourein in the Ledja area dating from 140 A.D. records the name of Atargatis,[127] and the same name was conjectured by Waddington in an inscription found at Nimra in the Djebel Druze dating back to the time of the Emperor Commodus (180-192).[128] A stele at Souweida, and originating from there, bears an inscription which records the construction of a cult-niche for Hadad and Atargatis.[129]

A basalt statue of a sitting Atargatis that once was part of a private collection, also attests the cult of the Dea Syria. The head was damaged already in antiquity and then restored.[130] A fragmentary relief in the Museum of Souweida, of which only the lower part has been preserved, representing an enthroned goddess between

---

[125] cf. R. Mouterde, Dea Syria en Syrie, *MUSJ* 25, 1942-43, 141f. and Pl. X, 3.

[126] I Macc. V, 42-44; II Macc. XII, 26; cf. R. Dussaud, *Topographie historique de la Syrie antique et médiévale*, Paris 1927, 328ff.

[127] *Syria, Publications of the Princeton University Archaeological Expedition to Syria in 1904-1905 and 1909*, III A, 792. cf. D. Sourdel, *Les cultes du Hauran à l'époque romaine*, Paris 1952, 41.

[128] *Waddington*, 2172 = IGR III, 1250 = Brünnow-Domaszewski, *Die Provincia Arabia* III, 319: [Ἔτους .. τοῦ κυρίου Αὐτο]κ(ράτορος) Κομόδ[ου .. | ...... τὸν] οἶκον ᾠκοδ]όμησεν .... | ...... ος γεγραμ(μ)έν[ος .... | ...... κφων· ἀπὸ ἔτους ..... | ..... Ἀτερ]γάτι ποιηθῆ τὰ ξε ... | .... Νάταμος ὀβαισα[θου..| .. καὶ Ὀβαί]σαθ(ος) ἀδελφ(ός)· etc...

[129] M. Dunand, *Le Musée de Soueida*, Paris 1934, no. 21:

> Ἀδάδῳ καὶ Ἀταρ-
> γατίδι τὴν (ψ)αλίδα
> ἐπόησεν ἐκ τῶν
> ἰδίων Σάλιμος
> Ἀννήλου τοῦ Σ(αλ)ί-
> μου ἔτει ....

[130] R. Mouterde, Dea Syria en Syrie, *MUSJ* 25, 1942-43, 140f., Pl. X, 2.

8

two lions, most probably shows Allat and not Atargatis, since it originated from a temple of Allat at Raḥa.[131]

In dispute is the identity of the deities to which the temple of Khirbet-Tannur in Jordan was dedicated. The excavator, N. Glueck, considers them Hadad and Atargatis, but there is no epigraphical evidence for such an identification.[132] The extant iconography of the deities worshipped is very similar, however, to the way Hadad and Atargatis are pictured elsewhere in the Syrian area so that—even if they actually are the local baʿal and his consort—their representations belong to the iconographical dossier of the Dea Syria and her consort. Restricting ourselves to the goddess the evidence can be listed as follows:

a) a relief showing the bust of the goddess wearing long tails and a veil decorated on top with two fish.[133] It is a counterpart of a relief showing exactly

b) the same goddess now accompanied by ears of grain identifying her as a fertility deity.[134]

c) A semicircular sculptured panel, once located above the crowning cornice of the east facade of the temple just above the main entrance to the inner temple-court, shows the long-haired bust of the goddess in a pattern of acanthus leaves and other fertility symbols like pomegranates and figs. The panel and its location prove the paramount position of the goddess at this sanctuary. The deity was crowned by an eagle in the same way as the goddess on the Nergal relief from Hatra.[135] The whole scene

---

[131] Dunand, *Le musée de Soueida*, no. 169, Pl. XXXIV; *cf.* J. Starcky, *SDB* VII, col. 1002; *cf.* Drijvers, De matre inter leones sedente, 348; N. Glueck, *Deities and Dolphins*, 283, n. 383 considers it a representation of Atargatis.

[132] N. Glueck, *Deities and Dolphins*, *passim*; *cf.* Sourdel's hesitation, Les cultes du Hauran, 42 and J. Starcky's important review of Glueck's book, Le temple nabatéen de Khirbet Tannur. À propos d'un livre récent, *RB* 75, 1968, 206-235. Starcky adduces convincing arguments that the god of Khirbet-Tannur is the ancient Edomite deity Qôs, who is not a typical Nabataean god.

[133] Glueck, *Deities and Dolphins*, 13, Pl. 1; *cf.* Starcky, *art. cit.* 226 for the iconography of the goddess of Khirbet Tannur.

[134] Glueck, *Deities and Dolphins*, 49, Pl. 25.

[135] Glueck, *Deities and Dolphins*, 65-67, Pl. 31-33.

shows great resemblance to a limestone relief from the temple of Khirbet Brak near Petra, where a similar goddess seemingly was worshipped.[136]

d) The goddess is pictured on one relief wearing a lion's torque, which should be related to the various complete and fragmentary representations of lions found in this sanctuary.[137]

e) The goddess apparently functioned as a Tyche since she is represented with a mural crown and a long veil; above her left shoulder part of what seems to be a kind of semeion is visible, and above her right shoulder a crescent is depicted. The whole bust is surrounded by a zodiac, so that the whole forms a medallion. The medallion was supported by a standing Nike, just as in some Palmyrene tombs standing Nikes support medallions with the busts of the dead.[138]

f) The same Tyche seems to be portrayed on two other rather damaged steles and

g) she also is pictured with a *cornucopia* on her right arm.[139]

Assuming that the whole range of reliefs represents the same goddess, of whom different aspects are illustrated, her whole personality as a fertility goddess and Tyche, having connections with lions and fish fits in very well with Atargatis' character as detected so far. N. Glueck puts great stress on the fish—in his view dolphins—and relates them to Nabataean contacts with the sea and sea-trade since otherwise there seems to be no single reason for picturing just fish in temples in extremely dry areas.[140] The dolphin motif—according to N. Glueck—should accordingly be attributed to the fact that "wherever they turned or might have visited, the Nabataeans were confronted with or would have seen

[136] cf. P. J. Parr, *ADAJ* IV-V, 1960, 134-136, Pl. XV, 1; Glueck, *Deities and Dolphins*, 292, 311.

[137] Glueck, *Deities and Dolphins*, 96, Pl. 44.

[138] Glueck, *Deities and Dolphins*, 108-110, Pl. 46-48; for Nikes supporting medallions with the busts of the dead in Palmyrene tombs, see Cumont, *Études syriennes*, 52f., 64, Fig. 29; Schlumberger, *L'Orient hellénisé*, Paris 1970, 88 and the Plates on 92-94; Drijvers, *The religion of Palmyra*, Pl. LXXIX 1, 2.

[139] Glueck, *Deities and Dolphins*, 97, Pl. 45a, b; 117, Pl. 55.

[140] Glueck, *Deities and Dolphins*, 334ff.

the dolphin symbol and from the beginning would have been impressed with its significance." [141] This argument rests on the supposition that the fish in question are dolphins, and since they live in the sea, the Nabataeans could only have become acquainted with them through their travels and traffic. The motif, consequently, would not belong to the original iconography of the goddess at Khirbet Tannur, but is a borrowing from various Mediterranean deities. Glueck therefore takes great pains in order to prove that the dolphins as fish from the sea have nothing to do with water and water supply in the usually dry Nabataean area. This seems rather curious since fish and water are one of the main characteristic traits of Atargatis, the goddess from Hierapolis, and Glueck rightly argues that the goddess venerated at Khirbet Tannur is Atargatis and, as at Hierapolis, together with Hadad. The fish at Khirbet Tannur, at Hatra and elsewhere, where they are related to Atargatis, have such a stylized shape, that it is hard to say if they really are dolphins. They are just fish or perhaps carps, like at Edessa. They symbolize the goddess' life-giving qualities expressed, in another way, by the ears of grain. This makes sense especially in the dry Nabataean area, where water and fish represent the most valuable things in life, and furthermore, it is in complete accordance with all the literary and iconographical traditions regarding the Dea Syria. We, consequently, do not consider the fish dolphins and reject the relation between the supposed dolphin at Khirbet Tannur and the Nabataean sea trade. They symbolize one of the features of the Dea Syria which became of utmost importance by their contrast in the desert area where the Nabataeans used to live and to worship their gods.

An altar from Beyrouth has, on the contrary, to do with travel in Syria and a temple in the Nabataean area near the Gulf of Aqaba, dedicated to Atargatis. Two sides of this altar are inscribed.

Inscription A:

θεᾷ 'Αταργάτε.	To the goddess Atargatis
τᾳ Γεράνων	of the *Statio*
'Αρτεμίδι	of the *Geranoi*

---

[141] Glueck, *Deities and Dolphins*, 353.

φωσφόρῶ

To Artemis
Phosphoros

Cladus D(ecii or ecimi) Claudii Poll(i)

Cladus a slave of Decius Claudius

onis Ser(vus) ac(tor) v(otum) s(olvit)

Pollio the actor fulfilled his vow.

Inscription B:

Veneri He

To Venus of Heliopolis

liopolitanae

et Deae Syriae

and the Dea Syria,

Geraneae sta(tionis)

Diana of the *Statio* of Gerana

Deanae Luc(ius) ser(vus) p(osuit)

Lucius the slave put (this altar) [142]

The *statio* of Gerana would be identical to the *Statio ad Dianam*, which occurs on the *Tabula Peutingeriana* and lies near the Gulf of Aqaba. Both slaves belonged to the personnel of this *statio*, which was part of the *portorium* of Syria. The goddess venerated there was called Atargatis and identified with Artemis Phosphoros and Diana. Especially the reading of inscription B makes clear that Atargatis-Dea Syria is identical with Diana-Artemis Phosphoros and not identical with the Venus of Heliopolis-Baalbek. The conjunction *et* should be stressed in this context.[143]

These inscriptions provide us with the opportunity to make more plausible that Artemis is equivalent to Atargatis in various inscriptions from Syria. An altar from Tell el-Ash'ari near Sheikh Sa'd in Batanea, the Qarnaim of the *Books of Maccabees*, is dedi-

---

[142] R. Mouterde, La *Statio ad Dianam* du *Portorium* de Syrie près le Golfe d'Aqaba, *CRAI* 1954, 482-487; cf. J.-L. Robert, *BÉ* 1956, 75: Nous faisons toutes réserves sur la transcription; cf. *AE* 1955, 85a-b.

[143] On Artemis Phosphoros see Nilsson, *Geschichte der griechischen Religion* I, 495; K. Hoenn, *Artemis*. Gestaltwandel einer Göttin, Zürich 1946, 98; *PW*, II, 1354, 1401; *Roscher's Lexikon* III, 2, 2441f.; Artemis Phosphoros is a moon goddess and usually represented with a torch; on Venus-Atargatis of Heliopolis-Baalbek see R. Fleischer, *Artemis von Ephesos und verwandte Kultstatuen aus Anatolien und Syrien*, EPRO 35, Leiden 1973, 273ff.; Y. Hajjar, *La triade d'Héliopolis-Baalbek* II, EPRO 59, Leiden 1977, 506ff. and *passim*.

cated to Ἀρτέμιδι τῇ κυρίᾳ.[144] Since there was an Atargatis temple nearby, Artemis in all likelihood is just another name of the *Dea Syria*. The same phenomenon occurs at Gerasa in the Dekapolis, where Artemis functioned as the Tyche of the city according to a whole range of coins.[145] Since she is called Deana on two altars the similarity to the Beyrouth altar is still more striking.[146] A terracotta figurine from a tomb at Gerasa might represent the goddess given the similarity to the portraits on the coins.[147]

Since Artemis is invoked in two inscriptions from Laodicea, both mentioning a priestess of the Lady Artemis (τῆς κυρίας Ἀρτέμιδος), which goddess is pictured on the local coins and probably called virgin (παρθένος) by Porphyrios, *De Abst.* II, 56, we may assume that she represents a local form of Atargatis assimilated to Artemis.[148] The Lebanon and the coastal area of Syria yielded more evidence of the cult of goddesses which are called Atargatis or Dea Syria. Atargatis had a small temple at Qalʿat Fakra in the Beqa, which can be dated to the time of Agrippa II and Berenice (49-100 A.D.) according to an inscription found in the *adyton*: ὑπὲρ τῆς σω|τηρίας Μάρ|κου Ἰουλίου | Ἀγρίππα κυρί|ου βασιλέως | καὶ τῆς κυρίας | βασιλίσσης | Βερενίκης θε|ᾷ Ἀταργάτει Σ[ατ]|ραβων ἀνέθηκε | διὰ Γαίου Μαν|σουήτου ἀρχιε|ρέως καὶ ἐπιμε|λητοῦ.[149]

---

[144] *IGR* III, 1163 = *Provincia Arabia* III, 310; Sourdel, *Les cultes du Hauran*, 42: Ὑπὲρ σωτηρίας καὶ διαμονῆς | Τίτου Αἰλίου Ἀδριανοῦ | Ἀντωνείνου Σεβαστοῦ Εὐσε|βοῦς καὶ τοῦ σύμπαντος αὐ|τοῦ οἴκου | Πάμφιλος Ἐρ[εν]νίου | βουλ(ε)υτὴς Ἀρτέμιδι τῇ | κυρίᾳ τὸν βωμὸν ἐκ τῶν | ἰδίων κατ' εὐ[χ]ὴν ἀνέγει|ρεν.

[145] *cf.* C. C. McCown, The Goddesses of Gerasa, *AASOR* 13, 1931-32, 129-166; O. Eissfeldt, *Tempel und Kulte syrischer Städte in hellenistisch-römischer Zeit*, AO 40, Leipzig 1941, 31f.; C. H. Kraeling, *Gerasa. City of the Decapolis*, New Haven 1938, 497ff. *cf.* A. R. Bellinger, *Coins from Jerash, 1928-1934*, NNM 81, 1938, 29-31, No's 40-47, Pl. II, III.

[146] C. B. Welles, The Inscriptions, in C. H. Kraeling, *Gerasa*, 390ff., no's 30 (*Deaniae Aug.*) and 31 (*Deanae*); *cf.* Eissfeldt, *Tempel und Kulte*, 18ff.

[147] C. C. McCown, The Goddesses of Gerasa, 165, Fig. 1; McCown considers Artemis of Gerasa a thoroughly Greek goddess imported from abroad by Greeks.... (p. 164), which seems utterly improbable.

[148] *IGLS* 1263, 1264; *cf.* Seyrig, *AS* I, 141.

[149] O. Puchstein - D. Krencker, *JDAI* 17, 1902, 107, n. 43; *Prosopogr. Imp. Rom.* II, Berlin 1897, 163, n. 89 and 226, n. 431; Krencker-Zschietzsch-mann, *Römische Tempel in Syrien*, 46ff.; Jalabert, *MFOB* 2, 1907, 302 rightly changed κυρίου βασιλείας into κυρίου βασιλέ ως.

The *adyton* of this Atargatis cella has benches along the north and the south wall, which seems unusual, at least if they were intended for sitting. The same kind of arrangement is to be seen in the cella of Allat at Palmyra; it may be suggested here that the benches were meant for putting ex votos on them like in temples at Hatra. It is an "Orientalizing" element in this Greco-Roman cella.[150]

A bronze plaque from the former collection de Clercq, now in the Louvre, that perhaps comes from Beyrouth is dedicated to the Dea Syria: *Deae Syriae Sacrum*, possibly an appellation for the Lady of Beyrouth, if indeed the plaque comes from there.[151] An inscription incised on the four sides of a stone found at Kafr Hawwar near the Hermon records that a slave Lucius was sent out by his mistress Atargatis, the Dea Syria from Hierapolis, to collect money, and apparently successful, he put up that altar. It reminds of Lucian, *De Syria Dea*, 35, which describes similar practices.[152]

A limestone plaque found at Kafr Yassif near Ptolemais-Accho records that a certain Diodotos with his wife Philista and their children dedicated an altar to "Hadad and Atargatis, the gods who listen to prayer" in order to fulfill a vow.[153] The editor M. Avi-Yonah is inclined, probably correctly, to date this inscription into the middle of the second century B.C. The cult of Hadad and

---

[150] Krencker-Zschietzschmann, *Römische Tempel*, 47: "Die Ausstattung eines Adytons mit Sitzen ist ungewöhnlich"; *cf.* Drijvers, Das Heiligtum der arabischen Göttin Allat im westlichen Stadtteil von Palmyra, *Antike Welt* 7, 1976, 34.

[151] A. de Ridder, *Catalogue de la collection de Clercq* III, Paris 1904, 380; *AE* 1905, no. 29: *Deae Syriae sacrum*
        Festiva et parhalia
        F. eius statili
        severi vot.
        L.A.S.

[152] *BCH*, 60, n. 68; *Waddington*, no. 1890.

[153] M. Avi-Yonah, Syrian Gods at Ptolemais-Accho, *IEJ* 9, 1959, 1-12:
        ['Α]δάδῳ καὶ 'Αταργάτει
        θεοῖς ἐπηκόοις
        Διοδότος Νεοπτολεμοῦ
        ὑπὲρ αὐτοῦ καὶ Φιλιστᾶς
        τῆς γυναίκος καὶ τῶν
        τέκνων τὸν βωμὸν
        κατευχήν.

Atargatis near Ptolemais can shed some light on the identity of
Zeus of Ptolemais, also identified with Jupiter Heliopolitanus in a
Greek inscription.[154] He often is reprented on the coins of Ptolemais with an ear of grain which symbol links him to other sky-gods
in Syria. His consort, the local Syrian goddess, is pictured on a coin
struck under Valerianus sitting on a stool flanked by two lions and
wearing a high *kalathos* and a veil.[155] She functions as a Tyche of
Ptolemais too, and as such, the goddess appears on the coins together with Zeus, bearing a *cornucopia*. In this inscription from
nearby Ptolemais the deities are addressed as Hadad and Atargatis,
which is in complete accordance with a general religious pattern
in Syria.

This pattern, as it appears from the bewildering variety of inscriptions, coins, sculptures, and terracottas which always per-
plexes the student of the religious history of Syria and Mesopotamia,
is mainly characterized by a certain interchangeability of divine
attributes among the various deities, for the reason that no cult
is exclusive. The various appearances of the Dea Syria show on
the one hand an endless range of different local variants, and on
the other a general pattern of an all-embracing mother goddess,
who gives water and fertility, protection and safety, who functions
as a good Tyche providing the cities with abundance of goods. It
may be assumed that every town of any importance in this area
originally had its own ba'al and ba'alat, a male deity of the heavenly
sky, of storm and rain, giver of fertility, and a female one representing security, at the same time a mother and a virgin, who protects
her children. Besides these two various other deities appear on the
scene in charge of special provinces in life. It is difficult and futile
to try to discern any systematic order in the wide range of different
deities which appear in our monuments, unless sheer accumulation
were to be considered a kind of systematizing. The only possible
order is of a sociological nature: different deities belong to different

---

[154] M. Avi-Yonah, *IEJ* 2, 1952, 118f. = *SÉG* 14, 832; *cf.* Seyrig, *AS* VI,
100ff.: Divinités de Ptolémais.

[155] Seyrig, *AS* VI, Pl. XIII, 2; *cf. idem*, Bractées funéraires, *Syria* 36,
1959, 57f. = *AS* VI, 30f., which are decorated with a bust of the Dea Syria
wearing a veil and a high kalathos.

groups of the population. Each brings in its own heritage, its own *theoi patroioi*, which in turn are assimilated to other deities already present or arriving later.

In this situation one god or goddess of a certain place sometimes gets a paramount position for one reason or another, as, for instance, Atargatis, the Dea Syria from Hierapolis. Her sanctuary became a place of pilgrimage and the character and iconography of the great goddess of Hierapolis influenced in its turn other local goddesses, or her cult even spread into other places. This is why it is often difficult to decide if the cult of Atargatis at a certain place is actually a branch of the sanctuary of Hierapolis or a local cult adapted to the practice and customs at Mabbug. Religious forms are not fixed in this area, but always change and develop, borrowing motifs from each other. The wide range of variants in the cult of the Dea Syria most appropriately demonstrates such a process of religious assimilation and articulation.

All this material provides us with a certain background for understanding the role of Atargatis at Edessa. She was the goddess of the life-giving springs near the citadel, where she had her temple. She was the Tyche of the city, where she had her priests and begging *galli* and was worshipped with ecstatic music and tremendous noise. Although her cult at Edessa may have been influenced by her centre at Hierapolis, it certainly belonged to the most authentic traditions of the city, which was founded close to her life-giving wells at a safe place in Northern Mesopotamia.

CHAPTER FIVE

THE CULT OF SIN LORD OF THE GODS
AT SUMATAR HARABESI

Sumatar Harabesi is an important watering-place with many wells situated in the Tektek mountains about sixty kilometres south-east of Urfa and about forty kilometres north-east of Harran. When H. Pognon visited the place in 1901 and 1905, it had no permanent inhabitants but functioned as a meeting-point of the beduins to water their herds.[1] In 1952, when J. B. Segal spent several days at Sumatar, the place had a few inhabitants and a gendarmery post.[2] In 1977 it had developed into a small village with several hundred inhabitants and a school.

H. Pognon recorded a number of Syriac inscriptions and reliefs in a cave but never made a thorough survey of the site. It was J. B. Segal who gave an exact description of various ruins scattered all over it and discovered a whole series of Syriac inscriptions engraved on the barren rock of a mount. These inscriptions and two reliefs carved at the north side of the mount near the summit established that the mount itself functioned as a cult site.[3] Some additional inscriptions and reliefs from Sumatar were published by the present author in 1973.[4] The increasing population of the site, usually attended by destruction of ancient monuments and their remains, makes it highly improbable that large finds will be made, although one or another inscription or relief might turn up.

---

[1] H. Pognon, *Inscriptions sémitiques de la Syrie, de la Mésopotamie et de la région de Mossoul*, Paris 1907, 23.

[2] J. B. Segal, Pagan Syriac Monuments in the Vilayet of Urfa, *AnSt* 3, 1953, 97ff.

[3] J. B. Segal, Pagan Syriac Monuments, 112ff. The religious Background of the Sumatar Monuments, Pl. VIII-XI; *idem*, Some Syriac Inscriptions of the 2nd-3rd Century A.D., *BSOAS* 16, 1954, 13-36; *cf.* Drijvers, *Old-Syriac Inscriptions*, no's 13-25.

[4] Drijvers, Some New Syriac Inscriptions and Archaeological Finds from Edessa and Sumatar Harabesi, *BSOAS* 36, 1973, 1-14.

The Central Mount

This natural mount dominates the whole site and is likely the reason for its religious function as a "high" place, a fairly common cult site in various Semitic religions (Pl. XXIV). On its northern slope near the summit are two reliefs accompanied by inscriptions (Pl. XXV). The relief on the left is a male bust set in a niche (Pl. XXVI). It is rather worn but behind its shoulders a crescent is visible as well as the folds in its dress. An inscription on the left of this bust reads:

[*br šyl*]ʾ	Son of Šila (?)
ʿ*bd šylʾ ṣlmʾ*	Šila made the image
lsyn ʾlhʾ ʿl ḥyy	to Sin the god for the life of
tyrdt br ʾdwnʾ wʿl ḥyy	Tiridates son of Adona and for the life of
ʾ*ḥwhy*	his brother.[5]

The inscription, therefore, identifies the bust in the niche as an image of Sin the moon god of Harran, an identification which is reinforced by the crescent behind its shoulders. This deity can simply be called "the god" as appears from another inscription on its right side:

br kwzʾ	Bar KWZʾ
dkyr zky wbnwhy	May be remembered ZKY and his sons
qdm ʾlhʾ	before the god.[6]

A relief to the right of Sin's bust shows a full-length male person dressed in a garment reaching to his knees (Pl. XXVII). His right hand rests on his hip and the left one seems to hold an object. The whole relief stands in an archivolted niche with pilaster columns at each side. The man seems to wear a headdress of large peacock's

---

[5] Segal, Some Syriac Inscriptions, 17f.; Drijvers, *Old-Syriac Inscriptions*, no. 14; to the left of inscription no. 14 is another nearly illegible one, Drijvers, no. 15.

[6] Segal, Some Syriac Inscriptions, 16f.; Drijvers, *Old-Syriac Inscriptions*, no. 13; an exact parallel to *qdm ʾlhʾ*—before the god, is found in a Syriac inscription on a votive stele with the representation of a sacred standard, which was found in the temple of Atargatis at Dura-Europos, *cf.* Drijvers, no. 63, where the relevant literature is given; Downey, *The Stone and Plaster Sculpture*, 178ff. gives the name of the dedicant as Khalīṣā instead of *wlgš* = Vologases (son of Seleucos), which is the correct reading.

(?) feathers as also occurs on a tomb relief in a cave tomb at Kara Köpru north of Urfa (Pl. XVIII).[7] To the right of this relief is an inscription:

hn' ṣlm' pqd	This image ordered (commanded)
'lh' lm'n' bywm 13	the god to Ma'na on the 13th day
b'dr šnt 476	of Adar (of the) year 476.[8]

The deity in question is again Sin, who ordered this relief in the month of Adar 476 of the Seleucid era = March 165 A.D. It is not clear who is portrayed here, whether Ma'na himself, or an unnamed person, or, as J. B. Segal suggested,[9] perhaps the god Sin. For the time being the question may be left open until a closer analysis of all relevant material has been carried through.

On the top of the central mount ten inscriptions were carved. Some of them are just memorial texts like, "may N.N. be remembered," but others yield more information. One memorial text contains a title of the deity, i.e., Mar°lahê = Lord of the gods.

dkyr 'bsmy' br 'dwn'	May 'Absamya son of Adona be remembered,
nwhdr' dkyr qdm	the military commander; may he be remembered before
mrlh' dkyr bbs	Mar°lahê; may BBS be remembered
wtyrdt bny (')bsmy'	and Tiridates sons of ('A)bsamya.[10]

---

[7] cf. Pognon, *Inscriptions sémitiques*, 179ff., Pl. XI; Drijvers, *Old-Syriac Inscriptions*, no's 58-61.

[8] Segal, Some Syriac Inscriptions, 19f.; Drijvers, *Old-Syriac Inscriptions* no. 16.

[9] cf. Segal, Some Syriac Monuments, 114f.; idem, *Edessa*, 59f.

[10] Segal, Some Syriac Inscriptions, 21f.; Drijvers, *Old-Syriac Inscriptions*, no. 18; for *nwhdr'* = military commander, see: G. Widengren, *Iranisch-semitische Kulturbegegnung in parthischer Zeit*, Köln 1960, 33; Altheim-Stiehl, *AAW* I, 1964, 623-638; A. Maricq, *Classica et Orientalia*, Paris 1965, 6, n. 1; D. Harnack, in: Altheim-Stiehl, *Geschichte Mittelasiens im Altertum*, Berlin 1970, 437-540; the title *mrlh'* = Lord of the gods is borne by different deities a.o. by Ba'alšamên at Palmyra, Gawlikowski, *Syria* 47, 1970, 316ff.; by the main deity of *qrqbš* cf. A. Caquot, *Syria* 40, 1963, 12-14; J. Teixidor, *Syria* 41, 1964, 273-279; Milik, *Dédicaces*, 394-398; B. Aggoula, *MUSJ* 47, 1972, 45ff.; by Zeus-Bel, cf. Išo'dad of Merw, *Livre des Sessions*, ed. C. van den Eynde, *CSCO* 229-230, ad Jud. 2, 13; by Bel and Marud (= Nimrod = Nebo), cf. Jacob of Edessa, *Hexaemeron*, ed. Chabot, 70, b, 8-71, a, 6, see above p. 74.

The Absamya mentioned in this inscription may be a brother of Tiridates, son of Adona, for whose life Šila made the image of Sin. 'Absamya held the function of *nwhdr*' = military commander, whereas his brother was "ruler of Arab," as appears from another inscription on the summit of the mount:

byrḥ šbt šnt 476	In the month of Shebat of the year 476
'n' tyrdt br 'dwn' šlyṭ' d'rb	I Tiridates son of Adona ruler of Arab
bnyt 'lt' hd' wśmt nṣbt' lmrlh'	built this altar and set up a *baetyl* to Mar^{e}lahê
'l ḥyy mry mlk' wbnwhy w'l ḥyy 'dwn'	for the life of my lord the king and his sons and for the life of Adona
'by w'l ḥyy dyly wd'ḥy wdbnyn	my father and for my life and of my brethren and our children.[11]

In this inscription dating from Shebat 476 Seleucid era = February 165 A.D., the deity in question is again addressed as Mar^{e}lahê = Lord of the gods, and is presented with an altar and a *nṣbt'* = *baetyl* about the same time in which the god ordered an image to Ma'na.[12] It is especially noteworthy that most of the texts quoted so far mention officials from military and civil ranks, who apparently were in charge at Sumatar during that year and had close relations to "my lord, the king," undoubtedly the King of Edessa. The only remaining relevant inscription on the central mount poses some difficulties in reading and interpretation:

---

[11] Segal, Some Syriac Inscriptions, 24f.; Drijvers, *Old-Syriac Inscriptions*, no. 23 gives a partly corrected reading; cf. Segal, *Edessa*, 57f.

[12] *nṣbt'* derives from a root *nṣb* = to erect, to dress; it occurs in Nabatean as *nṣb'* with the meaning stele, *baetyl*, cf. RB 43, 574, no. 16, l. 1 and Milik, *Syria* 35, 247; cf. Arabic *nuṣub*, pl. *anṣab* and T. Fahd, *Le panthéon de l'Arabie centrale à la veille de l'Hégire*, Paris 1968, 24ff.: Le culte des bétyles; H. Lammens, *L'Arabie occidentale avant l'Hégire*, Beyrouth 1928, 100ff.: Le culte des bétyles et les processions religieuses chez les Arabes préislamites.

bšbt šnt 476 byrḥ	In the month of Shebat of the year 476
ʾnʾ mnyš br ʾdwnʾ wmʿnʾ wʾlkwd	I MNYŠ son of Adona and Maʿna and ʿLKWD
wblbnʾ wʾlkwd ʾḥwhy	and BLBNʾ and ʾLKWD his brethren
śmn nṣbtʾ hdʾ bhnʾ ṭwrʾ	we set this *baetyl* on this blessed mount
brykʾ wʾqymn krsʾ lmn dntrsyhy	and we put a stool for him whom my ruler rears.
šlyṭy jhwʾ bwdr mn btr tyrdt šlyṭʾ	May he be *bwdr* after Tiridates the ruler.
wytl krsʾ lmn dmtrsʾ lh prʿnh	And may he (i.e., Tiridates) give the stool to him whom he rears.
mn mrlhʾ jhwʾ wʾn nkblʾ krsʾ	(Then) he will get his recompense from Marᵉlahê. But if he withholds the stool
wtthbl nṣbtʾ hw ʾlhʾ ydʿ	and the baetyl will be ruined, may he the god know (it).[13]

The inscription clearly is a counterpart of the foregoing one, according to which Tiridates set a *baetyl* on the sacred mount for the well-being of his lord the king (of Edessa), for his own well-being, and that of his closest male relatives. The last inscription makes clear that Tiridates set this *baetyl* in his function of *bwdr* of the god. His brethren, the other sons of Adona, in their turn set a *baetyl* on the sacred mount for Tiridates' successor as *bwdr*. Tiridates reared somebody to become his successor and to take his place on

---

[13] Segal, Some Syriac Inscriptions, 26-28; *idem, Edessa*, 57; Segal, Pagan Syriac Monuments, 102 and elsewhere suggested that the *krsʾ* = stool was intended to put the *baetyl* on, but that is very unlikely. *krsʾ* means chair or throne and is the seat of a ruler or a religious functionary. In *Old-Syriac Inscriptions* I had hesitantly read the last word of line 9 as *hy*, but a new inspection of the inscription *in situ* made clear that *ydʿ* is the only correct reading; see also A. D. H. Bivar - S. Shaked, The Inscriptions at Shīmbār, *BSOAS* 27, 1964, 288; Milik, *Dédicaces*, 348; on a possible meaning of the enigmatic *bwdr* see A. Maricq, *Classica et Orientalia*, Paris 1965, 141-144; Segal, *Edessa*, 57-59.

the stool, quite apparently an official seat of a religious functionary. If he were to hand over the stool to somebody whom he considers appropriate, then the god is invoked to recompense him for that. The last two lines seem to refer to a situation in which Tiridates is unwilling to hand over the function of *bwdr* and in token of his refusal has the *baetyl*, which was set up for his successor, destroyed. In that case the god is called upon to take notice of the situation and seemingly to take action. It is completely unknown whether the inscriptions refer to an exceptional situation or to a usual procedure of priestly succession. The political situation in and around Edessa in the year 165 A.D. seems to indicate a rather exceptional case connected with a political shift. Before we can reach more certainty on this point, however, some preliminary questions must be answered. Who is the god called Mar°elahê—Lord of the gods? What does the function of *bwdr* mean and what is its relation to the function of "ruler of Arab"? What body of persons is especially involved in the cult practiced at Sumatar Harabesi?

The deity worshipped at Sumatar Harabesi is called "Sin the god," or "the god" or "Lord of the gods." This last title occurs in the same inscription in which the deity in question is simply called "the god," which makes it very likely that the god, and Lord of the gods actually mean the same deity. The same phenomenon can be detected in the inscriptions to the left and right of the reliefs near the summit of the mount in which "Sin the god," and "the god" clearly designate the same deity. Combining this evidence already makes it very likely that all inscriptions refer to the same god, i.e., Sin the moon god of Harran. This conclusion is corroborated by external evidence concerning Sin and his various epitheta. The so-called Harran inscriptions of Nabonidus the last king of the Neo-Babylonian Empire (555-539 B.C.), who was a fervent worshipper of the moon god Sin, frequently address the god as *šar ilâni*—King of the gods or *bêl-ilâni*—Lord of the gods. The last title has an exact equivalent in Syriac *mrlh*, a contraction of *mr* *'lh*—Lord of the gods. The contracted form can be considered an indication of very common use of the title in question.[14] J. B. Segal,

---

[14] In the inscription of Eski-Harran Sin is called *šar-ilāni*, *cf*. Pognon, *Inscriptions sémitiques*, 5, II, 3, 19; C. J. Gadd, The Harran Inscriptions of

who reads the title as *Marilaha* = the Lord god—a reading not in accordance with the Harranian background of Sin's cult nor with the linguistic evidence—is inclined to identify the deity with Ba'alšamên, although with some hesitation, mainly because Ba'alšamên at Palmyra bears the title *mr*'—lord and at Hatra too was addressed as "king" and the "great god." He suggests that at Harran, Sin may have been identified with Ba'alšamên, but also remarks that "it is not profitable to speculate upon the precise identity of a godhead Marilaha.!......because "It is sufficient to observe that the general atmosphere over a large area of northern Mesopotamia and Syria during the first centuries of the Christian era favoured the conception of a single godhead." [15] This seems to imply a shift in the direction of monotheism that occurred especially during that particular period. It will appear, however, that it is more in accordance with all extant material to consider the cult of the "lord of the gods" at Sumatar and other cults in that partic-ular area as a continuation of indigenous cults without any essential change in comparison to an earlier situation. The title *mrlh*' = *bel ilani* already points to such a view, but the whole context of the Sumatar cult is only understandable in the light of the ancient cult of Sin the moon god at Harran, as the answers to our remaining questions will demonstrate.

The term *bwdr* occurs one time more in the Syriac tomb inscrip-tion from Serrin of a religious functionary dating from 73 A.D. The builder of the tomb was 'Ma'nu the priest, *bdr* of NḤY.' [16] If NḤY is the name of a godhead, which is very likely since *nḥy* occurs as theophorous element in some proper names from this area, the term *bdr* is a more precise definition of the function of Ma'nu the

---

Nabonidus, *AnSt* 8, 1958, 35-92: Hl, B, col. I, 7, 17, 33, 39, 44, col. II, 12, 21, 23, 28, 34: *šar ilani*; H2, A. col. I, 5: *bêl ilani*; col. II, 14: *bêlu ša ilani*; *cf.* also J. Starcky, *Bible et Terre Sainte* 119, 1970, 6; *cf.* W. Röllig, Er-wägungen zu neuen Stelen König Nabonids, *ZA* 56, 1964, 218-260, esp. 255; who gave a new translation of these texts and cleared their composition; *cf.* also Milik, *Dédicaces*, 349.

[15] Segal, *Edessa*, 60 and *idem*, Pagan Syriac Monuments, *AnSt* 3, 1953, 115f.

[16] *cf.* Pognon, *Inscriptions sémitiques*, 15-22; A. Maricq, *Classica et Orientalia*, 127-139 compares the inscription of Serrîn with the oldest Syriac inscription that of Birecik; A. Maricq, BDR DNḤY: dans l'inscription de Serrin, *Classica et Orientalia*, 141-144.

priest.[17] It is noteworthy that in Arabic records about the doctrine and practice of the so-called Sabians of Harran the term *bughdariy-yon* occurs as a designation of a special class of initiated male persons who assembled in a special house or temple, according to Mas'udi, an underground room.[18] It is interesting that the Arabic word occurs with different spellings, the most important variants being *bwḥdr* and *bḥdr*. If we assume that the guttural ḥ was not pronounced and therefore not written in Syriac, we have exactly the same variants in Arabic as in Syriac, namely *bwdr* and *bdr*. Leaving aside the whole complicated tradition about the Sabians of Harran, it can be stated that they represent a continuation of indigenous religion and that, however philosophically disguised their doctrines may be, the sources of Sabian belief and practice must be sought in the traditional religion of Harran.[19] The term *bwdr*, probably pronounced as Budar, therefore denotes a special religious functionary who likely gets this function through a certain process of initiation.[20] The inscription on the central mount at

---

[17] *'mtnḥy* = maid servant of NḤY and *'bdnḥy* = servant of NḤY occur on the Family Portrait Mosaic; *cf.* Segal, Some Syriac Inscriptions, 29f.; Drijvers, no. 47, LL. 5, 12; *'bdnḥy* = servant of NḤY is most likely to be found on the Mosaic of Zenodora, Drijvers, no. 44, L. 7; NḤY is probably identical with the Thamudic god Nahi, frequently mentioned together with Ruḍa in Thamudic texts. Both gods already appear in the texts describing how, after the conquest of Adumatu (which is Dūmat al-Ǧandal in the North-Arabian Ǧof), Sanherib deported thence a number of divine images, including those of Nuḫâa and Ruldain, *cf. Wörterbuch der Mythologie*, 456f.; M. Höfner in: H. Gese et al., *Die Religionen Altsyriens*, 374; R. Borger, *Die Inschriften Asarhaddons, Königs von Assyrien, AfO* Beiheft 9, 1956, 53, 10-12; *OrNS* 26, 1957, 10f.; *cf. ANET*, 291; for names composed with NḤY at Palmyra, *cf.* D. Schlumberger, *La Palmyrène du Nord-Ouest*, Paris 1951, 149, no. 16, L. 3; J. K. Stark, *Personal Names in Palmyrene Inscriptions*, 99 *s.v. NḤY'ZYZ* = NḤY is strong/powerful, *CIS* II, 4041; *cf.* Drijvers, The Cult of Azizos and Monimos at Edessa, *Ex Orbe Religionum*, Festschrift G. Widengren, Vol. I, Leiden 1972, 36of.; J. Levy, Naḥ et Rušpan, *Mélanges R. Dussaud* I, Paris 1939, 272-275; F. Vattioni, Appunti sulle iscrizioni siriache antiche, *Augustinianum* 11, 1971, 442.

[18] *cf.* Chwolsohn, *Die Ssabier* II, 45ff., 310, n. 378, 352ff.

[19] Drijvers, Bardaiṣan and the Hermetica. The Aramaic Philosopher and the Philosophy of his Time, *JEOL* 21, 1969-1970, 194ff.

[20] Note that one of the meanings of Syriac *bdr* = to sprinkle, spread salve on wounds, metaph. overspread, oint, *cf. Thesaurus Syriacus*, *s.v.*; has *bwdr/bdr* something to do with an initiation rite e.g. accomplished by an ointment ?

Sumatar dealing with Tiridates' successor as a *bwdr* might actually imply a kind of initiation since the successor is reared or brought up by Tiridates.

Besides being *bwdr* of the god Sin, Tiridates is ruler of Arab and has in this function close ties to the king (of Edessa), who is first mentioned in his inscription as "my lord the king." The "ruler of Arab" held sway over the desert area east of Edessa as far as the Tigris, which region was called Arab (*ʿrb*) by several Syriac authors.[21] Although it seemed to be dependent on Edessa and its king in the year 165, it may have had a ruler of its own in 114/115 A.D., when several princes paid their respects to Trajan during his sojourn at Edessa, among them Maʿnu of adjacent Arabia! [22] It is, however, by no means excluded that the same Maʿnu functioned as "ruler of Arab," had certain connections to the king of Edessa, but also a certain independence, just as later rulers of Arab may have had. In fact the only argument for a subordination of the ruler of Arab to the king of Edessa is that Tiridates built an altar and set a *baetyl* for the life or well-being of "my lord the king and his sons."

Sumatar Harabesi was an important center of these rulers of Arab and its semi-nomad population, as appears not only from the inscriptions of the central mount, but also from inscriptions and reliefs in a cave discovered by H. Pognon. This cave measures 5.10 meters by 4.30 meters, and has a large niche in the rear wall 1.80 m. wide, 1.20 deep and 2.40 high. Nowadays the cave is inhabited by a beduin family, but when Pognon came to Sumatar it was not used as such. The walls of the cave show several over life-size figures in relief which apparently are mentioned in the accompanying inscriptions. At both sides of the niche in the rear wall a relief is carved representing a horned pillar of oval shape, resembling a stylized human person wearing horns on his head. Between the horns a cross is carved evidently symbolizing a star.

---

[21] *cf.* the texts quoted by Pognon, *Inscriptions sémitiques*, 34f.; at Dura-Europos an *Arabarches* also functioned, *cf. Dura-Europos, Final Report V*, 1, *The Parchments and Papyri*, New Haven 1959, 115, no. 20, L. 5; this Arabarches, called Phraates, also held the office of tax-collector and governor of Mesopotamia and Parapotamia. *Thesaurus Syriacus*, s.v. *ʿrb*: (col. 2982): regio Mesopotamiae in vicinia Edessae.

[22] *Cassius Dio* LXVIII, 21; *cf.* Drijvers, *ANRW* II, 8, 873f.

An adjacent cave has the same kind of niche in the back wall, only one relief of an unknown person and illegible traces of a large Syriac inscription. The persons mentioned in the inscriptions in the main cave, and their respective functions, bear a certain relation to the inscriptions on the central mount since they record the same functions and partly the same persons. A survey of the relevant names and functions will make this clear.

Wa'el son of Wa'el ruler of Arab and Wa'el son of Wa'el the military commander of ŠWD/R (inscr. 4 and 5) are recorded in Pognon's cave. They quite apparently are father and son, the father being ruler of Arab and the son military commander. Bar Nahar son of R/DYNY is another recorded ruler of Arab. He seems to be subordinate to a certain Aurelius Ḥafsai son of Barkalba freedman of Antoninus Caesar, because Bar Nahar calls Aurelius Ḥafsai, of whom he had a relief made, his lord and benefactor (inscr. 6, 7, 10). Aurelius Ḥafsai surely was not a freedman of Antoninus Pius (138-161), as Pognon and Segal believe, since this would not be in agreement with his first Latin name Aurelius. There are four emperors who can be considered to have freed Ḥafsai son of Barkalba because both names Aurelius and Antoninus occur in their imperial titles: Marcus Aurelius Antoninus (161-180), Marcus Aurelius Commodus Antoninus (180-192), Marcus Aurelius Antoninus = Caracalla (211-217) and Marcus Aurelius Antoninus = Elagabal (218-222). Since both Marcus Aurelius (161-180) and Caracalla (211-217) were active in Edessean politics it is most likely that Aurelius Ḥafsai was a freedman of one of them. Since Adona son of Tiridates had a relief made in Pognon's cave of Aurelius Ḥafsai son of Barkalba, assuming that this Adona is a son of Tiridates ruler of Arab, a dating some time after 165 is most appropriate. Ḥafsai in this case would be a freedman of Marcus Aurelius, during whose reign the pro-Parthian King Wa'el was expelled from Edessa and Ma'nu VIII restored. If Adona son of Tiridates is another person, Aurelius Ḥafsai might have been a freedman of Caracalla who made Edessa into a *colonia romana* in 214 A.D., after having arrested King Abgar IX at Rome. In that case he might have been the father of the first Roman governor of Edessa appointed in 248 after the abolition of the kingdom, who was called Aurelianus son

of Ḥafsai.[23] But the whole Edessan political development in 165
and the years afterwards makes it more likely that Aurelius Ḥafsai
was a freedman of Marcus Aurelius.

One of Ḥafsai's relatives is probably recorded in a memento-
inscription on the central mount (inscr. 20). Besides Adona son of
Tiridates, Tiridates son of Adona, his father, ruler of Arab, who
occurs twice in the inscriptions on the central mount (inscr. 23, 24
and perhaps 17) is also mentioned in an inscription in the cave and
represented there, although his function remained unmentioned
(inscr. 12). The last ruler of Arab recorded on the cave is Abgar
(inscr. 9), for whom a relief was made by Maʿnu son of Moqimu.
These names seem to be connected with the royal dynasty of Edessa;
perhaps this Abgar is the same as King Abgar, who started his
reign in 177 A.D.

It is one of the most interesting features of these inscriptions that
the Adona family, recorded through various names and functions
on the central mount, is mentioned without any title in the cave,
where a son of Tiridates ruler of Arab honors a freedman of the
Roman emperor. The Adona family is represented on the central
mount by Tiridates the ruler of Arab (inscr. 14, 17, 23, 24), by
Absamya son of Adona the military commander (inscr. 18), and
by several of their brethren Maʿna (inscr. 16, 21, 24) MNYŠ (24),
BLBNʾ (24, 25) and ʾLKWD (24 and perhaps 17). Other members
of the family are ʾNʾ (17, 64), Maʿnu (17), Maʿta (17), BBS and
Tiridates sons of ʿAbsamya (18). This phenomenon may be explained against the background of the political events at Edessa
during the years 163-165 A.D. During that period Waʾel bar Sahru,
who was a puppet of the Parthians, reigned at Edessa and became
king with the support of the Parthian King Vologoses III. Waʾel's
predecessor Maʿnu VIII sought a refuge with the Romans. Rome

---

[23] cf. Michael Syrus, Chronicle V, 5, ed. Chabot, I, 120; the name Aurelius
Ḥafsai occurs in the Syriac deed of sale from Dura-Europos, LL. 20 and
Verso, L. 2, cf., which dates from 243 A.D.; cf. J. A. Goldstein, the Syriac
Bill of Sale from Dura-Europos, JNES 25, 1966, 1-16; Drijvers, Old-Syriac
Inscriptions, 54ff.; Bellinger-Welles, A Third-Century Contract of Sale from
Edessa in Osrhoene, YCS 5, 1935, 95ff., 132. On Aurelius see H. Chantraire,
Freigelassene und Sklaven im Dienst der römischen Kaiser, Studien zu ihrer
Nomenklatur, Wiesbaden 1967, 65.

took countermeasures and Avidius Cassius reconquered Edessa in 165, after the inhabitants had killed the Parthian garrison and let the Romans in. In the same year King Ma'nu VIII was restored to his throne by his Roman allies.[24] It is quite possible that Tiridates' resignation as *bwdr* of the Lord of the gods, which possibly implied his resignation as ruler of Arab too, was due to his being a supporter of the pro-Parthian King Wa'el, as might appear from the inscription on the central mount according to which Tiridates set a pillar for the well-being of "my lord the king." The pro-Roman party might have forced him to resign. The inscription dealing with the succession hints, in fact, at the fact that Tiridates might refuse a successor with the phrase "if he (i.e., Tiridates) withholds the stool and the pillar will be ruined (by Tiridates?)"! The spring of 165 A.D., the date of both inscriptions of Tiridates, certainly was a time of political trouble, a time when the Romans attacked Edessa and after having dislodged Wa'el restored Ma'nu. This also may be the reason that Tiridates son of Adona is recorded in the cave without any title, whereas his son even honors a freedman of the Roman emperor. The tensions between the pro-Parthian Tiridates and the pro-Roman party are reflected in this manner in the inscriptions on the central mount and in Pognon's cave.

The inscriptions in this cave seem to have been written down in a certain chronological order. The oldest ones are in honor of Wa'el ruler of Arab and his son, the military commander with the same name. Then follow the inscriptions dedicated to Tiridates son of Adona; next the inscription honoring Abgar ruler of Arab and Aurelius Ḥafsai son of Barkalba honored by Bar Nahar ruler of Arab and a son of Tiridates called Adona like his grandfather. If Tiridates gave up his position in 165 A.D., we might conclude that both Wa'els were in charge at an earlier time and Abgar perhaps was Tiridates' successor. If this Abgar is identical with the later King of Edessa Abgar VIII the Great (177-212) son of Ma'nu VIII, who was restored by the Romans in 165, then he would certainly have belonged to the pro-Roman party, which might explain his functioning as ruler of Arab after 165 A.D. Another possibility is

---

[24] *cf.* for all details Drijvers, *ANRW* II, 8, 975f.

that Bar Nahar was Tiridates' successor with Abgar coming after him. Bar Nahar surely was an adherent of the Romans too; otherwise his honoring Aurelius Ḥafsai freedman of Antoninus Caesar is hardly to be explained. It seems more likely, however, that Abgar was Tiridates' successor and Aurelius Ḥafsai and Bar Nahar were later functionaries; if our supposition is true that Aurelius Ḥafsai was a freedman of the emperor Marcus Aurelius, this might explain his first Roman name. We therefore assume that Bar Nahar became Abgar's successor as ruler of Arab after 177 A.D., when Abgar started his reign over Edessa. That no later rulers of Arab are mentioned in Pognon's cave might be linked up with the drastic curtailment of Abgar's kingdom by Septimius Severus in 197 A.D., because Abgar, together with other kings in Mesopotamia, had supported Pescennius Niger. Septimius Severus created the *provincia Osroene* in 197 A.D. and Abgar was left with the town of Edessa and its direct surroundings.[25] The area called Arab certainly was a part of the *provincia Osroene* and consequently had no more rulers who were dependent on the King of Edessa.

So far all inscriptions at Sumatar Harabesi refer to the political situation at Edessa and mirror major changes in that situation. B. Aggoula, on the contrary, expressed the view that the area of Arab once was dependent on Hatra and its kings since in his opinion an area "Arab of Wa'el" is recorded in a Hatrene inscription. The inscription in question is written on the socle of a marble statue of King Sanatruq II found in the ante-cella of the sanctuary no. 11 dedicated to Nergal.[26] It actually is a honorific text accompanying this piece of sculpture offered to King Sanatruq on the occasion of his birthday. The last line reads: *dkyrn l'lm' bḥtr' w'rbw'w* = may they (i.e., the dedicants) be remembered forever in Hatra and Arab and (?).[27] Whatever the explanation of the orthography *'rbw'w* may be, there is no reason for reading a *l* instead of the

---

[25] Drijvers, *ANRW* II, 8, 877ff. for details.

[26] Inscription no. 79, *cf.* A. Caquot, *Syria* 40, 1963, 2-6; J. Teixidor, *Syria* 41, 1964, 280f.; Milik, *Dédicaces*, 358, 364, 366, 379f., *mškn'*, however, does not designate a place Maškanê, but rather means 'temple', *cf.* Hillen, *BASOR* 206, 1972, 55ff.; B. Aggoula, Remarques sur les inscriptions hatréennes, II, *MUSJ* 47, 1972, 30ff.

[27] *cf.* Caquot's remarks, *Syria* 40, 1963.

last *w* and obtaining in this way *ʿrb wʾl*, which would have the
meaning of Arab of Waʾel. It is much more likely that the inscription
is not complete at the end, so that an appropriate reading should
be: *bḥtrʾ wʿrb wʾw...* = in Hatra and Arab and ʾw (?). Since this
inscription dates from after 230 A.D., Aggoula is obliged to change
the order of rulers of Arab in Pognon's cave in order to make
Waʾel and Sanatruq II contemporaries.[28] That rearrangement of
the most likely chronological order also does not fit in with the
order of the inscriptions and reliefs in the cave: Waʾel, Tiridates,
Abgar, and Bar Nahar. Aggoula dates Aurelius Ḥafsai and consequently Bar Nahar before Tiridates, assuming wrongly that
Aurelius Ḥafsai is a freedman of Antoninus Pius (138-161).

The political bonds between Hatra and Sumatar Harabesi as
wrongly reconstructed by Aggoula were, in fact, meant to explain
the occurrence at Hatra of some coins bearing the legend Sin
Marᵉlahê = Sin Lord of the gods.[29] If Sumatar was dependent on
Hatra and Sin Marᵉlahê was the paramount deity at Sumatar,
then there would be validity in having such coins struck at Hatra
which expressed religious practice in subordinate areas. The cult
of Sin is not attested at all at Hatra, so the coins cannot find an
explanation in the context of Hatrene religion. Since, however, the
supposed bonds between Sumatar and Hatra turned out to be
non-existent, we must assume for the time being that these coins
originate from another place in Northern Mesopotamia where the
cult of Sin was practiced, e.g., at Harran, and possibly at Singara.[30]

The worship of Sin at Sumatar appeared to have special links
with the functionaries, the discharge of their duties and their succession. The central mount was the place where an altar and *baetyls*
were put for Marᵉlahê and where the god was invoked to watch

---

[28] Aggoula, Remarques sur les inscriptions hatréennes II, 35; moreover,
he presents Segal's list of Rulers of Arab in the wrong order; according to
Segal, *AnSt* 3, 1953, 104f. the order is: 1. Waʾel; 2. Tiridates; 3. Abgar;
4. Aurelius Ḥafsai, and not 1. Tiridates; 2. Waʾel; etc.

[29] *cf.* J. Walker, The Coins of Hatra, *NumC.* 18, 1958, 167-172, Pl. XIV,
11, 12; Aggoula, Remarques II, 47-49.

[30] *cf.* Milik, *Dédicaces*, 362, 399; Drijvers, *ANRW* II, 8, 831f.; W. al-Salihi
wrongly identifies Bar Marên and Sin in order to explain the occurrence of
these coins at Hatra, *cf.* W. al-Salihi, New Light on the Identity of the Triad
of Hatra, *Sumer* 31, 1975, 75-80, Pl. 1-6.

over the proper procedure of Tiridates' succession as *bwdr*. The inscriptions do not record the dedication of a temple or the consecration of a shrine as a permanent religious building, but were carved in the mountain of the Lord of the gods for a special occasion.[31] The mountain itself was a cult place and there was never a temple on top of it.

What, however, was the function of the cave(s) with reliefs and inscriptions and the two horned pillars? Pognon considers it a temple dedicated to a god whose statue must have stood in the niche in the back wall. Segal does not express an opinion regarding the function of the cave. There are, in fact, numerous caves all over Sumatar and all are clearly tombs, since they have *arcosolia* and niches to put the dead in. At first sight, therefore, one is inclined to assume that this cave also functioned as a burial place for the rulers of Arab and related functionaries. This first impression is reinforced by some comparative evidence from Sumatar. On top of a hill situated about 250 metres east of the Central Mount a stele bearing a much-weathered inscription of six lines, and a bas-relief representing three women was found in 1971 and it is still there (Pl. XXXI). The stele lay in front of a stairway cut in the rock which led to a cave-tomb with *arcosolia* so that it can be assumed to be a funerary stele. The first line of the inscription reads: *hn' ṣlm' d'bd*—this is the image that made....[32] The same phrase, or a shortened form of it, occurs as the opening of all inscriptions in Pognon's cave.[33] Moreover, these texts do not show a single trace of a religious or honorific meaning as would be expected from reliefs in a temple or related buildings. Examples of statues erected in sanctuaries are especially abundant at Palmyra, but the accompanying inscription always says that the statue was erected to honor the person in question or was dedicated by the deity itself, i.e., from the proceeds of the temple. Thus far, the evidence therefore points in the direction of a funerary function of the cave.

---

[31] Segal, *AnSt* 3, 1953, 102, 107: "... the central mount .... At one time it must have had a temple; there are, however, no single traces of a former building on top of the barren rock".

[32] Drijvers, Some New Syriac Inscriptions, 6ff., Pl. IV.

[33] Inscription no. 5, L. 1: *hlyn ṣlm' d'bd*—these are the statues that made; no. 9, LL. 1f.: *hn' ṣlm' d'bd m'nw*—this is the statue that Ma'nu made; no. 10, LL. 1f.: *hn' ṣlm' (d'bd) ml'*—this is the statue (that) Male (made).

The horned pillars at both sides of the niche in the back wall of the cave are, in fact, the only argument to consider it a temple, or at least a room for non-funerary use. The horned pillar is the symbol of Sin the moon god of Harran and occurs as such on a coin from Harran struck under Septimius Severus. On its reverse it shows a temple with four columns, and in its central inter-columniation a conical *baetyl* surmounted by a crescent and standing on a base. (Pl. XXXII, 5). The temple on this coin certainly is a representation of the Sin temple at Harran and its main cultic image, i.e., the *baetyl* of Sin.[34]

It seems that the Edessene King Wa'el during his short reign from 163-165 A.D., of which we have only numismatic evidence, showed a particular reverence for a cult object similar to the *baetyl* of Sin at Harran. One of his bronze coins shows a temple with pediment and two columns in front and steps leading up to it. In the temple a cubic cult object—in fact a *baetyl*—on a base supported by two curved legs is to be seen. The coin bears the enigmatic legend usually read as *'lh 'lwl*, which is, however, very unlikely (Pl. XXXIII, 1).[35] The same temple recurs on a coin of Elagabal and Severus Alexander in reduced size between the busts of the two emperors (Pl. XXXIII, 4).[36] The Harran *baetyl* of Sin possibly was also represented on a stele discovered in 1956 in the pavement of the North entrance to the Great Mosque at Harran, which bears a copy of one of the Harran inscriptions of Nabonidus, the last King of the Chaldaean dynasty of the Neo-Babylonian Empire (555-539 B.C.) (Pl. XXIX). The inscription of the royal mother votaress of Sin at Harran is, in fact, broken at the top, but the lower part of the sculpture in the tympanum is still visible. It

---

[34] Hill, *BMC, Arabia*, 82, no. 4, Pl. XII, 4; see the drawing of the horned pillar, Segal, *AnSt* 3, 1953, 103, Fig. 2: the cross incised in the wall between the horns is surely a star, probably the Venus star, which very often occurs with the crescent on the *kudurru, cf.* Dhorme, *Les religions*, 84; a stele bearing a pillar standing on a base and crowned by the same crescent emblem of Sin was found about four miles from Harran on the road to Edessa, *cf.* Segal, The Sabian Mysteries in: *Vanished Civilizations*, 203.

[35] *cf.* P. Naster, Les monnaies d'Édesse révèlent-elles un dieu 'Elul?, *RBNS* 114, 1968, 6f., Pl. I, where the known copies of this coin are depicted; *cf.* Segal, *AnSt* 3, 1953, 115.

[36] Hill, *BMC, Arabia*, 103, no. 79 = Pl. XV, 8.

shows an object which is approached by other figures and that might be a low base upon which stood a pedestal in the form of a column.[37] A related symbol occurs on a relief of Bar-Rakkab of Zinjirli dating from the second half of the eighth century B.C. It is a pole with a tassel hanging down on either side and a crescent with disc on top of it. The inscription reads: My lord, Ba'al Ḥarran.[38] The cult of Sin, Lord of Ḥarran spread into this area of Aramaic kingdoms under Assyrian influence.

There being no doubt that the horned pillar symbolizes Sin of Harran, we are still left with the question of the function of the cave. All persons portrayed there are official functionaries who had special ties to the cult of Sin and even may have been his *bwdr*! This problem interferes with another one also dealing with the function of certain buildings at Sumatar. Mainly to the north and the west of the central mount is a group of partly ruined buildings of different shape (Pl. XXVIII). Below them there are grottos, the entrances of which more or less face the central mount. Some of the entrances are blocked, but those grottos that can be entered are without any doubt cave-tombs cut in the rock. They have *arcosolia* in vaulted chambers intended for placing the dead. The rather sumptuous upperstructures of these tombs, making them into a real *nefeš* in a Semitic tradition, are an indication that they were meant for rich and powerful people.[39] It is not too hazardous, therefore, to suppose that these tombs were the burial-places of the rulers of Arab and functionaries of equal rank and their families. If that should be true, then Pognon's cave was not a cave-tomb at all, but served other purposes. However similar the

---

[37] C. J. Gadd, The Harran Inscriptions of Nabonidus, *AnSt* 8, 1958, 37, Pl. I.

[38] Y. Yadin, Symbols of Deities at Zinjirli, Carthage and Hazor, *Essays in Honor of Nelson Glueck. Near Eastern Archaeology in the Twentieth Century*, ed. J. A. Sanders, N.Y. 1970, 210f. Fig. 21; *cf. KAI* 218; R. Degen, *Altaramäische Grammatik*, *AKM* 38, 3, 1969, 9, Barr. III.
Bel Harran often occurs in Neo-Assyrian onomastics from the time of Sargon on till the end of the Neo-Assyrian empire, *cf.* Pomponio, *Nabû*, 89; according to Yadin Ba'al-Ḥarran is parallel to (or even replaces) Ba'al-Ḥamman, *cf.* also *Wörterbuch der Mythologie I*, 271f., *s.v.* Baal-Ḥammōn.

[39] *cf.* Gawlikowski, *Monuments funéraires de Palmyre*, Warszawa 1970, 9ff. for a discussion of the various types that occur in Syria.

cave may be to cave-tombs, there is one great difficulty in considering it a tomb, and that is that all functionaries recorded in the inscription surely belonged to different families and even might have been of different origin. It is hardly conceivable that they all were buried in the same tomb since people of a certain social rank and their families used to have a tomb of their own.

The cult place of Sin, however, was the central mount, the blessed mount as it is called, so that the cave actually was not a temple, as Pognon thought. The recording of the various functionaries and their portrayals in relief on the walls—all centered, in fact, round the niche in the back wall—and the symbols of Sin are an indication that the cave most likely was the place where these functionaries were invested with their offices, which were at the same time civil and religious ones: they were rulers of Arab and Budars of Sin. The relation between Sin and the ruler of Arab is also hinted at in the decoration on the tiara of King Abgar VIII of Edessa as represented on his coins. The tiara is adorned with a crescent and star in it, which is Sin's symbol (Pl. XXXIII, 2, 3).[40] Is this to be considered a reminiscence of his former function of ruler of Arab? There is much to be said for that, especially as the tiara of a later King Abgar X, who is represented on coins together with Gordian III, is not decorated with the crescent. Sin's symbol, therefore, did not belong to the usual paraphernalia of the Edessene kings, but was only pictured on the tiara of those among them who once functioned as ruler of Arab and as such had close religious relations to Sin.

J. B. Segal once considered the buildings with grottos below them to be planet temples centred around the blessed mount of the Lord of the gods, based on a report on the Sabians of Harran by a famous Islamic author from the tenth century A.D., Mas'udi. Mas'udi's account gives a description of the various temples of the Sabians dedicated, e.g., to the First Cause, to Reason, to Fate and

---

[40] cf. Hill, BMC, Arabia, 94ff. no's 14ff., Pl. XIII, 15, 16; XIV, 1-9; Segal, AnSt 3, 1953, 108 remarks: "That the moon deity was worshipped at Edessa is shown by the crescent symbol on the coins" and refers to Hill, BMC, 94; in fact the crescent symbol only occurs as decoration on Abgar's tiara and is not further attested on Edessene coins.

Soul and to the various Planets.[41] The last ones in particular would all have a different shape and this was the main ground for Segal to identify the buildings at Sumatar with the Sabian planet temples, and to describe the cult at Sumatar as fundamentally a planet-worship. Two major objections can be formulated against this view: first of all the buildings clearly are tombs; and secondly, Mas'udi's account actually describes religious, philosophical and astrological entities that played a role in the doctrine of the Sabians, and in order to formulate this in an appropriate way he assigns a temple to each of them. The cult at Sumatar Harabesi consequently is not a planet cult, but in principle, the local cult of Sin the moon god of nearby Harran connected with high civil and military functionaries in that area. As such it is, in fact, a continuation and survival of an ancient indigenous cult and conceptions related to it.

The name of the moon god Sin actually is a borrowing from Sumerian and in the famous Sumerian city of Ur the god was highly venerated together with his spouse Nin-gal the great Lady. On the well-known stele of Ur-Namma, founder of the third dynasty of Ur (2112-2095), the god is represented enthroned with staff and sceptre in his right hand, Nin-gal is seated to his right and the king in front of them. The staff and the sceptre are the *insignia* with which the god invests the king.[42] These are, in fact, close ties between the moon god and kingship in Mesopotamia. The physical appearance of the crescent looks like a royal crown and Sin consequently is called "Lord of the Crown" (*bel agi*) in the Babylonian creation epic *Enuma Elish*.[43] The Codex Hammurapi states that Sin will deprive the transgressor of Hammurapi's laws of "the crown, of the throne of kingship," and Hammurapi himself is called "seed of the royalty, which the god Sin has created." In an ode to Hammurapi the first line reads: Sin assigned the primacy

---

[41] See Chwolsohn, *Die Ssabier* II, 366ff.; Segal, *AnSt* 3, 1953, 112ff.; *cf.* J. Hjärpe, *Analyse critique des traditions arabes sur les Sabéens Ḥarraniens*, Diss. Uppsala 1972, 68ff. and esp. 90-92.

[42] *cf.* Dhorme, *Les religions*, 55, 83f.; G. Contenau, *Manuel d'archéologie orientale* II, 777, where the stele of Ur-Namma is depicted; *cf.* J. Lewy, The late Assyro-Babylonian Cult of the Moon and its Culmination in the Time of Nabonidus, *HUCA* 19, 1945-46, 478.

[43] Dhorme, *Les Religions*, 85; *cf.* Tallquist, *Akkadische Götterepitheta*, 41, 232; *cf. Codex Hammurapi*, Recto II, 13ff.; Verso, XXVII, 41ff.

to you.[44] Sin in general gets all epitheta and characteristics of a deity of the first rank; he is the Lord of the month and reigns over time together with Shamash the sun. He is the chief of the gods, the only august one, etc. What is important in our context and for our purposes is Sin's close ties with human rulers, a theme which recurs in the Harran inscriptions of Nabonidus. This last king of the Neo-Babylonian empire had a special veneration for Sin of Harran and restored his famous sanctuary E-ḫul-ḫul there, as appears from one of his Harran inscriptions: E-ḫul-ḫul the temple of Sin anew I built, I finished its work. The hands of Sin, of Ningal, Nusku and Sadarnunna from Suanna my royal city I clasped, and with joy and gladness I made them enter and dwell in their lasting sanctuary.[45] Sin called Nabonidus to the kingship, as it is often stated in these texts. The inscription of the royal mother votaress of Sin at Harran phrases it as follows: Sin, king of the gods, looked upon me and Nabu-na'id (my) only son, the issue of my womb, to the kingship he called, and the kingship of Sumer and Akkad from the border of Egypt (on) the upper sea even to the lower sea all the lands he entrusted hither to his hands.[46] The way Nabonidus' reign is described reminds of the proud title "king of the totality of the country" that was conferred to the rulers of Ur by the moon god of their city when they succeeded in extending their power beyond the immediate neighborhood of their city-state. The title was later transformed and applied to rulers of world empires like the kings of Akkad. Even in the late period, when Sargon and the Sargonids emphasized their devotion to Sin of Harran, and Esarhaddon and Ashurbanipal had themselves crowned in that city, these two rulers were given by Sin the "kingdom of the totality of the countries" according to Nabonidus.[47] It seems that the cult of Sin at Harran implied the notion of a kingdom of the totality of

---

[44] Dhorme, *Les religions*, 85; for the Ode to Hammurapi see *idem*, *La religion assyro-babylonienne*, 163, 177, n. 115.

[45] Gadd, The Harran Inscriptions, *AnSt* 8, 1958, H2 Col. III, 21-25; *cf.* W. Röllig, *ZA*, NF 22, 1964, 223ff.

[46] Gadd, The Harran Inscriptions, H1. B. Col I, 39-44; *cf.* Col. II, 1; H2 A and B. Col. I, 10-11; Col. III, 35-37; *cf.* Röllig, *ZA* 1964, 241, n. 61.

[47] J. Lewy, The Assyro-Babylonian Cult of the Moon, 481f.; *cf.* Gadd, The Harran Inscriptions, 72.

the land, which was given to the rulers at Harran, just as in ancient times it was given to the rulers of Ur. Nabonidus' veneration for Sin consequently would have had political aspects having to do with his nostalgic aspirations of restoring a large realm. Omitting consideration of all problems connected with Nabonidus' reign and his ten-year stay at Tema in Northern Arabia, it can be stated that his fervent veneration of Sin actually was a politico-religious attitude and a continuation of ancient views of kingship and rule given by Sin the Baʿal of Harran.[48]

It is quite possible that the same notions played a role in Waʾel's supposed worship of Sin and the flourishing of the god's cult during his short reign. In fact the cult of Sin at Sumatar is only attested shortly before and after Waʾel's kingship and the first recorded ruler of Arab Waʾel son of Waʾel even may have been one of his relatives or sons, as we saw before. Waʾel's endeavour to become independent of Rome with the help of the Parthians consequently harked back to a special cult connected with claims on an independent rule of the totality of the land between Euphrates and Tigris. Even on a restricted scale this politico-religious conception holds true for the close ties between the rulers of Arab and the moon god Sin, which find their real explanation and meaning against the background of ancient religious notions connected with the cult of Sin at Harran. Sin's worship spread over the whole of Syria already in the time of the Neo-Assyrian kings, and perhaps still earlier, and therefore the god and his companions are often found in Aramaic inscriptions from the beginning of the first millenium B.C. on. The inscription of Bar-Rakab son of Panamuwa who calls the Baʿal Harran his Lord has already been mentioned. Sin and Ningal occur in a whole list of deities which are witnesses to the treaty between King Bar-gaʾja of KTK and Matiʿ-el of Arpad.[49] On two basalt funerary steles from the seventh century B.C.,

---

[48] cf. esp. W. Röllig, *ZA* 1964, 234ff.: Die Herkunft Nabonids. Babylonische Reaktion and 243ff.: Aufenthalt in Arabien; W. G. Lambert, Nabonidus in Arabia, in: *Proceedings of the fifth Seminar for Arabian Studies held at the Oriental Institute*, Oxford, 22nd and 23rd September 1971, London 1972, 53ff.

[49] *KAI* 222, LL. 8-13 and the commentary *KAI* Vol. II, 244ff.; cf. J. A. Fitzmyer, *The Aramaic Inscriptions of Sefîre*, Rome 1967, 13f., 33ff.; R. Degen, *Altaramäische Grammatik*, 9f.; cf. A. F. Key, *JBL* 84, 1965, 20-26.

originating from Nerab near to modern Aleppo, ŠHR, Šamaš, Nikkal and Nusku are listed as the gods who are invoked to revenge whomever may damage the tomb. In this list ŠHR—the moon god clearly replaces Sin the moon god of Harran, if we take into consideration that Ningal/Nikkal and Nusku in particular are also worshipped at Harran together with Sin.[50]

It is very likely that Nabonidus brought the cult of Sin with him to the oasis Tema because an Aramaic inscription found there on a stele from the fifth or fourth century B.C. mentions int. al. the god SNGL'; the best explanation of this name is to consider it a composite name of Sin and GL' = heap of stones.[51] This interpretation is even more likely, as the relief on the stele is very similar in style and representation to the reliefs on Nabonidus' Harran inscriptions.[52]

The cult and gods of Harran survived till late in the Christian era, and even in Muslim times the city was famous for its pagan beliefs. The *Doctrina Addai* mentions the worship of Bath-Nikkal = daughter of Nikkal, certainly a designation of Ishtar-Venus. Jacob of Saruġ's *Homily on the Fall of the Idols* lists the gods of Harran as follows: He (i.e., Satan) led astray Harran by Sin, Baʿalšamên and Bar Nemrê, by my Lord with his Dogs and the goddesses Tarʿatha and Gadlat.[53] Some of these gods are also mentioned in Isaac of Antioch's two homilies on the conquest of Beth Ḥur by the Arabs dating from the fifth century.[54] Beth Ḥur was situated

---

[50] *KAI* 225, 226; and the commentary *KAI* Vol. II, 275; Sin, Šamaš, Ningal und Nusku were the most outstanding deities of Harran, *cf. Vorderasiatische Bibliothek* 4, 1912, 222, 18-21; 290 II, 5f. referring to texts of Nabonidus; on Ningal see Dhorme, *RB* 1928, 382ff.; P. Jensen, Nik(k)al in Harran, *ZA* 11, 1896, 293ff.; for Ugarit see W. Herrmann, *Yariḫ und Nikkal und der Preis der Kuṭarat-Göttinnen, BZAW* 106, Berlin 1968; *Wörterbuch der Mythologie* I, *s.v.* Nikkal, p. 302f.; on Nusku, see Dhorme, *Les religions*, 111f.; H. and J. Lewy, *Or* NS 17, 1948, 146-159; *Wörterbuch der Mythologie* I, 116f. *s.v.* Nusku.

[51] *KAI* 228; *cf.* J. Lewy, *HUCA* 19, 1945-46, 446, n. 183; *cf.* R. Degen, Die aramäischen Inschriften aus Taimā' und Umgebung, *Neue Ephemeris f. Sem. Epigraphik* 2, 1974, 79ff.

[52] Gadd, The Harran Inscriptions, 41f., Pl. IIIb gives a detailed discussion.

[53] *cf.* Ch. II, n. 69.

[54] Baʿalšamên in Isaac's 1st Homily on the Conquest of Beth Ḥur, ed. G. Bickell, 67ff.; Gadlat, Šamaš and Sin, *ibidem*, 167-170.

near Nisibis and founded by Harran, so that both cities surely had
religious institutions in common. Sin, Ba'alšamên and Gadlat occur
in both texts. My Lord of his dogs is a designation of Nergal and
there is good reason, therefore, also to consider Bar Nemrê a local
appellation of a certain god. Two possibilities actually present themselves if we take as our starting-point the meaning in Akkadian of
the root *nmr*, namely, shine, radiate: *namra-ṣit* = rise of shine,
and as such is an epitheton of Sin,[55] and *namurru* means shining,
radiating. The supposed meaning of *nmr*' as crown [56] and Syriac
nemro = leopard or panther, all derive from the basic meaning of
the root; in the case of the leopard we may assume a correlation
between the shining yellow color of its skin and the root *nmr*.
Bar NMR' therefore has the meaning "Son of the Shining one" or
"Son of Shine." If by the "Shining one" or "Shine" Sin, who bears
the epitheton *namra-ṣit*, is meant, Bar NMR' should be considered
Nusku, the god of fire, who at Harran sometimes functions as son
of Sin.[57] His emblem was the lamp and often Nusku himself is
called "light" (*nuru*) or "god light," because he embodies the new
light of the new moon.[58] Another epitheton expressing the idea of
shine is "bearer of the shining sceptre" (*naš ḫaṭṭi elliti*). As Nusku,
together with his spouse Sadarnunna, belongs to the cultic environ-
ment of Sin, Bar NMR' (perhaps Bar Namura?) can designate him,
so that Jacob of Saruǧ really preserves an authentic designation
applied to Nusku, like Lord of his Dogs is an appellation of Nergal.
Another possibility which, however, is less likely in my view, is to
consider Bar NMR' a circumscription of Šamaš the sun god. The
Syriac *bar* can be used as an expression for any close relation, sub-
jection or similarity and consequently has a wider sense than just
"son." Bar NMR', therefore, can have the meaning of "a shining
one" like *bar nwhr*' means "an enlightened one." The shining one
par excellence is the sun and Bar NMR' may denote therefore the

[55] *cf. AHW* II *s.v. nawāru(m), namāru.* Dhorme, *Les Religions,* 56, 85;
Tallquist, *Akkad. Götterepitheta,* 214, 387.

[56] *cf.* Landersdorfer, *Die Götterliste,* 31; S. Ronzevalle, *MUSJ* 22, 1939,
107-121; R. Dussaud, *Syria* 25, 1946-48, 161-162.

[57] Dhorme, *Les Religions,* 59, 112-132.

[58] Gadd, The Harran Inscriptions, 40; Tallquist, *Akkad. Götterepitheta,*
143.

sun god, who also is recorded in Isaac of Antioch's homily on Beth Ḥur. It seems strange, however, that so common a god as the sun god is circumscribed in this unusual way, which has no similarity to any of the epitheta of Šamaš that occur in cuneiform texts. For the time being the problem cannot be solved definitely, but it seems more likely that Bar NMR' denotes Nusku. It should be noted that there was a close connexion between Nusku and Nabu/Nebo, so that consideration has been given to whether they were not essentially and functionally the same.[59]

The second century cult at Sumatar Harabesi, the *Doctrina Addai*, and Jacob of Saruğ's homily turned out to preserve authentic Harranean religious ideas related to its ancient cults. We cannot detect any fundamental change which would have occurred in the second century A.D. or later, but only a tenacious survival of existing ideas. Such a conclusion fits in with the general picture of pagan religion in and near Edessa which we have so far acquired. The city had various relations with other important places like Hierapolis, Antioch, Harran and even Babylon and showed these relations in its religious pattern. Moreover, various groups of its population diversified this pattern even more since not only the ancient cult-centers of Syria and Mesopotamia, but also the inhabitants of the desert contributed to the variety of its beliefs.

---

[59] H. and J. Lewy, The God Nusku, *Or.*, 1948, 146ff.; Gadd, The Harran Inscriptions, 40, n. 4; Pomponio, *Nabû*, 203f.

CHAPTER SIX

THE CULT OF AZIZOS AND MONIMOS AND OTHER ARAB DEITIES

In December 362 the Emperor Julian, the last of the Hellenes, delivered at Antioch his famous oration on King Helios, describing the sovereign might of Sol Invictus. This was his contribution to the festivities of the Solis Agon, celebrated in Rome on December 25.[1] In Antioch Julian is involved in various difficulties with the adherents of Jesus Christ, whose birthday would afterwards be commemorated on the twenty-fifth of December, when the pagan Sol Invictus was superseded by the Christian Sol Salutis.[2]

It is not surprising that in this context the emperor remarks upon the religion of Edessa, according to legend the earliest Christian state in the world, but according to him devoted to the cult of Helios from time immemorial. The Christianity of the Edessenes greatly annoyed the emperor, who even refused to enter the town on his campaign against the Persians "from hate of its inhabitants, who had long been converted to Christianity in great numbers."[3] Julian states that his remarks on the cult of the Sun at Edessa derive from the sages of Phoenicia, whose conceptions he learnt from Iamblichos, who is known to be of Syrian birth.[4]

After some information regarding Aphrodite, who according to the Phoenician sages shares in the creative power of the Sun—

---

[1] L'Empereur Julien, *Oeuvres complètes* II, 2, éd. C. Lacombrade, Paris 1964, 75ff.

[2] cf. G. Downey, *A History of Antioch in Syria*, Princeton 1961, 38off.; H. Rahner, *Griechische Mythen in christlicher Deutung*, Zürich 1957, 125ff.: Das christliche Mysterium von Sonne und Mond; G. H. Halsberghe, *The Cult of Sol Invictus*, EPRO 23, Leiden 1972, 174.

[3] Sozomenos, *Hist. Eccl.*, VI, 1, 1; Theodoretus, *Hist. Eccl.* III, 26, 2; according to *Zosimos* III, 12, 2 Julian did pass through Edessa on his campaign against the Persians, cf. Segal, *Edessa*, 111.

[4] Iamblichos was born at Chalcis in Coele Syria about 250 A.D. and died at Daphne near Antioch ca. 325, cf. Downey, *Antioch* 332, n. 63; Alan Cameron, *Hermes* 96, 1968, 374-376; E. des Places, *Oracles chaldaïques*, Paris 1971, 24.

Aphrodite meaning the planet Venus—Julian continues as follows:
"Ἔτι μετριάσαι βούλομαι τῆς Φοινίκων θεολογίας· εἰ δὲ μὴ μάτην, ὁ
λόγος προϊὼν δείξει. Οἱ τὴν Ἔδεσσαν οἰκοῦντες, ἱερὸν ἐξ αἰῶνος Ἡλίου
χωρίον, Μόνιμον αὐτῷ καὶ Ἄζιζον συγκαθιδρύουσιν. Αἰνίττεσθαι δέ
φησιν Ἰαμβλίχος, παρ' οὗπερ καὶ τἆλλα πάντα ἐκ πολλῶν σμικρὰ
ἐλάβομεν, ὡς ὁ Μόνιμος μὲν Ἑρμῆς εἴη, Ἄζιζος δὲ Ἄρης, Ἡλίου
πάρεδροι, πολλὰ καὶ ἀγαθὰ τῷ περὶ γῆν ἐποχετεύοντες τόπῳ. "I desire
to mete out still more of the theology of the Phoenicians, and
whether it be to some purpose my argument as it proceeds will
show. The inhabitants of Edessa, a place from time immemorial
sacred to Helios, associate with him Monimos and Azizos. Iamblichos, from whom I have taken this and all besides, a little from a
great store, says that the secret meaning to be interpreted is that
Monimos is Hermes and Azizos Ares, the assessors of Helios, who
are the channel for many blessings to the region of our earth." [5]

Further on, connecting Helios with Rome, Julian states that the
city's founder, Romulus, is called the son of Ares: Ἐγὼ δὲ ὅτι μὲν
Ἄρης Ἄζιζος λεγόμενος ὑπὸ τῶν οἰκούντων τὴν Ἔδεσσαν Σύρων
Ἡλίου προπομπεύει, καίπερ εἰδὼς καὶ προειπὼν ἀφήσειν μοι δοκῶ.
"Now I am aware that Ares, who is called Azizos by the Syrians
who inhabit Edessa, goes before Helios in the procession,..." [6]

According to the text of Julian's oration on King Helios, then,
the Edessenes worship the Sun, flanked by Azizos and Monimos,
whom Iamblichos identifies with Ares and Hermes, respectively.
Azizos, the Sun's precursor, is the Morning Star (he goes before
Helios in the procession), and Monimos consequently is the Evening
Star, although this is not explicitly stated. Julian's text seemingly
presents a few problems that complicate matters. Following Spanheim, many scholars considered these references to a cult of the
Sun more applicable to Emesa than to Edessa, and in agreement
with the German philologist, corrected Julian's text accordingly,
although all manuscripts unanimously read Edessa. Scholars emi-

---

[5] Julian, 150 C-D = Oeuvres complètes II, 2, 128; the English translation
is given after W. C. Wright, Julian I, 413 (ed. Loeb) with some minor
alterations; Wright reads Ἔμεσαν instead of Ἔδεσσαν and he translates
συγκαθιδρύουσιν as 'they associate in their temples'.
[6] Julian, 154 B = Oeuvres complètes II, 2, 133; Wright, Julian I, 421-423.

nently acquainted with the religions of Syria and Mesopotamia in
Graeco-Roman times, such as R. Mouterde,[7] R. du Mesnil du
Buisson [8] and D. Sourdel,[9] follow Spanheim without hesitation.
J. G. Février leaves the matter undecided,[10] but H. Seyrig did
not then commit himself. Publishing in 1950 a limestone altar from
Emesa dedicated to the god Azizos, he wrote of Spanheim's con-
jecture: "Cette correction se fonde sur ce que la ville en question
est qualifiée de description qui a paru convenir mieux à Emèse
qu'à Édesse. Elle a été adoptée par les editeurs de Julien." [11]
C. Lacombrade, however, who prepared a new edition of Julian's
oration in 1964, did not follow Spanheim, but stuck to the reading
of all manuscripts. In 1970 Seyrig's opinion is altered (because of
Lacombrade's edition?), for he then writes: "Arès.....était à
Édesse l'appariteur (πρόπομπος) d'Hélios." [12] J. B. Segal writes in
his history of Edessa: "We should no doubt read 'Emesa', which
was celebrated for its cult in honour of the sun, for 'Edessa'; it
may be observed that Ephraim, the contemporary of Julian, makes
no mention of sun worship at Edessa." [13] Others, again, hold to
Julian's text as a source of knowledge for the religion of Edessa. Thus
F. Cumont,[14] R. Duval,[15] I. Levy,[16] H. Th. Bossert,[17] J. Rendel

---

[7] R. Mouterde, Cultes antiques de la Coelésyrie et de l'Hermon, *MUSJ*
36, 1959, 76-78: an altar from Moʿallaqat Zaḥlé with a representation of
the sun god and—according to Mouterde—Azizos and Monimos; it was
published anew by J. Rey-Coquais, *IGLS* VI, 2962, who also accepts the
correction. He does not, however, think, we can be certain of the identity
of the gods depicted.

[8] R. du Mesnil du Buisson, *Les tessères et les monnaies de Palmyre*, 333f.

[9] D. Sourdel, *Les cultes du Hauran à l'époque romaine*, 75.

[10] J. G. Février, *La religion des Palmyréniens*, Paris 1931, 16-19; *cf.*
idem, Un aspect du Dioscurisme chez les anciens Sémites, *JA* 229, 1937,
293-299.

[11] Seyrig, *Syria* 27, 1950, 237 = *AS* IV, 132 = *IGLS*, 2218.

[12] Seyrig, Le culte d'Arès en Syrie, *Syria* 47, 1970, 111.

[13] Segal, *Edessa*, 106, n. 1.

[14] F. Cumont, *RevArch.*, 1888, 95-98; *idem*, *Études syriennes*, 269; *idem*,
Les religions orientales dans le paganisme romain, 4th ed., Paris 1929, 104;
idem, *PW* XX[1], 656 *s.v.* Phosphoros.

[15] R. Duval, *Histoire politique, religieuse et littéraire d'Édesse jusqu'à la
première croisade*, Paris 1892, 74.

[16] I. Levy, Cultes et rites syriens dans le Talmud, *REJ* 42, 1901-186ff.

[17] H. Th. Bossert, *Altsyrien*, Tübingen 1951, 162, Fig. 528.

Harris,[18] H. Gese,[19] M. Höfner,[20] L. R. Bailey,[21] J. Starcky,[22] E. T. Newell,[23] and R. Dussaud.[24] The latter gives the following qualification of Spanheim's correction: "La correction, qu'à la suite de Spanheim on adopte généralement en substituant Émèse à Édesse, dans Julien, *Orat.*, IV, p. 150 et 154 ne constitue pas une erreur grave, car des princes arabes étaient installés à Émèse aussi bien qu'à Édesse, mais elle est le type des corrections abusives et inutiles, déplaçant arbitrairement un renseignement confirmé par des auteurs contemporains comme Isaak d'Antioche (voir Wellhausen, *Reste arab. Heidentums*, 2e ed., p. 40) qui mentionne, dans la régions de la Haute-Mésopotamie, le même culte arabe sous la forme 'Ouzza." [25] Leaving aside the question whether the cult of 'Uzza is in fact the same as the cult of Azizos and Monimos, Dussaud actually shows us the way to verify Julian's notice: the identification of other Arab elements in the religion of Edessa, thus rendering the cult of the Arab gods Azizos and Monimos credible and understandable.

This does not preclude the cult of Azizos and Monimos also being celebrated at Emesa. The Greek inscriptions found near this town frequently contain the names Azizos and Monimos as personal

[18] J. Rendel Harris, *The Cult of the heavenly Twins*, Cambridge 1906, 105ff.; *idem, Boanerges*, Cambridge 1913, 255ff.; *cf.* Cumont, *Études syriennes*, 353.

[19] H. Gese et al., *Die Religionen Altsyriens, Altarabiens und der Mandäer*, Stuttgart 1970, 81; according to Gese Azizos and Monimos correspond with Šaḥr and Šalim in the mythology of Ugarit, as pointed out before by J. G. Février, Un aspect du Dioscurisme; *cf.* P. Xella, *Il Mito di Šḥr e Šlm. Saggio sulla mitologia ugaritica. Studi Semitici* 44, Roma 1973; I. Trujillo, *The Ugaritic Ritual for a sacrificial Meal honoring the good Gods*, Ph. Diss. Johns Hopkins Univ. 1973, a commentary on *CTA* 23, *cf.* p. 180 for more details; *cf.* also J. Henninger, Zum Problem der Venussterngottheit bei den Semiten, *Anthropos* 71, 1976, 142ff.

[20] M. Höfner, in: W. Haussig, *Wörterbuch der Mythologie* I, 425 *s.v.* Ares.

[21] L. R. Bailey, The Cult of the Twins at Edessa, *JAOS* 88, 1968, 342-344.

[22] J. Starcky, art. Pétra et la Nabatène, *SDB* VII, col. 995.

[23] E. T. Newell, *Western Seleucid Mints*, 66, n. 68, who refers to coins of Seleucus III from Nisibis with representations of the Dioscuroi.

[24] R. Dussaud, Notes de mythologie syrienne 2, *RevArch.* 1903 I, Azizos et Monimos parèdres du dieu solaire; *idem, Les Arabes en Syrie avant l'Islam*, Paris 1907, 132; *idem, La pénétration des Arabes en Syrie avant l'Islam*, Paris 1955, 101, 142.

[25] Dussaud, *La pénétration*, 101, n. 4.

names.[26] An altar dedicated to Azizos was also found at Emesa, and, moreover, Azizos is the name of one of its rulers.[27] The cult of the sun-god of Emesa is well-known, so that Spanheim's conjecture, in fact, may not be inaccurate. The question is merely whether it is necessary, and that question can only be solved in the way indicated above.

The second problem posed by Julian's remarks, is the precise identity of Azizos and Monimos. Since R. Dussaud's *Notes de mythologie syrienne 2*: Azizos et Monimos parèdres du dieu solaire,[28] they are generally held to be twin gods, sprung from a process of reduplication causing all gods identified with the planet Venus to appear in two hypostases, representing the Morning and the Evening Star. Thus there is a male form of Venus, ʿAṭtar, occurring in the South-Arabian pantheon, in Northern Arabia and in the Syrian and Phoenician area, redoubled in these two forms under the names Azizos and Monimos. Dussaud puts it thus: "Les deux hypostases de ʿAthtar ont pénétré jusque dans le monde gréco-romain sous les noms d'Azizos et Monimos. On les a signalés dans le Ḥauran et jusqu'à Édesse. Ils furent naturellement identifiés à Phosphoros et à Hespéros,..." [29] In 1955 Dussaud expressed the same opinion and he literally repeats what he wrote half a century before.[30] This thesis, that Azizos and Monimos are twin gods, two aspects of the same phenomenon, is generally accepted and, variously phrased, repeated by many authors. F. Cumont thought at first that the two gods are Phosphoros and Hesperos belonging to the cult of Mithras, and so identical with Cautes and Cautopates; [31] but later he only spoke of Phosphoros and Hesperos as

---

[26] Azizos: *IGLS* 256A, 269², 310B, 1631, 1671, 2184, 2251, 2303, 2565, 2566; Monimos: *IGLS* 2079 (?), 2187, 2382, 2383, 2383bis, 2563, 2595.

[27] Dussaud, *Les Arabes en Syrie*, 10; F. Altheim, Der arabische Sonnengott, *AAW* III, Berlin 1966, 126ff.; *cf.* C. Chad, *Les dynastes d'Émèse*, Beyrouth 1972, 67, 69; Azizos' reign was from 47-53 A.D.

[28] *RevArch* 1903 I, 128-142.

[29] Dussaud, *Les Arabes en Syrie*, 132.

[30] Dussaud, *La pénétration des Arabes en Syrie*, 142; see also A. Kammerer, *Pétra et la Nabatène*, Paris 1929, 415.

[31] F. Cumont, Le culte de Mithras à Édesse, *RevArch* 1888, 95-98.

reduplication of the planet Venus.[32] J. G. Février,[33] J. Rendel Harris,[34] H. Seyrig,[35] D. Sourdel,[36] E. Kirsten,[37] T. Fahd,[38] E. Merkel,[39] and others, however, consider Azizos and Monimos as twin gods, Morning and Evening star as two aspects of the Venus star. Some even speak of Azizos and Monimos as the Dioskouroi, a thesis particularly defended by Rendel Harris. The only one to oppose this generally accepted view was Drexler, who in *Roscher's Lexikon* gave Monimos and Azizos as the Aramaic names of Nabu and Nergal, who "als Schirmherren über die Planeten Merkur und Mars walten." [40]

The whole question of the identity and function of the Venus star in the religions of the Semites was discussed at length, and in almost every detail, by J. Henninger in 1976.[41] His conclusions seem so convincing, that it is worthwhile summarizing them in this context in order to make clearer the role of Azizos and Monimos. Among all groups of Semites there existed, from the third millenium B.C. onwards, Venus star deities who were partly male and partly female. Their names ('Attar, Ištar, et al.) all derive from a common root. In Northern Arabia as well as in Southern Arabia a male Venus star deity was worshipped who usually was represented under two aspects as Morning and Evening star. In South Arabian religion, e.g., the god 'Attar functions as Morning star and then he is called 'Attar šariqan = the Eastern 'attar and is considered to be a warlike protecting god. Therefore he sometimes is called

---

[32] F. Cumont, *Études syriennes*, 269, n. 2.
[33] J. G. Février, *La religion des Palmyréniens*, 17.
[34] J. Rendel Harris, *Boanerges*, 256f.
[35] H. Seyrig, *AS* IV, 54; 106, n. 2.
[36] D. Sourdel, *Les cultes du Hauran*, 75.
[37] E. Kirsten, Art. Edessa, *RAC* IV, 564; *cf. RAC* I, 1096, *s.v.* Baal.
[38] T. Fahd, *Le panthéon de l'Arabie Centrale à la veille de l'hégire*, Paris 1968, 83, n. 5; 94; 119; see for this book the extremely critical review by A. Caquot, *Syria* 1970, 187-191, without which it cannot be used.
[39] E. Merkel, in: *Wörterbuch der Mythologie* I, 426, 428, 433.
[40] *Roscher's Lexikon* II, *s.v.* Monimos with a reference to E. Meyer, *Geschichte des Altertums* I, 179, par. 148.
[41] J. Henninger, Zum Problem der Venussterngottheit bei den Semiten, *Anthropos* 71, 1976, 129-168; Henninger had in principle already expressed the same views in: Über Sternkunde und Sternkult in Nord- und Zentral-Arabien, *ZE* 79, 1954, 82-117.

ʿAttar ʿazizan = the strong ʿAttar. As Evening Star ʿAttar is a
god of the life-giving water.[42] The two hypostases of an originally
male Venus star occur in the Palmyrene pantheon as Azizu and
Arṣu, and in the Northern region of the Syrian desert as Azizos
and Monimos. These pairs have an analogon in the Ugaritic deities
Šaḥr and Šalim, so that they may go back to an earlier period and,
in fact, may belong to a religious stratum common to all Semites.

In addition to the twin deities personifying the Venus star, a
female Venus deity has a paramount position in the North-Arabian
area. She is called al-ʿUzza = the Strong One or simply the Star
or the Bright Star, especially by Syriac authors.[43] Her name is
derived from the same root ʿzz = being strong, of which Azizos
is derivate, and this already can be considered an indication of
some relation between both deities, at least as to their origin. The
question whether the Venus star deity originally was a male god
who later on became female, as is stated by Henninger, may be
left out of consideration for our purpose. It is sufficient to state
that the cult of al-ʿUzza and of Azizos and Monimos is attested at
the same time in the same area, i.e., the northern part of the Syrian
and Mesopotamian desert.

Taking for certainty that Azizos and Monimos represent Venus
as Morning and Evening Star, respectively, we are left with the
question what could have induced Iamblichos to identify Azizos
and Monimos with Ares and Hermes, who are certainly not twins,
let alone Dioskouroi. Iamblichos was a Syrian by birth, and well
informed as to religious phenomena in his mother country.[44] The
religions practiced in the Syrian and Mesopotamian desert might
yield some evidence to elucidate this question.

---

[42] Henninger, Zum Problem 133; cf. M. Höfner, in: Gese et al., Die
Religionen Altsyriens, 257, 268, 270, 290.
[43] Henninger, Zum Problem 136; cf. The Doctrina Addai, which mentions
the cult of the Bright Star (Phillips, 24); Ephrem Syrus, Hymni contra
Haereses VII, 4 (the Star), VIII, 10 (the Star), VIII, 12, 14; XLI, 4; Isaac
of Antioch, Homily II on the conquest of Beth Ḥur (ed. Bickell) 407ff. (the
Star), 463ff. (the Star) etc.
[44] cf. M. P. Nilsson, Geschichte der griechischen Religion II, München
1950, 428ff.; J. Bidez, Le philosophe Jamblique et son école, REG 32, 1919,
29ff.

Although often it is simply stated that the relation of Edessa to Arabic culture and language is a fact sufficiently established,[45] it is desirable for the purpose of our inquiry to set forth this relation both in general and in connection with the cult of the sun god. "Arabic" in this context does not refer to the inhabitants of Arabia Felix, but to the semi-nomadic population of the northern Syrian-Mesopotamian desert, who kept flocks and had a little agriculture.[46] In Edessene onomastic there are a great many Arabic names; most of them are paralleled in the onomastic of Palmyra, Hatra and the Nabataeans.[47] The commonest names in the ruling dynasty of Edessa were Abgar and Ma'nu, which show its Arabian origin.[48]

There is consequently also marked Arabic influence in religious matters. To quote once again the *Doctrina Addai* on the religion of the Edessenes:

> Behold there are those among you who adore.....and the Eagle as the Arabians, also the Sun and the Moon, as the rest of the inhabitants of Harran, who are as yourselves. Be ye not led away captive by the rays of the luminaries and the Bright Star.

Here we have explicit mention of Arabic religious influence and also of the cult of the Sun. Moreover, the *Doctrina* records the veneration of the *Bright Star*, which certainly refers to the Venus Star *al-'Uzza*, widely worshipped throughout Northern Mesopotamia.

Other evidence regarding Arabic cults at Edessa comes from the *Apology of Pseudo-Melito*. Directly after the passage on Hadad and 'Athi, discussed in a former chapter, the Apology reads: The people of Mesopotamia also worshipped *KWTBY*, a Hebrew woman, who rescued Bakru, a patrician of Edessa, from his enemies.[49] The Apol-

---

[45] J. Teixidor in: J. T. Milik - J. Teixidor, New Evidence on the North-Arabic Deity Aktab-Kutbâ, *BASOR* 163, October 1963, 24.

[46] *cf.* R. Dussaud, *La pénétration*, 14ff.; F. Gabrieli, *L'antica società beduina*, Roma 1959, 56; J. Henninger, *Über Lebensraum und Lebensformen der Frühsemiten*, Köln-Opladen 1968, 30ff.

[47] *cf.* names like 'WY, 'YW, 'SW, BRKLB', BRŠWM', BRŠMŠ, GYW, GRMW, W'L, ZYDLT, KWKW, MQYMW, 'BDLT etc. see the Index of Proper names in Drijvers, *Old-Syriac Inscriptions*.

[48] *cf.* the list in Segal, *Edessa*, 16.

[49] *Apology of Pseudo-Melito* in W. Cureton, *Spicilegium Syriacum*, London 1855, 44, LL. 31-33 (transl.) 40, LL. 8-20 (text).

ogy was known to Theodore bar Koni, a Nestorian author of the
late eighth century, who in his *Book of Scholia* gives the following
text: The Mesopotamians worshipped KWZBY, an Arab (goddess
or woman) and GTY of Adiabene who sent his daughter PLṬ, a
doctor, to cure the daughter of the king of the Damascenes.[50] On
the one hand it makes plain that Theodore was acquainted with
the text of the *Apology*, and on the other hand it calls her an Arabian
(goddess or woman). Since the difference between Hebrew and Arabian in Syriac is just the metathesis of *r* and *b* (*'bryt'* and *'rbyt'*), and
a deity al-Kutba' is mentioned in Nabataean and Lihyanite inscriptions, Theodore's reading is to be preferred to the text of the
Apology, so that KWTBY, in fact, denotes an Arabic deity, worshipped by the Mesopotamian population. The people of Mesopotamia are the inhabitants of Edessa, Nisibis and Maḥuze, as is
stated by Ishodad of Merw in his commentary on the Book of
Genesis.[51] The worship of al-Kutba' appears int. al. in the Nabataean inscription no. 17 oft he Wadi Ramm, which is inscribed under
two rock-cut *baetyls*: *'lktb' dybgy' 'l'z' 'l'z'* = al-Kutba' who is in
Gaia, al-'Uzza'. Gaia most likely denotes modern el-Ği situated
near the entrance of Petra. Al-Kutba' and al-'Uzza, therefore, are
represented as baetyls.[52] The name of al-Kutba' is also recorded
in a Nabataean inscription from Tell esh-Shuqafiyeh in Egypt
which commemorates the building of a temple to her in the first
century B.C.[53] Shuqafiyeh is an important road junction in the
Wadi Ṭumilat, one of the main trade routes of the Nabataeans.
An altar was dedicated to al-Kutba' in a temple at Qaṣrawet
according to the most likely reading of an inscription on an altar
found in a temple there: *ḥwyrw br grm l'lktb'* = HWYRW son of

---

[50] Theodore bar Koni, *Liber Scholiorum* II, 287, LL. 19-24, ed. A. Scher,
CSCO 66, Louvain 1912.

[51] Ed. C. van den Eynde, *CSCO* 126, Louvain 1950, 177, L. 3; *cf.* Milik-
Teixidor, New Evidence on the North Arabic Deity Aktab-Kutbâ, 24.

[52] See J. Strugnell, The Nabataean Goddess al-Kutba' and her Sanctuaries,
BASOR 156, Dec. 1959, 29ff.

[53] First published by Clermont-Ganneau, *Recueil d'archéologie orient.*
VIII, 1924, 229ff.; *cf.* E. Littmann - D. Meredith, Nabataean Inscriptions
from Egypt, *BSOAS* 16, 1954, 227-230; J. Starcky, *Syria* 32, 1955, 155ff.;
Strugnell, *BASOR* 156, 31ff., where F. M. Cross' improved reading of the
inscription is given.

GRM to al-Kutba'.[54] In Petra itself the name of the deity was read by J. T. Milik as part of an inscription in a circular triclinium hollowed out in a rock: *qdm kwtb' 'lh' dnh* = before Kutba' this god.[55] It should be noted that the sex of al-Kutba' is not clear. Only the inscription from Shuqafiyeh makes plain that we have to do with a goddess. The inscriptions from the Wadi Ramm and from Qasrawet do not contain an indication of the deity's sex and the Petra inscription clearly refers to a god. A male form of the same deity is the Lihyanite god han-'Aktab.[56] The text of the *Apology of Pseudo-Melito* and consequently Theodor bar Koni in his *Book of Scholia* explicitly mention a goddess. This ambiguity in the tradition has an exact parallel in the sex of the Venus star which can be male as well as female, and probably is caused by the original representation of these deities in the form of a *baetyl* that shows no clear signs of a well-defined sex, nor of a specific character of the deity in question. The name of al-Kutba', deriving from the root *ktb* = to write, indicates that he or she could have something to do with intellectual activities like writing, etc. We will return to this question after a while.

Another example of an Arab deity worshipped in or near Edessa is the mysterious figure of the god NHY, whose name appears in a Syriac tomb inscription at Serrin dating to 73 A.D. and which, moreover, forms the theophorous component of a few Edessene personal names: *'bdnhy* and *'mtnhy*.[57] NHY probably is identical with the Thamudic god Nahi frequently mentioned together with Ruda in Thamudic texts. Both deities already appear in the cuneiform records describing how, after the conquest of Adumatu (which is Dūmat al-Ǧandal in the North-Arabian Gulf), Sanherib (704-681) deported thence a number of divine images, including

---

[54] *cf.* Starcky, *Syria* 32, 1955, 156; Strugnell, *BASOR* 156, 34f.

[55] Milik, in: Milik-Teixidor, New Evidence, 22f.

[56] *cf.* Strugnell, The Nabataean Goddess al-Kutba', 30; F. V. Winnett - W. L. Reed, *Ancient Records from North Arabia*, Toronto 1970, 76.

[57] The Inscription of Serrîn, Drijvers, *Old-Syriac Inscriptions*, no. 2, L. 3; *'bdnhy* is perhaps seen on the so-called mosaic of Zenodora, *cf.* Drijvers, *Old-Syriac Inscriptions*, no. 44, L. 7; *'bdnhy* and *'mtnhy* occur on the Family Portrait Mosaic, Drijvers, *Old-Syriac Inscriptions*, no. 47, LL. 5, 12; see also A. Maricq, BDR D NHY dans l'inscription de Serrin, *Classica et Orientalia*, 141-144.

those of Nuḫâa and Ruldain.[58] The spelling ḥ instead of ḫ is preserved in the inscription at Serrin and the Syriac proper names.
In a Thamudic inscription published by Winnett and Reed the
god is invoked together with Ruḍa and ʿAttarsam: O Ruḍa and
Nuhai and ʿAttarsam, help me in the matter of my love.[59] NHY
might have been a name of the Sun god, write Winnett and Reed,
in view of the Thamudic text Hu. 327: "By Nuhai, exalted Sun!
By Yahthi." [60] ʿAttarsam, a short form of ʿAttarsamin = ʿAttar of
Heaven, most likely is a male personification of the planet Venus.[61]
If Nuhai - NHY, therefore, is really a Sun god, he appears in this
inscription flanked by Ruḍa and ʿAttarsam = Venus, which will
presently prove significant. The tomb inscription of Serrin refers
to a *bdr* (= Budar) of NHY, which denotes a certain priest and
has a parallel in the *bwdr* (= Budar) of the god Sin at Sumatar
Harabesi. This also might be interpreted as an indication that NHY
is an astral or planetary deity like Sin himself. However that may
be, the cult of the god NHY at Edessa and its environs also has
direct parallels in the religion of the Arab tribes of the Syrian desert.

Worship of the Sun in Edessa, as stated by the *Doctrina Addai*,
is further confirmed by the topographical names of the city. The
southern gate is called the Harran gate or Gate of Beth Semes =
Gate of the Temple of the Sun, showing that there must have been
such a temple there. According to their *Acta* the Edessene martyrs
Gurya and Shmona are required to do obeisance to the sun, which
they refuse.[62] This detail, too, may be regarded as evidence of a

---

[58] For Nahi see *Wörterbuch der Mythologie* I, 456f.; M. Höfner in: H. Gese
et al., *Die Religionen Altsyriens*, 374; R. Borger, *Die Inschriften Asarhaddons,
Königs von Assyrien*, *AfO* Beiheft 9, 1956, 53, 10-12; *Or.* N.S. 26, 1957,
10f., *cf. ANET*, 291; NHY appears once as a personal name in a Palmyrene
inscription from the Palmyrène, *cf.* Schlumberger, *La Palmyrène du Nord-
Ouest*, Paris 1951, 149, no. 16, L. 3; *cf.* Stark, *Personal Names in Palmyrene
Inscriptions*, 99; the name NHYʿZYZ = NHY is strong occurs in a Palmyrene tomb inscription *CIS* II 4041. *cf.* also A. van den Branden, *Histoire
de Thamoud*, Beyrouth 1966, 104ff.
[59] Winnett-Reed, *Ancient Records*, 80f., no. 23.
[60] Winnett-Reed, *Ancient Records*, 81.
[61] *cf.* Henninger, Zum Problem der Venussterngottheit, 147ff. and notes
75, 77, 79; *Wörterbuch der Mythologie* I, 427f.; T. Fahd, *Le panthéon* 47, 144.
[62] *cf. Chronicon Edessenum*, *CSCO* 3, 4, 7; see L. Hallier, *Untersuchungen
über die Edessenische Chronik*, *TU* 9, 1, Leipzig 1892, 114; the Acts of Gurya

Sun-cult at Edessa. There are also a number of Edessene personal
names composed with - šmš = sun, which may be adduced as
additional evidence.[63]

Ephrem Syrus' *Hymni contra Haereses* yields information of a
more general kind on planetary worship and astrology, which he
considers a great danger to orthodox belief in God's omnipotence
and human free will. Ephrem does not mention any special pagan
cult, but he is dealing with religious deformation of orthodoxy as
found in the heretics Marcion, Bardaiṣan, Mani, and the teachings
of the Chaldaeans, which may be linked with Christian beliefs and
in fact often present themselves as such. Actual paganism is less
of a threat because it is clearly recognisable, but when disguised
in a Christian garment it is much more dangerous to Ephrem. In
such a context he frequently mentions the cult of the Star =
Venus and all sexual indulgence connected with it.[64] Quoting some
fragments of Bardaiṣan's hymns Ephrem states:

> He looked at the Sun and the Moon; with the Sun he compared
> the Father
> With the Moon the Mother; male and female (ones).[65]

Father and Mother in this context mean the Father and Mother
of Life, the divine couple giving birth to a divine Son and to other
descendants, probably the planets. Whatever the explanation of
Bardaiṣan's poetical fragments may be, which show all kinds of
connections with later Manichaean imagery, it is clear that his

---

and Shmona, ed. F. C. Burkitt, Euphemia and the Goth with the Acts of
Martyrdom of the Confessors of Edessa, London 1913, 102, ch. 42; 43; it is
noteworthy that the sun is called *mrn* = our Lord, like at Hatra.
cf. O. von Gebhardt, *Die Akten der edessenischen Bekenner Gurjas, Samonas
und Abibos, TU* 37, 2, Leipzig 1911, 42, 8; 43ff.; Segal, *Edessa*, 83ff.

[63] *int. al.* ŠMŠGRM, in whose house Bardaiṣan's Dialogue on Fate, the
so-called *Book of the Laws of Countries*, is supposed to be held, *cf. PS* I, col.
536, 1.; BRŠMŠ, Drijvers, *Old-Syriac Inscriptions*, no. 30, L. 2, 49, L. 4;
ʿBDŠMŠ, no. 47, L. 8; ŠMŠGRM, no. 28, L. 4; ŠMŠYHB, P.L. 21; although
the inscription of Amaššemeš is considered not to be Old-Syriac, the name
Amaššemeš = maidservant of the Sun actually occurred at Edessa, *cf.*
J. Pirenne, Aux origines de la graphie syriaque, *Syria* 40, 1963, 109-115.

[64] Ephrem Syrus, *Hymni contra Haereses*, ed. Beck, VII, 4; VIII, 10, 12,
14; XLI, 4.

[65] Ephrem Syrus, *Hymni contra Haereses* LV, 10.

semi-Christian conception of a Father, Mother and Son of Life
was partly based and inspired by pagan mythology about Sun and
Moon as a divine couple, the moon representing the female part.[66]
Ephrem Syrus, too, knows about the sexual aspects of the cult of
the Moon, when in the *Hymni contra Haereses* he calls both Moon
and Venus adulteresses.[67]

The same conception of Sun and Moon as a divine couple is
recorded by Isaac of Antioch in his homilies on Beth Ḥur: "For the
eyes of the Sun they were exposed, who worshipped the Sun and
the Moon." (the Syriac text uses the name Sin!) ... The pagans
erroneously made Sun and Moon into a couple....[68] The worship
of the Sun seems to have been the main cult at Beth Ḥur, for Isaac
stresses the relation of the name of the place with the cult of the
Sun by deriving the element Ḥur from the root ḥr = to look at:
"The founders of the place encouraged it by its very name to ex-
change God for the Sun.... Look at the Sun, your Saviour, O city,
that came forth from Harran!" [69] The combination of the indigenous
cult of the Sun with Arab religious practice is best expressed by the
following statement of Isaac: "The Persians spared her not, for
with them she served the Sun; the Beduins left her not, for with
them she sacrificed to ʿUzzai.[70]

It can therefore be taken as certainty that the cult of the Sun
was part of the religious pattern at Edessa, as stated by the *Doctrina
Addai*, and confirmed by various other evidence. It is of special
interest that the *Doctrina* considers the cult of the Sun and Moon
a link between Edessa and Harran, whereas Isaac of Antioch,
writing in the fifth century and describing the same kind of cult
at Beth Ḥur, also explicitly mentions the religious bonds between
Beth Ḥur and Harran, the former city being founded by the latter
one. This can be taken again as an indication that the historical
reliability of the *Doctrina Addai* in matters of pagan religious history
is much greater than is usually assumed since there is not a single

---

[66] *cf.* Drijvers, *Bardaiṣan of Edessa*, 147ff.
[67] Ephrem Syrus, *Hymni contra Haereses* VIII, 12, 14.
[68] Isaac of Antioch, *Homily on the Conquest of Beth Ḥur* I, ed. Bickell,
159-184.
[69] *Homily on the Conquest of Beth Ḥur* I, 51-62.
[70] *Homily on the Conquest of Beth Ḥur* I, 99-102.

trace of literary dependence on Isaac's part on the text of the *Doctrina Addai*.

Resuming the results obtained so far—evidence of Sun worship and a strong Arab streak of religious feeling—it is entirely unnecessary to alter Julian's text and to remove the cult of the Sun with Azizos and Monimos from Edessa to Emesa. That conjecture indeed is a "correction abusive et inutile" (R. Dussaud).

After having formally established that cult at Edessa, the next problem is: who actually are Azizos and Monimos and what qualities led Iamblichos to identify them with Ares and Hermes?

Azizos is a god found especially in the Palmyrene pantheon; the name frequently appears in the Palmyrene onomastic as well as the Greek inscriptions of the Near East as a proper name.[71] There are, however, but a few monuments of his cult in the extant iconography of Palmyra's religion. There is a bas-relief, probably dating from 213 A.D. and originating from the Palmyrene, depicting a rider on a mehari and a horseman. The meharist goes ahead and the horseman follows; both have a long lance in their right hands and are turned to the left, where the dedicant stands. It is clear from the inscription on the plinth of the relief that the meharist is Arṣu and the horseman Azizu. They are called *'lhy' ṭby' wskry'* = good and rewarding gods. The relief was dedicated by a certain Baʿlai son of Yarhibola *'pkl' dy ʿzyzw 'lh' ṭb' wrḥmn'* = priest of Azizu the good and merciful god.[72]

A fragmentary relief from Khirbet Semrin in the Palmyrene shows the Arab warrior god Abgal as a soldier with a spear in his right hand and a shield in his left. To the right of his head we read Abgal, to the left Azizu. Most probably, therefore, the warrior depicted is Abgal, while Azizu was portrayed in similar fashion on

---

[71] cf. Stark, *Personal Names in Palmyrene Inscriptions*, 44, 105; H. Wuthnow, *Die semitischen Menschennamen in griechischen Inschriften und Papyri des vorderen Orients*, Leipzig 1930, 13; above n. 26; A. Caquot, Sur l'onomastique religieuse de Palmyre, *Syria* 39, 1962, 252, n. 8.

[72] cf. J. B. Chabot, *Choix d'inscriptions de Palmyre*, Paris 1922, 68f., Pl. XXII; the two reliefs combined by Chabot actually do not belong together; *CIS* II, 3974; Ingholt, *Berytus* 3, 1936, 116, Pl. XXIV; Seyrig, *AS* IV, 63; Milik, *Dédicaces faites par des dieux*, 22; Drijvers, *The Religion of Palmyra*, Pl. LXVIII.

the part that is lost.[73] Until recently these were the only monuments of Azizu. The Polish excavations in Palmyra have revealed a bas-relief of a god on horseback in whom we must recognize Azizu, according to the accompanying inscription.[74] We see, then, that Azizu is either portrayed as a warrior with lance or shield, or as an armed horseman, and that he occurs either alone or together with other deities of the same character like Abgal and Arṣu. There are quite a number of such divine pairs of armed meharists and/or horsemen known under different names, e.g., Abgal and Ašar, Maʿn and Šaʿd/r, Ašadu and Šaʿd/r, Šalman and ʿRGYʾ, which were recently discussed by Seyrig.[75] It seems that the various gods can appear in different combinations, e.g., Abgal and Azizu, Abgal and Ašar, Azizu and Arṣu, all expressing the same idea, namely divine escort and protection. The way they are represented expresses the idea of functional equipment. Azizu is one of these gods of the steppe, where danger is always present, and his main task is to keep its inhabitants safe. There may be gods with the integral characteristic of riding a mount, but Azizu is not one of them, as already became clear from his iconography. He sometimes is depicted as a horseman because that is most practical for doing his work! "Les dieux sont représentés à cheval 'pour les besoins de leur action'." [76] These mounted gods, therefore, are found all over the Syrian and Mesopotamian desert, Palmyra, Dura-Europos, Homs, etc. A relief from Tell Halaf, now in the Museum of Aleppo and showing a mehari-rider with lance and shield, is generally considered to represent Azizos too.[77] The very name Azizu is derived

---

[73] Schlumberger, *La Palmyrène du Nord-Ouest*, 58, Pl. XXIII, 4; 147, inscr. no. 10; *cf.* Seyrig, Les dieux armés et les Arabes en Syrie, *Syria* 47, 1970, 77ff., fig. 2, pl. IX, 1; Drijvers, *The Religion of Palmyra*, Pl. LXIV, 2.

[74] *cf.* K. Michalowski, *Palmyre*. Fouilles polonaises 1960, 138, fig. 153; *cf.* for a correct reading of the Inscription, M. Gawlikowski, *Recueil d'in-scriptions palmyréniennes provenant de fouilles syriennes et polonaises récentes à Palmyre*, Paris 1974, no. 151; the reading by Bounni and Schlumberger, *MUSJ* 46, 1970, 214, n. 1 is incorrect; *cf.* Milik, *Dédicaces faites par des dieux*, 22f.; Drijvers, *The Religion of Palmyra*, Pl. LXVI, 2.

[75] H. Seyrig, Les dieux armés et les Arabes en Syrie, *Syria* 47, 1970, 77ff.

[76] E. Will, *Le relief cultuel gréco-romain*, Paris 1955, 124; Seyrig, *Syria* 1970, 82, 92.

[77] H. Th. Bossert, *Altsyrien*, 162, fig. 528; *cf. Syria* 10, 1929, 31, fig. 1.

from the root '*zz* = being strong, and consequently means "the strong one." He is the masculine form of the deity whose feminine aspect was al-'Uzza, who represents the martial aspect of the Arabic Venus Star. Azizos' main function, therefore, is escorting and protecting caravans and travellers in the desert as well as the Sun in its daily course. Whether Azizos originally was Venus as Morning Star, the "prodomos' of the Sun, and hence also considered the protecting escort of his worshippers by analogy, is difficult to decide. We will return to this question after having discussed Azizos' partner Monimos.

The very name Monimos, also frequent in onomastic, is the Greek form of the Arabic *mun'im*, derived from the root *n'm* = to be pleasing. Hence *mun'im* means "the favourable one." [78] Clermont-Ganneau remarked long ago that *mun'im*-Monimos is an exact equivalent of the god Arṣu whose name, derived from the root *rṣ'* = to be pleasing, also has the meaning of "the favourable one." There was no known representation or inscription of a god Mun'im-Monimos, however, to confirm Clermont-Ganneau's hypothesis.[79] In 1972 J. Starcky published a bas-relief from the Palmyrene which was at that time in a private collection at Beyrouth. It represents a god on horseback with a lance in his left hand. His right hand is folded over his breast and holds an indistinct object (a globe?). He has a quiver at his hip and wears a fluttering mantle. On the right stand the dedicators in front of an altar with burnt sacrifice. The relief dates from 138 A.D. The Palmyrene inscription states that this stele was dedicated *lmn'ym gny' ṭb' wskr'* = to Mun'im, the good and rewarding god.[80] The Palmyrene *gny'* is a synonym of *'lh'* = deity, and means, therefore, *numen*, deity. It is the Arabic *djinn*, that has passed into Palmyrene.[81]

---

[78] *cf.* above n. 26; Wuthnow, *Menschennamen*, 78, 152; G. Ryckmans, *Les noms propres sud-sémitiques* I, 142.

[79] Clermont-Ganneau, Le dieu Monimos, *Recueil d'archéologie orientale* IV, 165-167.

[80] J. Starcky, Relief dédié au dieux Mun'im, *Semitica* 22, 1972, 57-65, Pl. I, II.

[81] *cf.* Schlumberger, *La Palmyrène du Nord-Ouest*, 135-137; J. Starcky, *Syria* 26, 1949, 249-257; Schlumberger, Le prétendu dieu Gennéas, *MUSJ* 46, 1970-71, 209-222.

After this, it would not be at all surprising if one day a relief
were to appear showing Azizu and Mun'im together as "good and
rewarding gods" or "good and rewarding Genii/Djinns." For this
pair is fully analogous with Azizu and Arṣu and other pairs of gods
riding a horse or camel or represented as warriors. In this context
it is usual to speak of twin gods, that is of gods who are completely
identical, both in their depiction and in their function. That is,
however, not the case with Azizos and Monimos, whose names are
completely different, probably an indication also of partly different
functions, and who are identified with Ares and Hermes, in fact,
completely different deities. It seems better, then, to speak of
divine pairs, each of which has more or less the same function, in
this case protecting and escorting the inhabitants of the desert and
the Sun, but which, on the other hand, might represent different
aspects of the one Venus Star deity as Morning and Evening Star.
The doubling of the Venus planet actually might not result in two
wholly identical deities, but rather in two gods, who express best
its varied character. The fact that these gods often are invoked
alone and not in pairs is a token of that, and also of Iamblichos'
identification. Now if Iamblichos tells us on the one hand that
Azizos = Ares and Monimos = Hermes, and on the other, that
Azizos opens the procession of the Sun, while both gods "are the
channel for many blessings to the region of our earth," then he is
contemplating several of the foregoing qualities of Azizu and
Mun'im at the same time. The identification of Azizos with Ares
is rather obvious: Azizu's appearance with arms recalls the way
Ares is depicted: with shield, lance and sword.[82] Just as al-'Uzza
has a militant warrior aspect, especially in her function as Morning
Star, so has Azizu. The precursor of the Sun is his main protector
just as the vanguard of a caravan is. Their protective function is
also rendered by the role they play in taking oaths. Al-'Uzza, like
Allat the other Arab warrior goddess, is very often invoked in
taking oath; so also is Ares.[83] The gods of war often become avengers
of injustice, hence their role in the swearing of oaths. Making war

---

[82] P. Grimal, *Dictionnaire de la mythologie grecque et romaine*, Paris 1958,
44.

[83] *cf.* Nilsson, *Geschichte der griechischen Religion* I, 518f.

has, in fact, two aspects, a destructive one and a protecting one. The identification of Azizu with Ares lays stress on the protective and defending qualities of the god of war. It is perhaps for this reason, therefore, that Azizu and Mun'im are called *ṭb' wskr'* = good and rewarding, which is paraphrased by Iamblichos in the statement that they are "the channel for many blessings to the region of our earth." Azizos is a militant protective god as "prodromos" of the Sun as well as the escort of the caravans and travellers in the desert. Iamblichos' identification is the fruit of his correct understanding of the nature of Azizos.

The identification of Monimos with Hermes poses more difficult problems than that of Azizos with Ares. To solve them J. Teixidor suggested we assume the goddess Kutbai, whose cult is attested in Edessa, to be identical with the god Nebo, also worshipped in Edessa, since both have to do with script and writing: "That Nebu and Kutbai are identical seems obvious." [84] Nebo/Kutbai would then be identical with Hermes/Mercury as god of writing, from which it follows that Monimos, as Hermes or Mercury, is identical with Nebu-Kutbai. Considering that al-Kutba appears together with al-'Uzza in the Nabataean inscription Wadi Ramm 17, this identification demands further study of Julian's text according to which the Edessans think that Monimos is Hermes and Azizos Ares! This suggestion of Teixidor follows a view J. Starcky had formerly communicated to J. Strugnell, who, however, received it somewhat sceptically: "Monimos (*Mun'im*) is, however, usually held to be an epithet of 'Arṣu, the companion of Azizos. Although there is no formal epigraphic attestation of this equation, it is probable, and the text of Julian is not sufficiently unambiguous to enable us to identify Mon'mos with Al-Kutba'—we can safely infer only an association of Monimos and Azizos, who seem elsewhere to be Hesperus and Phosphorus, with the possibility that Monimos had some other similarity to Greek Hermes, not necessarily connected

---

[84] J. Teixidor, *BASOR* 163, 1961, 25; his remark: "The *Liber Legum Regionum* of Bardesanes also speaks of Ares/Azizos, *Patrol. Syr.* II, col. 593, 18" is not correct; it is probably taken from J. G. Février, *La religion des Palmyréniens*, 21: "L'assimilation se retrouve chez les auteurs syriaques, Cureton, *Spic. Syr.* 13, 24", which is also erroneous; in fact the passage in question calls the planet Mars strong (*'rs 'zyz'*).

with his scribal activity." [85] Before looking for the other similarity
of Monimos to Hermes, it seems appropriate to discuss Starcky's
viewpoint in more detail.

His starting-point is Herodotus III, 8, where the Greek historian
describes the Arab cult of Orotalt and Alilat, by whom the desert-
dwellers take oath. According to Herodotus, Orotalt is Dionysos
and Alilat Urania. With Milik, Starcky rightly regards Orotalt as
the god Ruḍa, who appears in Thamudic and Safaitic inscriptions
as Raḍu and is the same whom the people of Adumatu in the
seventh century B.C. called Ruldaiu according to the Annals of
Sanherib.[86] Since, according to Herodotus, Alilat is identical with
Venus, Ruḍa cannot be so. In contrast with, e.g., Ryckmans and
Dussaud, and in agreement with M. Hofner, Winnett and Reed,
and A. Jamme, Starcky rightly regards Ruḍa as a male deity, and
not a goddess.[87] With regard to his identification of Kutbai with
Nebo/Mercury, which last is accounted a "planète bénéfique" [88]
Starcky wonders whether this planet-god is not the same whom the
people of Adumatu called Ruldaiu = the Favourable one, who in
turn is the same god as Ruḍa and Arṣu. The influence of the cult
of Nebo would then have been so strong, that the name of "Writer"
was given to Ruḍa, the "Mercure des Arabes septentrionaux." The
cult of Venus and Mercury is shown in this manner among the Arab
tribes, just as Azizu and Arṣu are also Venus and Mercury.[89] For

---

[85] J. Strugnell, *BASOR* 156, 1959, 36.

[86] *cf.* Starcky, *SDB* VII, 988ff.; *Semitica* 22, 1972, 62ff.; Milik, *Dédicaces faites par des dieux*, 49.

[87] G. Ryckmans, *Les religions arabes préislamiques*, 2nd ed., Louvain 1951, 18, 21f., n. 165; Dussaud, *La pénétration*, 142ff.; M. Höfner in: H. Gese et al., *Die Religionen Altsyriens*, 374f.; *Wörterbuch der Mythologie* I, 463f. Winnett-Reed, *Ancient Records*, 75f.; A. Jamme, Safaitic Vogué 402; *JNES* 31, 1972, 16-21.

[88] Starcky, *SDB* VII, 988ff.; K. Tallqvist, *Akkadische Götterepitheta*, *Studia Orientalia* 7, Helsingfors 1938, 384ff.; in Palmyra Nebo is called "good and rewarding" (ṭbʾ wskrʾ), *cf.* A. Bounni - N. Saliby, *AAS* 15, 1965, 126ff.; this text is lacking in Stark, *Personal Names*, 60, *s.v.* NBW; J. Henninger, Über Sternkunde und Sternkult in Nord- und Zentral-Arabien, *ZE* 79, 1954, 82-117 demonstrated that the planet Mercury in Arabia is totally unknown.

[89] J. Starcky, *SDB* VII, 995; *idem*, La civilisation nabatéene: États des questions, IX Congrès international d'archéologie classique, *AAAS* 21, 1971, 81; *Semitica* 22, 1972, 62f.

this last, Starcky finds evidence in the cult of Azizos and Monimos at Edessa, since Iamblichos identifies Monimos with Hermes.

This whole series of identifications rests upon two hypotheses: a) the intellectual aspects of all these gods are dominant, since all are linked with Nebo, the god of scribes and wisdom; b) all these gods may be identified as representing the *planet* Mercury. The whole argumentation, in fact, started off from Julian's text in order to explain why Iamblichos identified Monimos with Hermes. The god Hermes/Mercury as companion of the Sun, that is as a planet, has become the centre on which the reasoning turns.

Two major objections to Starcky's reconstructed series of identifications can be raised: a) the planet Mercury is totally unknown in Northern and Central Arabian cultures and religions, as J. Henninger's investigations have pointed out; [90] b) the only other known identification of one of these deities with a Greek god is Arṣu, who is assimilated to Ares (and not to Hermes!) in at least two Palmyrene bilingual inscriptions and in a Greek inscription found in Rome.[91] Notwithstanding the meaning of his name "The Favourable one" Arṣu just like Azizu is assimilated to Ares, the god of war. There are therefore all kinds of reasons to look for the other similarity of Monimos to Hermes which can explain their assimilation without a detour by way of Nebo.

In examining the identification of Azizos with Ares, we found that it can be explained by Azizos' appearance, his characteristic iconography, and consequently by his function of an armed escort. We may well suppose the identification of Monimos with Hermes to have proceeded along similar lines. The analogy between Munʿim-Monimos and Arṣu and Ruḍa, which has a sound linguistic foundation (these gods are all called "the pleasing one"), can be maintained both from their iconography and from their function. We can best approach the nature of Munʿim-Monimos, then, from our knowledge of Arṣu and Ruḍa.

---

[90] J. Henninger, Über Sternkunde und Sternkult, *ZE* 79, 1954, 82ff.

[91] *cf.* C. Dunant, *Museum Helveticum* 13, 1956, 216ff.; *eadem, Le sanctuaire de Baalshamin à Palmyre* III. *Les Inscriptions*, Rome 1971, no. 45; an unpublished bilingual inscription from the excavations of the sanctuary of Allat in honor of the same Soados Boliades; *IG*, XIV, 962, *cf.* Milik, *Dédicaces faites par des dieux*, 16.

The great frequency in Palmyra of personal names with Arṣu as theophorous element, shows he was one of the gods most venerated in Palmyra and especially in the Palmyrene.[92] His important position in the Palmyrene pantheon is also shown by his being represented on two reliefs, one from the Palmyrene and the other from the Temple of Bel, next to the triad of Bel.[93] Another relief originating from the Wadi Arafa, about thirty kilometres northwest of Palmyra, represents the major deities of Palmyra, Aštarte, Bel, Ba'alšamên, et. al., and among them, Arṣu.[94] The mural paintings in the so-called temple of Bel at Dura-Europos also picture Arṣu next to the triad of Bel or to Aglibol and Yarhibol, Bel's companions.[95] Arṣu usually is represented in military dress with a long lance or sceptre in his right hand, a small round shield at his left arm, and wearing a helmet. As a typical warrior god he consequently also occurs on the well-known relief from Bel's temple among the gods who fight against the chaos monster.[96] If Arṣu is represented alone, he is either portrayed as a standing warrior in indigenous dress with a lance in his right hand, a sword, and the small round shield,[97] or on horseback, or as a meharist riding a camel.[98] Arṣu, then, can be represented as a horse-rider like Azizu

---

[92] cf. A. Caquot, Sur l'onomastique religieuse de Palmyre, 239, n. 4: the name TYMRṢW appears 70 times; for GDRṢW see Caquot, art. cit., 242, n. 5; see also Stark, Personal Names, 13, 55f.

[93] A. Bounni, Mélanges offerts à Kazimierz Michalowski, Warszawa 1966, 314-316, Fig. 3; H. Seyrig, Syria 48, 1971, 90, Fig. 1; Drijvers, The Religion of Palmyra, Pl. IX, 1; the relief from the Temple of Bel: Seyrig, AS I, 27f., Pl. XLII, cf. Seyrig, Syria 48, 1971, 90, n. 1; Drijvers, The Religion of Palmyra, Pl. VII.

[94] A. Bounni, Mélanges Michalowski, 316ff., Fig. 4; Seyrig, Syria 48, 1971, 97, Fig. 4; Drijvers, The Religion of Palmyra, Pl. X, 2.

[95] Cumont, Fouilles de Doura-Europos, 86-114 and Pl. L, LI; Seyrig, Syria 13, 1932, Pl. XLIII; Cumont, Fouilles de Doura-Europos, 122-134 and Pl. LV; Perkins, The Art of Dura-Europos, 36ff., Pl. 12, 13.

[96] Seyrig, Syria 15, 1934, 165-173, Pl. XX, XXIV, 1; Drijvers, The Religion of Palmyra, Pl. IV, 2; cf. Du Mesnil du Buisson, Le bas-relief du combat de Bêl contre Tiamat dans le temple de Bêl à Palmyre, AAAS 26, 1976, 83ff.

[97] Schlumberger, La Palmyrène du Nord-Ouest, 88-89, Pl. XLI, 4 (most likely Arṣu, but the mutilated stele is not inscribed); Downey, The Stone and Plaster Sculpture, 53ff., Fig. 42, cf. 195ff.

[98] Perkins, The Art of Dura-Europos, 98-100, Pl. 40, cf. Downey, The Stone and Plaster Sculpture, 196f. Fig. 43; J. Starcky, Relief palmyrénien

on the relief of Arṣu and Azizu discussed earlier, that portrays Arṣu on camel-back. The iconography of Arṣu, consequently, is not exclusive in all aspects but, on the contrary, the type of the militant escorting deity shows some variants that are freely distributed, especially when they are represented as a pair. This may be interpreted as an indication that each represents a certain aspect of the Venus star irrespective of his exact name. That these deities also are considered to function in a cosmic setting becomes clear from the astral symbols that sometimes accompany them on the reliefs.[99]

The *tesserae* are fully analogous with the results obtained so far. Arṣu appears on these as a warrior with helmet, lance and shield, or riding a camel.[100] *Tessera* 169 shows his bust identified as such through an inscription, with a star over his right shoulder. The *tesserae* 175, 176, and 190 show only a camel with a crescent or a star; a dedication to Arṣu makes clear that these *tesserae* in fact were dedicated to him and his feasts. *Tessera* 174 shows Arṣu as a standing warrior and on the reverse side Hermes with a laden camel, expressing the idea of escorting a caravan.

Arṣu's militant character is the reason why in Palmyra he is equated with Ares in a bilingual inscription of 132 A.D. found in the temple of Ba'alšamên. This inscription deals with the dedication of four statues in four different sanctuaries, one of them being the temple of Arṣu which the Greek version calls ἱερὸν Ἄρεος.[101] This identification is confirmed by a still unpublished inscription dealing with the same subject found in Allat's sanctuary at Palmyra and perhaps by a Greek inscription from Rome dating back to

---

dédié au dieu Ilahay, *Mélanges bibliques André Robert*, Paris 1957, 370-380, cf. Milik, *Dédicaces faites par des dieux*, 21 for the correct reading of the inscription.

[99] cf. e.g. the bas-relief of Abgal and Ašar, Schlumberger, *La Palmyrène du Nord-Ouest*, 56, Pl. XXII, 1 and Downey, *The Stone and Plaster Sculpture*, Fig. 43; Downey's commentary on pp. 196f. is not convincing, cf. Drijvers, Mithra at Hatra ?, 182ff.

[100] Ingholt-Seyrig-Starcky, *Recueil des tessères de Palmyre*, no's 169, 170, 174, 175, 176, 177, 182, 185, 186, 187, 190, 192, 193, 194, 195, 196, 197, 497 (?); cf. the Model Article by P. Lallemant, *s.v.* Arṣu for Vol. I of the *LIMC*, who in essence repeats Starcky's views.

[101] C. Dunant, *Museum Helveticum* 13, 1956, 216ff. and *eadem*, *Le sanctuaire de Baalshamin à Palmyre* III, *Les Inscriptions*, no. 45.

133 A.D. that contains a dedication by a certain Lucius Licinius
Hermias to Ἄρῃ θεῷ πατρῴῳ ἐπηκόῳ.[102]

On the one hand Arṣu is therefore identified, like Azizos, with
Ares, on the other he seems to have some relation to Hermes regarding *tessera* 174. Hermes with a laden camel suggests that we
are dealing with Hermes ὅδιος or Hermes ἡγεμόνιος, who protects
travellers on their journey.[103] The way Arṣu is portrayed in a
helmet may also have helped to identify him with Hermes, because
the helmet of Arṣu greatly resembles the winged helmet of Hermes,
int. al. upon the *tesserae* 169, 170, 173, 182.[104] Two *tesserae* (175,
176) provide Arṣu with the epithet *r'yy'*, which may have the
meaning of "shepherd" or "herdsman." [105] This gives another link
with Hermes in his function of νόμιος or ἐπιμήλιος, the god especially
entrusted with the care of the flocks of sheep and goats. In fact,
this epithet of "shepherd" expressed a variant of the idea of
guiding and escorting that is fundamental to Arṣu's character.
Arṣu, therefore, can be viewed in different ways depending on what
aspect of his personality is focused on. When his militant aspect is
mostly stressed, Arṣu is equated with Ares; when his protecting
and guiding qualities are present, he is assimilated to or identified
with Hermes, the guide under the gods *par excellence*. The most
appropriate explanation of Iamblichos' identification of Azizos and
Monimos with Ares and Hermes, respectively, therefore seems to
be that just as Azizos and Monimos themselves are the two aspects
of the Venus star, representing the Morning and the Evening star
and at the same time Venus' militant and protecting qualities, so
Ares and Hermes stand for the same two main aspects of Venus.

---

[102] *IG*, XIV, 962, *cf.* Seyrig, *Syria* 1970, 111; the inscription is intended
for Hadrian's well-being; this emperor kept friendly relations with Palmyra,
which he visited in 129 A.D.

[103] *cf.* Nilsson, *Geschichte der griechischen Religion* I, 507f.; Grimal, *Dictionnaire de la mythologie grecque et romaine*, 207.

[104] The editors of the Recueil des tessères call this helmet of Arṣu a
'casque à aigrettes'; du Mesnil du Buisson, *Les tessères et les monnaies*, 236
speaks of a 'végétation aquatique sortant de la tête d'un dieu' in accordance
with his chthonic interpretation of Arṣu, whose name he derives from *'rṣ* =
earth, which is absolutely impossible.

[105] *cf. Recueil des tessères*, 182f.; *r'yy'* can derive from *r'y* = to lead, to
pasture and is in that case a substantive based on a *nisbe*-form.

These are expressed by a process of doubling, resulting in two gods, each one bearing one of Venus' most conspicuous characteristics. In fact, it does not make much difference which quality of Venus each represents. Arṣu can be assimilated to Ares, but so can Azizu. We are therefore fully justified in considering the couple Arṣu and Azizu also, respectively, as Ares and Hermes, just as we do in the case of Azizos and Monimos.

That Monimos and Arṣu should be identified with Hermes via Nebo also seems unlikely, because Arṣu and Nebo are totally unconnected in Palmyra; neither are they linked in the *tesserae*. The identification of Nebo and Kutbai even seems questionable. Nebo and Bel form part of the old "Babylonian" stock in Edessene religion, whereas Kutbai, on the other hand, belongs to its "Arabic" component and was perhaps worshipped more by the population of Arab descent. A certain social stratification must be allowed for here. Nebo and Kutbai may well have had more or less the same characteristics and fulfilled the same function, but this does not imply they are the same gods. Iamblichos' knowledge of the religion of Edessa and other towns with a strong Arab component thus sufficiently appears from what Julian records about Azizos and Monimos in a cosmic setting, and as Ares and Hermes, who best express their respective qualities. It is not astonishing in this whole process of assimilation and cross-cultural identifications, that pairs of such gods can be equated with Castor and Pollux, the Castores, as appears, e.g., at Khirbeit Semrin in the Palmyrene, where Abgal and Ashar were identified with them.[106] Numerous bas-reliefs from Syria representing two youths flanking a Sun god express more or less the same idea.[107] Two busts of young male persons bearing a torch, which are to be seen in bas-relief in the wall of a sheikh's house in 'Ire, are one of the most well-known examples.[108]

---

[106] *cf.* Schlumberger, *La Palmyrène du Nord-Ouest*, 56, no. 17 and Pl. XXI, 4; see also 126f.; *cf.* Seyrig, Genneas et les dieux cavaliers en Syrie, *Syria* 26, 1949, 236.

[107] *cf.* Dussaud, *RevArch* 1903, I, 124ff. = *Notes de mythologie syrienne* I, 2, 9-14; *idem*, *Syria* 23, 1942-43, 63, n. 4 (relief of Khirbet Haman), 74; Sourdel, *Les cultes du Hauran*, 75; Dunand, *Le musée de Soueida*, no's. 37, 38, 38bis.

[108] See Sourdel, *Les cultes du Hauran*, 29f., Pl. II, 1.

Just as in Palmyra Arṣu was the most venerated god of the two,
so Azizos was at Edessa and elsewhere.[109] It seems that his militant
qualities were especially attractive to soldiers from Syria serving
in the Roman army at the Danubian limes in Dacia and elsewhere.
A series of Latin inscriptions attests to his cult, which was evidently
practiced in the various camps. From Apulum in Dacia a range of
inscriptions, all dating from the time of Commodus and later, are
dedications to *bono puero* (CIL III, 1131, 1134, 1137 and 7652
originating from Torma in Dacia), *bono puero phosphoro* (CIL III,
1136), *deo bono puero phosphoro* (CIL III, 1130), *bono deo puero
phosphoro* (CIL III = 1132), *puero phosphoro d(eo) o(ptimo)
m(aximo)* (CIL III, 1135), *deo bono puero phosphoro Apollini Pythio*
(CIL III, 1133), and *deo bono phosphoro Apollini Pythio* (CIL III,
1138).[110] The same god was venerated in the camp at Lambaesis
according to a dedication to *deo bono puero pro salute d(omini)
n(ostri) L. Domiti Aureliani etc.* set up by the prefect of *Legio III
Augustae Aerelianae* and his wife between 270 and 275 A.D.[111] The
identity of *bonus puer* appears from an inscription from Potaissa
in Dacia: *Deo Azizo bono p[uero conserva]tori pro salutem d(ominorum)
[n(ostrorum) Valeriani et Gal]lieni Aug(ustorum) et Valeri[ni no-
biliss(imi) Caes(aris) et Corneliae Salonina [e Aug(ustae) et Genio]
leg(ionis) V Mac(edonicae) III piae fidelis. . . . Donatus praef(ectus)
leg(ionis) eiusde[m . . . . .templum inceptum perfecit. . . .*[112] Azizos,
therefore, had a temple in or near the camp at Potaissa. It may not

---

[109] See *e.g.* an altar in the museum at Soueida; on one side there is a bust
over which an eagle spreads his wings. Ἀζείζῳ is written above the bust.
On the opposite side there is a different bust, regarded by Dussaud as
Monimos, but by Dunand as the dedicator of the altar, which is more likely,
cf. Dunand, *Le musée de Soueida*, 8, Pl. IX, 8; *CIG* 4617.

[110] *cf.* in general; *PW* XX¹, 656 *s.v.* Phosphoros and *Roscher's Lexikon* I,
743 *s.v.* Azizus; Cumont, Les noms des planètes et l'astrolatrie chez les
Grecs, *L'Antiquité Classique* 4, 1935, 6, 2; *idem*, *Mélanges Bidez*, 1933, 153;
cf. M. J. Rostovtzeff, *JRS* 23, 1932, 107ff.

[111] *CIL* VIII, 2665, *cf.* A. von Domaszewski, *Aufsätze zur römischen
Heeresgeschichte*, repr. Darmstadt 1972, 144.

[112] *CIL* III, 875; *cf.* Z. Kádár, *Die kleinasiatisch-syrischen Kulte zur
Römerzeit in Ungarn*, *EPRO* 2, Leiden 1962, 24; A. von Domaszewski, *Die
Religion des römischen Heeres*, Trier 1895, 64ff.; L. W. Jones, *The Cults of
Dacia*, UCPCP 9, 8, 1929, 285ff., 296ff.; *cf.* also F. Altheim, *Niedergang der
Alten Welt* II, 450f., n. 275-288.

be mere accident that from Potaissa also come two short dedications by the same man: *Marti amico et consentienti sacrum. Hermias dedicavit idemq. vovit* (CIL III, 897 = ILS 3161), and *Mercurio consentienti sacrum. Hermias dedicavit idemq. vovit* (CIL III, 898 = ILS 3194).[113] Mars and Mercurius are without any doubt similar to Ares and Hermes and consequently to Azizos and Monimos, of whom the cult of the first is attested to by the other inscription from Potaissa. These short dedications, then, can be considered an indirect confirmation of Iamblichos' identifications. The last inscription of interest in this context is a dedication from Intercisa, a military camp at the *limes* in Pannonia: *Deo Aziz[o p]ro salute d.n. [in]vi(c)ti Aug. et Iulia [e] [A]u[g]ustae Iulius [Fir]manus.*[114] It is just another testimony to the cult of the Syrian god in the time of Severus Alexander.

The epithets given to Azizos clearly characterise him as the youthful Morning Star Phosphoros, who represents the protecting warrior qualities of Venus which naturally are of special interest in a military atmosphere. Hence Azizos/Mars is called *amicus*, friend of the soldiers, who is of the same feeling as they are (*consentiens*). This last epithet, *consentiens* = agreeing, accordant, expresses especially the connotation of very close bonds between Hermias, the dedicator, and the god.

It seems that *bonus puer* also had a predictive function, otherwise his equation with the oracle god Apollo Pythios is a bit strange—unless we take into consideration that the Morning Star as such predicts that the Sun soon will rise, which function was a sufficient ground for the equation.[115]

---

[113] cf. Kádár, *Die kleinasiatisch-syrischen Kulte*, 25; Rostovtzeff, *JRS* 23, 1932, 107ff.; it may be the same Hermias who is mentioned in *IG* XIV, 962.

[114] *AÉ* 1910, no. 142; cf. Kádár, 23f., whose interpretations, however, are in need of correction. He reads the proper name of the dedicant as Firmianus, which is incorrect, interprets the name Aziz as 'liebenswürdig, freundlich', whereas the name means 'powerful', 'mighty', and considers Azizos as a sun god (Azizos erscheint hier also als der Sonnengott mit den zwei Gesichtern); cf. also J. Fitz, *Les Syriens à Intercisa*, Coll. *Latomus* 122, 1972, 182, 184, who quotes Kádár.

[115] Th. Klauser, *RAC* I, 1071 considers Apollo Pythios the god of the dawn; according to *Roscher's Lexikon* III, 3386 Apollo Pythios occurs on a coin of Emesa, cf. *Hunter*, 3, 197, 11, and *BMC*; Galatia, 240, 21; in fact,

The epithet *conservator* given to Azizos in the inscription from
Potaissa leads into a vast field of related concepts. *Conservator*
means "protector" or "defender" and is, therefore, a precise definition of Azizos' main characteristics. The epithet is often given to
Jupiter and then is usually provided with a complement in order
to indicate what the god is supposed to protect.[116] Since Azizos
actually is one of a pair, sometimes identified with the Castores or
Tyndarides, it is of interest that an inscription from Rome calls
the deities, who sometimes escort Jupiter Dolichenus, *Castores
Conservatores*: *I.o.s(ancto) p(raestantissimo) D(olicheno) et Iunoni
sanctae Herae Castorib(us) et Apollini Conservatoribus.*.[117] The
Castores of Jupiter Dolichenus originally were portrayed as busts
rising from a mount and represent the idea of cosmic stability
since they flank the god of Doliche, who is a mountain god and at
the same time the god of heaven, giver of storm and rain.[118] They
are also pictured as armed horsemen on several monuments from
the cult of Jupiter Dolichenus, of which the best-known is an altar
from Mainz,[119] the manner of representation of which brings them

the coin represents an urn, so that the equation with Apollo Pythios is rather
dubious; A. Alföldi, Apollo Pythius Aziz, *Vjestnik Hrv. Archeol. Društva*
(N.S.), 1928, 223ff., Pl. V discusses some coins of G. Vibius Trebonianus
Gallus Aug. or of G. Vibius Vilusianus and interprets the second part of
the legend: *ARN-AZI* as Azizos, since the coins represent Apollo with an
olive branch and a snake standing on top of a mountain; that seems a rather
dubious interpretation, *cf.* B. Pick, *JdI* 13, 1898, 170, n. 117; R. Hanslik,
Apollo Pythius Azizus and sein Kult, *VigChr* 8, 1954, 176-181 proposes to
read Azizum instead of acystum in the *Hist. eccl. trip.* of Cassiodorus-
Epiphanius and identifies Azizus with Attis, which seems rather fantastic.

[116] *cf. e.g.* Dessau, Index *s.v. Iupiter conservator imperii, d.n. imper.,
municipii* etc.; Dessau, 3668: *conservator horreorum*; 3356: *conservator
viniarum*; 3018; *conservator possessionum*; 3016; *conservator omnium rerum*;
see E. Will, Les castores dolichéniens, *MUSJ* 27, 1947-48, 35.

[117] P. Merlat, *Répertoire des inscriptions et monuments figurés du culte de
Jupiter Dolichenus*, Paris 1951, no. 202; *cf.* Will, *art. cit.*, 35.

[118] *cf.* Ch. Pichard, *RHR* 109, 1934, 73ff.; P. Merlat, *Syria* 1951, 230ff.
and *idem*, Orient, Grèce, Rome. Un exemple de syncrétisme? Les "Castores"
dolichéniens, *Éléments orientaux dans la religion grecque ancienne*, Paris
1960, 77ff.

[119] See Merlat, *Répertoire*, no's 152, 206, 311; *cf.* Seyrig, *MUSJ* 23, 1940,
91-94; Merlat, *Syria* 28, 1951, 232, fig. 1; E. Will, *MUSJ* 27, 1947-48, 33;
see also Will, *Le relief cultuel*, 110, where a stele from Zinjirli is discussed
representing the sun god Šamaš flanked by two horses, *cf. Syria* 1920-21,
87, fig. 105; Merlat, Orient, Grèce, Rome, 83ff.

closer to the Tyndarides and divine pairs like Azizos and Monimos, or Arṣu and Azizu. Although Jupiter Dolichenus and his Castores are not comparable in all aspects to the Sun god and his armed escort of Morning and Evening Star, both conceptions finally express the same idea of cosmic order and stability on which man can rely and which protects him. A possible link between the two conceptions is suggested by a recently published stele from Qaryatein, eighty kilometres south-east of Homs. It represents an eagle with outstretched wings on top of a mountain and to its left the god Arṣu in standing position with helmet, cuirass, in his right hand a lance, and on his left arm a round shield. The identity of the god is indicated by a Palmyrene inscription; over the eagle under a garland is written '*lhgbl* = the deity Mountain.[120] The deity Elahagabal reminds very strongly of the god Jupiter Turmasgades = Jupiter, Mountain of the Sanctuary, of which we possess some evidence from Davia, Trier and Rome and who shared a sanctuary with Jupiter Dolichenus at Dura-Europos.[121] The name Turmasgades, in fact, might be another designation of Jupiter Dolichenus himself, who actually was a mountain god. The same phenomenon occurs at Palmyra, where the god Ba'alšamên was also known as Duraḥlun.[122] An inscription from the Dolichenum at Dura-Europos identifies Jupiter Turmasgades with Helios Mithras, which might be significant in this context since Mithras had its own acolytes Cautes and Cautopates, perhaps also symbolizing the Morning and Evening Star.[123]

The concept of *Deus Azizus bonus puer conservator* therefore appears to have various connections with the religions of Syria and Anatolia, from where a good many of the soldiers in the Roman army originated, especially in the second and third century A.D.

---

[120] *cf.* J. Starcky, Stèle d'Elahagabal, *MUSJ* 49, 1975-76, 503-520.

[121] *cf.* J. G. Gilliam, Jupiter Turmasgades, *Actes du IXe congrès intern. d'études sur les frontières romaines*, Köln-Wien 1974, 309-314; *cf. The Excavations at Dura-Europos, Prel. Report of 9th Season*, Part III, 97-134, Milik, *Biblica* 48, 1967, 568ff. on deified mountains like Karmel, Hermon, etc.

[122] *cf.* P. Collart - J. Vicari, *Le sanctuaire de Baalshamin à Palmyre* I, Rome 1969, 215-218.

[123] *Dura Prel. Report* IX, 3, 114, no. 974 = *Bull. épigr.* 1953, 206 = *AÉ* 1954, 267 = *CIMRM* I, no. 70; *cf.* Gilliam, *art. cit.* 312f.

It provides us with a good example of how these soldiers brought with them the traditional religious ideas of their homeland and adapted them to the special needs of their military life in the various *castra* of the Roman empire. This process usually is called syncretism, but that seems too simplistic. It is, in fact, more a process of expressing religious conceptions of one culture with the vehicles of another culture in order to keep the world identifiable. Such a process is both determined and limited by the possibilities of recognition one culture finds in the other. Iamblichos' identification of Azizu and Mun'im, gods of his Syrian homeland, with Ares and Hermes, is an excellent example of such a cross-cultural process of mutual recognition.

CHAPTER SEVEN

EDESSAN RELIGION, PAGANISM IN THE ROMAN EMPIRE, AND EARLY CHRISTIANITY

The foregoing chapters—on the various deities worshipped at Edessa during the first centuries A.D. and earlier, on the religious conceptions connected with their cults and the origins and spread of some of them—yield only a partial insight into religious practice and what it meant to the inhabitants of the city. Our sources merely provide us with a superficial knowledge of current religious ideas but do not allow a deeper understanding of the varieties of religious experience as expressed in the formal language of myths and ritual in the temples of Edessa, not to speak of the even more personal religious expressions in prayers and hymns. It is not until the final victory of Christianity in the empire that we are able to lay hands on such evidence of religious language in the soon so abundant literature of the Syriac-speaking church, the same that has preserved the scanty and depreciating remarks on pagan religion as a Satanic institution.

Even if we were right in assuming that the same fervour and religious devotion that is found in Christian Syriac literature must already have existed in pagan practice—emasculations and ecstatic experiences in the cult of the Dea Syria may be cited as one instance of a possibly more general pattern—there is no way of proving it. We only see the divine names and stereotyped expressions in which feelings and emotions ultimately are congealed, especially if they are described by opponents. The available evidence is, however, still sufficient to list at least some general and main characteristics of Edessan religion in pagan times.

The most impressive feature of the Edessan pantheon is that it consists of various deities of a different cultural origin. Besides gods of a clearly Babylonian origin like Nebo and Bel, probably the theoi patroioi of Edessa, Atargatis and Hadad from Hierapolis occur, and the traditional deities of Harran also played their role at Edessa. Gods of Arab origin had an equally important share in the religious life of the city: the eagle worshipped by the Edessans finds its parallel in Mar^{e}n NŠR' = Our Lord the Eagle, who had a temple of his own in Hatra. The cult of the female Venus star actually comprises the worship of al-ʿUzza and all lascivious practice connected with it. The cult of the male Venus star appears in the twin gods Azizos and Monimos the accompanying escorts of the Sun, who belong to the religious inheritance of the Arab desert population. Grosso modo we therefore can discern three main components of Edessa's religion in pagan times: Babylonian deities, divinities worshipped in the Syrian area that belong mainly to the traditional religions of the Aramaic-speaking population of that region, and Arab gods. The strong appeal of astrology, which is attested by several sources, *int. al.*, the *Doctrina Addai* and the polemical works of Ephrem Syrus, is further evidence of the strong influence of Mesopotamian religious practice and priestly wisdom. The composite nature of the city's pantheon is identical with that found in other cities in the Syrian-Mesopotamian area during the same period. Palmyra, e.g., shows the same religious pattern. Bel and Nebo were venerated there on or near the ancient tell like some other deities of Mesopotamian origin. The other component comprises the gods of Aramaic and West-Semitic origin like Yarhibol, Aglibol, Malakbel Baʿalšamên, Atargatis, *et al.* The last component consists of Arab gods like Šamš, Allat, Arṣu, Azizu, *etc.* The pantheon of Hatra has fundamentally the same composite structure: in addition to Mesopotamian deities like Nergal, we find Aramaic gods like Baʿalšamên and Atargatis, whereas the Arab gods form the kernel of Hatra's religious life centering around the worship of the triad of Mar^{e}n, Mart^{e}n and Bar-Marên, the first being the Arab Sun god Šamš, the last a deity comparable to Nabataean Dusares or Hermes/Mercurius at Baalbek.[1]

The various panthea of these and other cities actually are not products of priestly and theological speculation which always tries to bring some order even into a divine chaos, but more the result

---

[1] *cf.* Drijvers, *ANRW* II, 8, 828ff.: Hatras Religion als synkretistische Erscheinung; *idem*, Mithra at Hatra?, 158ff.; on the young god Hermes at Baalbek see Y. Hajjar, *La triade d'Héliopolis-Baalbek* II, *EPRO* 59, Leiden 1977, 507ff., 517ff.

of the different cultural and even ethnic influences long at work in that area. Just as the human population consists of various groups, each with its own religious inheritance, so the divine population of the temples reflects the sociological structure of the city. Accumulation of deities goes together with the accumulation of the city's population and mirrors the enormous intermingling that characterizes the Syrian and Mesopotamian areas particularly in Greco-Roman times.

It is of particular interest in this context that there is no evidence of Iranian religious influence at Edessa. Several words of Iranian origin occur in the Aramaic dialect of Edessa, which developed into Syriac with all characteristics of Eastern Aramaic.[2] It is, however, very hard to determine, if these words were already in use in Official Aramaic, the language of the Achaemenid chancelleries, or whether they were borrowed in Parthian times. Parthian dress was very fashionable at Edessa, as at Palmyra and Hatra, especially among the higher ranks of the society that had themselves portrayed in that way, but it is very dubious whether such a phenomenon might be considered a real proof of profound Iranian cultural influence.[3] It is also doubtful whether the main characteristics of what is usually called Parthian art, actually have anything to do with Parthia itself. This art is mainly restricted to the Syrian and Mesopotamian desert area and the cities on its edge which all show a rather homogeneous cultural pattern with local variations.[4] It

---

[2] cf. Widengren, *Iranisch-semitische Kulturbegegnung in parthischer Zeit*, 25ff.: Die sprachlichen Verhältnisse; on the development of the Aramaic dialect of Edessa, in its written form a kind of Standard Literary Aramaic, see K. Beyer, Der reichsaramäische Einschlag in der ältesten syrischen Literatur, *ZDMG* 116, 1966, 242-254; Drijvers, *Old-Syriac Inscriptions*, Introduction XIff.; J. Greenfield, Standard Literary Aramaic, *Actes du Premier Congrès International de linguistique sémitique et chamito-sémitique*, ed. A. Caquot - D. Cohen, The Hague-Paris 1974, 289 drew attention to the fact that the Edessean area throughout the Neo-Assyrian, Neo-Babylonian and Achaemenian periods was densely settled with Aramaic speakers, so that the inscriptions might show traces of Western or North Syrian.

[3] H. Seyrig, Armes et costumes iraniens de Palmyra, *Syria* 18, 1937, 4-31 = *AS* II, 45-73 is still fundamental.

[4] cf. D. Schlumberger, Descendants non-méditerranéans de l'art grec, *Syria* 37, 1960, 131-166; 253-318; *idem*, *L'Orient hellénisé*, Paris 1970, 68ff., 198ff.; Drijvers, *ANRW* II, 8, 86of.; E. Will, Art parthe et art grec, *Études d'archéologie classique* II, Paris 1959, 125-135; M. A. R. Colledge, *Parthian Art*, Ithaca, N.Y. 1977, 138ff.: 'Parthian' art.

is much more likely that its traditions and special features partly go back to Hellenistic traditions existing in the Near East since Alexander the Great, and partly are due to the development of artistic traditions of a special character that came into existence since the beginning of the first century A.D., when Rome ruled the East. During the first century B.C., e.g., frontality in the visual arts was not prevailing, but became so since the beginning of the first century A.D., as various finds at Palmyra make clear.[5] There is no reason to assume that the situation at Edessa was fundamentally different. The often-adduced Iranian influence on symbolism and ideas connected with the nativity of the Saviour in Eastern Christianity is only detectable from the fifth century on, when Christianity spread on a large scale in the Sassanian empire and is, therefore, more likely due to polemics against Iranian conceptions than to Iranian influences on the theology of the Syriac-speaking churches.[6] For the time being the problem of Iranian religious influence in Syria and Mesopotamia must be left open. It is, however, very doubtful whether, if, apart from very little isolated evidence, it ever can be substantiated.[7]

In contradistinction to other places in Syria the Edessan pantheon shows no sign of any systematization grouping the deities into dyads or triads. At Palmyra Bel and Ba'alšamên as kosmokratores were flanked, respectively, by Yarhibol and Aglibol, and Malakbel and Aglibol representing Sun and Moon. This formation of an astrological triad goes back to the beginning of the first century A.D. and

---

[5] cf. H. Seyrig, Remarques sur la civilisation de Palmyre, *Syria* 21, 1940, 328-337 = *AS* III, 115-124; *idem*, Sculptures palmyréniennes archaïques, *Syria* 22, 1941, 31-44 = *AS* III, 124-137; Colledge, *The Art of Palmyra*, London 1976, 126ff.

[6] The main champion of this theory is G. Widengren, *Iranisch-semitische Kulturbegegnung*, 62ff.: Die Geburtstätten des Erlöserkönigs; see also U. Monneret de Villard, *Le leggende orientali sui magi evangelici*, Studi e Testi 163, Roma 1952, passim. I am preparing a publication on Syriac traditions concerning the Magi and their role in the Nativity story. Widengren summarised his views in Culture Contact, Cultural Influence, Cultural Continuity, and Syncretism, in: *Religious Syncretism in Antiquity*. Essays in Conversation with Geo Widengren, ed. by Birger A. Pearson, Scholars Press, Missoula 1975, 1ff.

[7] cf. Drijvers, Mithra at Hatra? Some remarks on the problem of the Irano-Mesopotamian Syncretism, 151-186.

is likely due to priestly speculations on the nature of the god of heaven.[8] The Hatrene triad of Mar^{e}n, Mart^{e}n and Bar-Marên shows all the peculiarities of West-Semitic and especially Phoenician triads grouping the gods into a family consisting of father, mother and son.[9] Still it should be noted that Mar^{e}n and Bar-Marên were by far the most venerated deities, so that the triad as such seems to be a rather artificial construction. At Edessa nothing of this kind can be detected. Since Nebo and Bel are always mentioned together and come from the same religious tradition, it might be ascertained that they have close bonds and very likely represent a divine Father and his Son. On the other hand it is completely unproven that the Edessan Atargatis formed a couple together with Bel, as is often stated.[10] Atargatis as the most important half of the Hierapolis dyad functioned as Tyche of Edessa as of other cities, but does not seem to have relationships to Bel. The only other instance of a certain systematization is the worship of the Sun flanked by Azizos and Monimos as Morning and Evening Star.

Although the whole varied pantheon is not a systematic concept with clear interrelations and interdependencies, it covers more or less the whole field of nature and culture. Bel represents the kosmokrator, creator of order out of chaos, ruler of the luminaries and the stars, warrant of the well-organized kosmos in which human life has its own place. Nebo as god of wisdom actually is the initiator of human culture, messenger of divine wisdom and holder of human fate. He might function as a divine guide connecting Bel's heaven with human earth. It is not likely by accident that Nebo holds a predominant position at Edessa, which is called the 'Athens of the East' in Syriac sources.

Atargatis symbolizes the female aspect of human life and culture, the care-giving and protecting mother, life-giving and fertilizing, warrant of the city's prosperity, but also the seductive virgin to

---

[8] *cf.* Seyrig, Bêl de Palmyre, *Syria* 48, 1970, 89ff.

[9] *cf.* W. W. Baudissin, *Adonis und Esmun*, 15ff.; *cf.* Seyrig, *Syria* 27, 1960, 247ff.; H. Gese, Die Religion der Phönizier, in: H. Gese et al., *Die Religionen Altsyriens*, 182ff., who adduces examples of various triads; in fact these triads are less consistent and uniform than is usually believed, see Seyrig's prudent remarks.

[10] *e.g.* by Th. Klauser, *RAC* I, 1084, n. 43 *s.v.* Baalat von Osrhoene.

whom a man can sacrifice his virility in a last effort to unite himself
with her. Atargatis' links with water and its life-giving qualities,
which are described by Lucian in *De Dea Syria*, surely apply to the
situation at Edessa, where the river Daiṣan provided the city with
water, but also with several floods, the earliest recorded in 201 A.D.
in the *Chronicon Edessenum*.[11] Atargatis' role as Tyche of Edessa
gives a strong identity to the urban walled area in distinction to
the rural country outside. We may assume that her temple near
the springs at the foot of the citadel was one of the most appealing
religious centers of the city marking this quarter out as the real
kernel of urban life, where the citadel gives protection and the
wells give life and fertility—actually the only requirements for
founding a city.

All the other deities recorded for Edessa were most likely linked
to special groups of various origins in the population and, therefore,
strengthening their identity without, however, becoming exclusive.
The worship of Sun, Moon, Planets and Stars could have been part
of Bel's cult in his role as kosmokrator. An indication of this is a
similar situation in the cult of Bel at Palmyra and possibly elsewhere in Syria, and the concept of a creator god ruling over Planets
and Stars that is found in the second-century semi-Christian philosophical kosmology of the Edessan philosopher Bardaiṣan.[12] On
the other hand the Sun at least seems to have had a temple of its
own at Edessa, most likely outside the walls, since the Harran gate
is also called the Gate of the Temple of the Sun. According to the
Doctrina Addai the Edessans shared the cult of the Sun with the
inhabitants of Harran, so that a Sun temple situated outside Edessa
in the direction of Harran would fit in very well. Since the worship
of the Sun in Syria and Mesopotamia is mainly an Arab cult, the
same may be the case at Edessa.[13] This view is strengthened by its
being escorted by Azizos and Monimos, both deities of clearly
Arab character, and by the very location of the Sun temple. Sanc-

---

[11] *cf.* L. Hallier, *Untersuchungen über die Edessenische Chronik, TU* 9, 1,
Leipzig 1892, 84-87, 91; Drijvers, *ANRW* II, 8, 864f. on the floods at Edessa.
[12] *cf.* the passage in Bardaiṣan's *Book of the Laws of Countries, PS* II,
col. 568 and col. 572; for a commentary Drijvers, *Bardaiṣan of Edessa*, 83ff.
[13] Seyrig, Le culte du Soleil en Syrie à l'époque romaine, *Syria* 48, 1971,
339.

tuaries of Arab deities, which in a sense form a link between religious practices in the cities and the cult of the desert population and, consequently, between the Arabs settled in the urban area and their semi-nomadic relatives outside the cities, are often situated *extra muros*. Such was the original situation, e.g., at Palmyra, where the Arab gods had their shrines at the West side of the city outside the trace of the oldest walls.[14] The manner in which religions arrange urban space, and mark special places with a certain sacredness by building temples or shrines, often reflects a complicated network of underlying social relations. The exact locations of pagan temples at Edessa are practically unknown, but we may assume that their various places are connected with the living quarters of special groups of the population and with regard to Nebo, Bel and Atargatis with the real urban center, where the solidarity among the population was formed and strengthened and found its symbolic expression in the cults of the theoi patroioi.

The religious ordering of space and time, which finds its symbolic expression in processions that link sacred places, and in feasts that highlight certain times and periods, is unhappily enough also practically unknown. In the great Spring festival linked with the cult of Bel and held in Nisan/April certainly was one of the most important religious feasts during which processions took place. Its importance is also marked by the attention paid to it by the *Acts of Sharbel* which clearly refer to processions held during that feast. It may be taken for certainty that these processions involved lots of people with all kinds of musical instruments accompanying the divine statues that were carried around.[15]

---

[14] *cf.* Gawlikowski, *Le temple palmyrénien*, 87ff.; the so-called Transverse Colonnade was built from the beginning of the first century A.D. on along the trace of the former city wall. The sanctuary of Allat, the most important of the Arab temples, already existed in the first century B.C. and was at that time situated outside the walls.

[15] *cf.* Isaac of Antioch on the cult of Baʿalshamên at Nisibis, where processions in his honor were held with the music of horn and tambourine; First *Homily on the Conquest of Beth Ḥur*, ed. Bickell, 76ff.; Seyrig, *AS* II, 111ff.; where all kinds of processions in Syrian cults are mentioned; H. Lammens, Le culte des bétyles et les processions religieuses chez les Arabes préislamites, *L'Arabie occidentale avant l'Hégire*, Beyrouth 1928, 101ff.; at Palmyra processions were held between the temple of Bêl and the sanctuaries in the Western quarter of the City.

It should be stressed in this context that pagan religions in the Near East in Roman times—and as a matter of course also in other regions and periods—do not show a single sign of mutual exclusiveness based on a special doctrine or practice. On the contrary paganism is tolerant, not by virtue of special human qualities, but rather by its own character, as it deals with all the various aspects of human nature and culture without resolving the contradictions existing among them. *Au fond* it confirms the existing order even when certain religious phenomena make the impression of a radical effort to change it. This stabilizing effect of religious practice as it comes to light especially in rituals, feasts and processions in which very often the whole hierarchical structure of a society is mirrored, must have been very strong in these Near Eastern cities with their mixed population and various cults. This idea of a fundamentally unvariable order established and maintained by all deities *ab origine*, was even strengthened by prevailing astrological concepts, according to which human fate was determined by the divine order in the kosmos. To feel easier men consulted oracles to learn beforehand what was disposed to them, and what they could not alter. The greatest human virtue and wisdom consequently was to live in accordance with that order in daily practice, philosophical reflections, mystical experience, orgiastic feasts and observance of certain rules.

The foregoing lines are partly based on study of other societies and cities, partly on the impression some ruined cities in Syria and Mesopotamia make even today. The ruins of Palmyra, e.g., with the temples in the various quarters of the city connected by the monumental colonnades, give only a faint idea of how an ancient city once functioned to keep the body social stable. The hundreds of different tesserae attest to a very complex social structure, which expresses itself, int. al., in the meals of the thiasoi to which the tesserae gave admission.[16] In the case of Edessa we can only guess at what happened there in reality, but we may be sure that our

---

[16] *cf.* H. Seyrig, Les tessères palmyréniennes et le banquet rituel, *Mémorial Lagrange*, Paris 1940, 51-58; J. Greenfield, The Marzeaḥ as a social Institution, *Acta Ant. Acad. Scient. Hung.* XXII, 1-4, 1974, 451-455.

outer knowledge is the very surface of a highly complex religious situation that lasted for several centuries, influenced Roman paganism, and at last succumbed to victorious Christianity.

Syrian slaves, merchants and soldiers going abroad often stuck to their traditional religion. In this way the cult of Atargatis, of Jupiter Dolichenus and of the Edessan Azizos spread into the Roman empire and contributed to its varied pattern of religions. So Syrian soldiers brought the cult of Azizos bonus puer to Pannonia. It is of particular interest that the cult of Azizos at the Danubian *limes* was fundamentally similar and identical to the same cult at their hometown neither undergoing important changes, nor assimilating to other cults. The Latin inscriptions cover a traditional Arab cult to which many soldiers were attached.

Another good example of the same process is the often-mentioned cult of Balti(s) = My Lady which occurs in the Danubian provinces too.[17] An inscription from Aquincum mentions the construction of a temple dedicated to Balti and the Dea Syria: *Balti diae divinae et Diasuriae templum f.T.Fl.*[18] The inscription seems to be incomplete; the remaining part might have been engraved into another block. A relief found at Aquincum, unhappily enough only fragmentarily preserved, shows a nude god standing in a niche that seems to form the central representation of the whole relief. He has a thunderbolt in his right hand and a long sceptre in his left. An eagle sits to his right. Thunderbolt and eagle identify the god as Zeus or his Syrian equivalent Hadad, although it seems a little odd that he is portrayed nude. In a niche at the left side of the relief a standing goddess is pictured with a mural crown and spindle and distaff. Between Zeus and the goddess a lion walks to the right and above the lion the first part of an inscription can be read. To the right of Zeus there was clearly another niche, the second part of the inscription in question which is partly visible, and below it what seems to be a sphinx. The inscription is therefore

---

[17] *cf.* Cumont, *Les religions orientales*, 4th ed., 1929, 104; *idem*, art. Baltis, *PW* II, 2, 2842f.

[18] *CIL* III, 10393 = *ILS* 4277; *cf. RAC* I, 1084; *PW* II, 2, 2842; Kádár, *Die kleinasiatisch-syrischen Kulte*, 6, n. 2; Diasuriae instead of Deae Syriae is not unusual, *cf. CIL* III 10964, *ILS* 4280.

fragmentary and reads: *Deae Syr. et .... ae pro salu......*[19] It seems that the whole relief was dedicated to at least two goddesses, of which the second one is unknown. It is, however, remarkable that the inscription does not seem to mention Zeus-Hadad, although he is represented in the central niche. Kádár's supposition that the relief might portray Balti and the Dea Syria is therefore completely unproven, whereas even the ending-*ae* of the second divine name in the inscription does not say much for this identification, unless we supply the missing text as follows: *Deae Syr. et (Balti De)ae pro salu....* In this case, however, we would have nine letters in the upper line of the second part of the inscription, whereas both lines in the first part only have seven—also a serious objection against the proposed interpretation. For the time being, therefore, we omit from our evidence this relief from Aquincum which likely should be explained in another way. If we could read, e.g., in the second part: *et Dian* providing the reading *et Dianae*, it would fit in better with the length of the line and other evidence.[20]

That the cult of Balti is known in that area also becomes clear from two other inscriptions. One was found in Kornye between Brigetio and Aquincum: *deae Balti Flavia Victorina pro se et pro suis om.v.t.l.m.*[21] Near Aquincum an altar was found dedicated to *Balti Aug(ustae)*.[22] Another altar was dedicated to Balti by Cocceia Marcia in Brigetio and was found there.[23] Whether a relief of a sitting goddess with long hair, dressed like an amazone with a double axe in her left hand and a shield in her right, represents Balti is extremely doubtful. It was found at Brigetio in Pannonia, but the inscription is only partly preserved: *.....] i aug sac.* The

---

[19] *cf.* V. Kuzsinsky, *Aquincum*, 99ff. No. 363, Fig. 100; Kádár, *Die kleinasiatisch-syrischen Kulte*, 6ff., Pl. I, 1; Kádár's reading *Deae Syri* seems incorrect since the *i* of Syri is nowhere to be seen.

[20] *cf. e.g. CIL* IX 4187 = *ILS* 4281 dedicated to Deanae Syri(ae); the identification of the Dea Syria with Deana is stated by Lucian, *De Syria Dea*, 32.

[21] *CIL* III 10964 = *ILS* 4278; *cf.* Kádár, *Die kleinasiatisch-syrischen Kulte*, 56, n. 6, where he mentions publications regarding the cult of Balti at Brigetion, which, however, do not adduce new evidence.

[22] *CIL* III 10574.

[23] St. Paulovics, *Laureae Aquincenses*, Budapest 1944, 131, no. 14. Pl. XVI, 1; *cf.* Kádár, *Die kleinasiatisch-syrischen Kulte*, 56, n. 5.

editors supplement the letter *i* to *balt]i* assuming that the accompanying relief actually pictures this goddess. It is, however,
much more likely that, judging from the iconography, it represents
Diana so that we can leave it out here.[24] To the West of Brigetio at
Gyor, ancient Arrabona, an altar came to light which is dedicated
to *Balti et Arvi deabus*.[25] Arvis seems to be a local fertility goddess
having to do with agriculture judging from her name which is
related to *arvum* = field. This altar is an indication of a certain
assimilation of Balti to local goddesses of the same character.

The solid evidence for the cult of Balti in Pannonia along the
Danubian *limes* consists, therefore, of the foundation inscription
of a temple dedicated to her and the Dea Syria at Aquincum, and
of four altars, one of which also mentions the local goddess Arvis.
The most interesting aspect of this material is the distinction
between Balti and the Dea Syria as it appears from the foundation
text of the temple at Aquincum. It is exactly the same distinction
as found at Edessa and in the area of Osrhoene: the Dea Syria is
Atargatis, the goddess of Hierapolis; Balti is identical with the
Arab goddess al-ʿUzza, and Greek Aphrodite, as stated by Isaac of
Antioch in his homilies on Beth Ḥur.[26] In the *Doctrina Addai*, as
in Isaac's homilies, she is also called the *Star*, i.e., Venus. In her
cult sacred prostitution is common, in contradistinction to the
worship of Atargatis of Hierapolis. Balti, therefore, is not the female
companion of a Baʿal of Edessa or of any other Syrian city, as
stated, e.g., by Z. Kádár and F. Cumont, but she is the goddess
of love and fertility worshipped in the whole North Mesopotamian
area and known there under different names: Balti, al-ʿUzza,
Aphrodite, the Star. The Dea Syria on the other hand, however
much she may have in common with Balti, represents mainly the

---

[24] *CIL* III, 10973; see also Kádár, *Die kleinasiatisch-syrischen Kulte*, 57.

[25] St. Paulovics, *Laureae Aquincenses*, Budapest 1944, II, 122, 131; *cf.*
Kádár, *Die kleinasiatisch-syrischen Kulte*, 60 and Pl. VI, 12.

[26] Isaac of Antioch, *First Homily on the Conquest of Beth Ḥur*, ed. Bickell,
I, 97-102, 129; a marginal remark in Isaac's Second Homily on the Conquest
of Beth Ḥur, 407ff. identifies al-ʿUzza and Aphrodite; on al-ʿUzza see
J. Wellhausen, *Reste arabischen Heidentums*, third ed., Berlin 1961, 34-45;
J. Noiville, Le culte de l'étoile du matin chez les Arabes préislamiques,
Hespéris 8, 1928, 363-384; T. Fahd, *Le panthéon*, 163-182; M. Höfner, in:
Wörterbuch der Mythologie I, 475f.

strong emotional ties of the Syrians with their hometown, of which she is the symbol and protectress pictured as she is with a mural crown. The same functional division of tasks and roles between both goddesses that are attested in our Syriac sources reappears in the Pannonian inscriptions and reliefs. This is another piece of evidence, like the cult of Azizos in Pannonia, that Syrian cults were brought by Syrian soldiers, slaves and merchants to the various places where they went or were obliged to go, without undergoing any fundamental change, but more or less representing the local religious situation in their homeland. In the Roman empire, with its strong unifying, uniformalizing and centralizing tendencies, the various religions of foreign origin mainly served to help the strangers to keep their own identity. There are some traces of assimilation, e.g., in combining Balti and Arvis or in the identification of Azizos and Apollo Pythius, in the use of Latin in the inscriptions as a concession to the language of the Roman army, but in general Syrian cults remained restricted to people of Syrian origin or birth and kept their local characteristics.

This does not mean that religious concepts at Edessa had only their own purely local character without any influence from elsewhere. Besides particularistic tendencies in religious practice there are other influences at work in order to connect people's own experiences with those of others, to keep the world understandable and orderly, and not to succumb to alienation. Late antique philosophy shows these unifying tendencies to a high degree, and philosophy and philosophers were at home at Edessa. Bringing philosophy into this context does not mean introducing a sharp division between the religion of the lower classes, adhering to local traditions and inherited practices and the elevated and sophisticated views of an elite, bringing folk religion on a higher level. It does mean that religion as a composition of convictions, mental dispositions and ritual behaviour always has two aspects on every level of experience: an intellectual one and a practical one. It always tries to combine action and reflection, however different they may be in mutual proportion.[27]

---

[27] F. Cumont, Les religions orientales, 111ff. and J. Teixidor, The Pagan God, 3-6 drew a sharp distinction between popular belief and theological

Conceptions of After Life, as far as they become transparent from preserved funerary reliefs and mosaics, tomb inscriptions and literary sources, are particularly appropriate to demonstrate reflection on this main issue of human life in a religious or sometimes purely profane context, where the value-system of a culture, and therefore the main source for action, often essentially sounds through.

Nearly all the tomb inscriptions and the greater part of the known mosaics covering the floor of the cave tombs express a strong solidarity among the members of a family and an intense alliance with forefathers and posterity. A tomb is always made by somebody for himself, his relatives and posterity. Out of ten known mosaics six represent a real family scene: Zenodora is represented with her children; the mosaics of Aptuḥa and Belai bar Gusai show all the members of a family; the Family Portrait Mosaic pictures a whole family of seven persons gathered around the pater familias Moqimu (Pl. XIII); the Tripod shows six members of a family with the father in the middle holding a branch or leaf in his right hand, outstretched over an incense altar (called Tripod) (Pl. XIV).[28] The solidarity between the living members of a family, their ancestors, and progeny is strikingly expressed by the epigram on this mosaic:

> *whoever removes*
> *the sorrow of posterity*
> *and mourns the forefathers,*
> *he shall have a good end.*[29]

The most striking examples of these family scenes are representations of the so-called funerary banquet, which occur in some cave-

---

thought, the first stressing the importance of the latter, the second giving all his attention to so-called popular beliefs.

[28] For all literature see Drijvers, *Old-Syriac Inscriptions* No's 44 (Zenodora), 45 (Aptuḥa), 46 (Belai bar Gusai), 47 (Family Portrait Mosaic), 48 (The Tripod Mosaic), 51 (The Funerary Couch Mosaic); *cf.* J. Leroy, Mosaïques funéraires d'Édesse, *Syria* 34, 1957, 307-342; *idem*, Nouvelles découvertes archéologiques relatives à Édesse, *Syria* 38, 1961, 159-169.

[29] For this epigram see J. Naveh, Remarks on Two East Aramaic Inscriptions, *BASOR* 216, December 1974, 9ff,

tombs in and near Edessa, and on one mosaic (Pl. XVII, XVIII, XIX).[30] A reclining figure in relief on the wall of a tomb tower at Deir Yakup near Edessa belongs to the same genre.[31] Its closest parallel is a similar relief in the tomb tower of Kithot at Palmyra.[32] The funerary banquet is one of the commonest themes in Palmyrene funerary art and very often forms the central representation in a tomb tower or hypogaeum. It pictures the pater familias, often identical with the founder or builder of the tomb, in the midst of his family lying on a couch with a cup in his hand usually with his wife sitting at the head of the couch. Servants serve him, and his children all stand around their father lying on his couch. An Edessan mosaic dated A.D. 278 represents fundamentally the same scene with the father Zaidalat son of Barbaʿsamên, who built the tomb, in the center surrounded by his wife and six children. Contrary to what has often been said, the scene of the funerary banquet does not bear upon a religious or metaphysical concept of, e.g., a meal in the beyond or a meal held in honor of the dead, who are supposed to be present. On the contrary, the scene illustrates the happiness and wealth of a man in the midst of his family as one of the highest values of earthly life.[33] It hints at the dominant position of men in that society and gives an idea of the hierarchy within a family, but does not picture an ideal state in the beyond. The Tripod mosaic pictures the family centered around an incense altar, worshipping the gods and in this way symbolizes another value of life. The people gazing at us from the reliefs and the mosaics are the wealthy members of the upper level of society who often embody the strongest traditional values of ordinary life.

---

[30] cf. Pognon, Inscriptions sémitiques, 76f.; Segal, Edessa, 27 and Pl. 25b; Pognon, Inscriptions sémitiques 179ff. and pl. XI: a cave tomb with a funerary banquet at Kara Köpru; The Funerary Couch Mosaic dating from 277/8 A.D., cf. Segal, New Mosaics from Edessa, Archaeology 12, 1959, 150-157; idem, Edessa, 55 and Pl. 2.

[31] Segal, Edessa, Pl. 39b.

[32] cf. E. Will, Le relief de la tour Kithot et le banquet funéraire à Palmyre, Syria 28, 1951, 70-100; cf. J.-M. Dentzer, l'Iconographie iranienne du souverain couché et le motif du banquet, AAAS 21, 1971, 39ff.

[33] cf. H. Seyrig, Le repas des morts et le "banquet funèbre" à Palmyre, AAS I, 1951, 32-41; Will, Le relief de la tour Kithot et le banquet funéraire à Palmyre, Syria 28, 1951, 70-100.

Another idea expressed in the funerary inscriptions is that the dead body should not be removed from the tomb. Violators of the tomb are threatened with having no offspring to throw dust on their eyes, i.e., to fulfill the usual funerary rites, and with not getting a tomb themselves.[34] The deity Marᵉlahê is invoked in one inscription to curse anyone who removes the body from the tomb.[35] Esteem for a corpse has nothing to do in this context with the expectation of a bodily resurrection but is another way of expressing the solidarity among living and dead members of a family. The tomb is the very place where the living ones meet the dead, where the visual representations and the inscriptions express the bonds between them, and where the dead are present in the form of their corpses and effigies. Whoever breaks these bonds by removing the dead will himself be removed from the society of the living and the dead, because no son will throw dust on his eyes after his death, and he will get no burial place which means that he will completely disappear from the memory of mankind.

Two mosaics seem to express other concepts of after-life. One represents Orpheus playing on his lyre among the animals and is dated A.D. 228 (Pl. XV). The other pictures the Phoenix bird standing on an upright stele and dates from A.D. 235-36 (Pl. XVI).[36] Orpheus as well as Phoenix are identified as such by the accompanying Syrian inscriptions on the mosaics. Both inscriptions are rather stereotyped, mention the founder of the tomb who built it for himself and his family, but do not say a word on special expectations of after life that are suggested by the Phoenix bird as well as by the figure of Orpheus. The only peculiarity in both inscriptions is that they call the tomb itself *byt ῾lm᾿* = house of

---

[34] *e.g.* in the inscription of Serrîn, Drijvers, no. 2; Maricq, *Classica et Orientalia*, 127-139; *cf.* A. Parrot, *Malédictions et Violations de Tombes*, Paris 1939, 25ff. for parallels in the Syrian area.

[35] The inscription comes from a cave-tomb at Kirk Mağara, one of the cemeteries of ancient Edessa, *cf.* Pognon, *Inscriptions sémitiques*, 80-82; Drijvers, *Old-Syriac Inscriptions*, no. 35 with an improved reading.

[36] Segal, *Edessa*, Pl. 43, 44; *idem*, The Sabian Mysteries. The Planet Cult of ancient Harran, in: *Vanished Civilizations*, ed. E. Bacon, London 1963, 208 (reproduction in colour of the Phoenix mosaic), 209 (the Orpheus mosaic in colour); for the inscriptions: Drijvers, *Old-Syriac Inscriptions*, no's 49 and 50.

eternity, which will last *lywmt ʿlmʾ* = till the days of eternity, which phrase further only occurs in the inscription of the mosaic of Aptuḥa and nowhere else in Syriac funerary texts.[37] Another designation of a tomb is *byt qbwrʾ* = *house of burial*, which seems to be older than *byt ʿlmʾ* = house of eternity.[38] It is therefore possible that the various expressions in combination with the visual representations indicate a certain shift in the concepts of life, burial and after-life, but our sources actually are too limited to allow solid conclusions, and a phrase like 'till the days of eternity' is also ambiguous. Does it mean forever, or does it imply the notion of a consummation of this world which will come to its end at a certain day, the day of eternity?

The expression as such seems to point in the direction of the last explanation. There also are no clear indications that these mosaics were made for the tombs of Jews or Christians who surely lived at Edessa in the third century. On the contrary, it is more likely that, like all the other funerary monuments and inscriptions that have been preserved, these mosaics were made for the tombs of pagans, although the Phoenix bird and Orpheus occur in Christian literature and symbolism.[39] To deal with the Phoenix first, it can

---

[37] The Mosaic of Aptuḥa is now on view in the Museum of Istanbul; see Segal, *Edessa*, Pl. 17a; J. Leroy, Mosaïques funéraires d'Édesse, *Syria* 34, 1957, 309-311; Drijvers, *Old-Syriac Inscriptions*, no. 45; on the notion of *byt ʿlmʾ* = house of eternity see Parrot, *Malédictions et Violations de Tombes*, 165ff.: La "domus aeterna".

[38] *byt qbwrʾ* occurs in the inscription of Birecik, L. 4, the oldest known Old-Syriac inscription dated 6 A.D., in inscr. no. 26 from Harran, in inscr. 31 dated 201 A.D., in inscr. no. 35 and in inscr. 51 on the Funerary Couch Mosaic dated 277/8 A.D.

[39] *cf.* R. van den Broek, *The Myth of the Phoenix according to classical and early Christian Traditions*, EPRO 24, Leiden 1972, 423ff.; on Orpheus in Christian literature and symbolism see A. Wrzésniowski, The Figure of Orpheus in Early Christian Iconography, *Archeologia* 21, 1970, 112-123; Sister Charles Murray, The Christian Orpheus, *CAr* 26, 1977, 19-27, a discussion with H. Stern, Orphée dans l'art paléochrétien, *CAr* 23, 1977, 1-16 on a supposed Jewish origin of the christian Orpheus, which is maintained by Stern. On Orpheus in a Jewish milieu see: A. Dupont-Sommer, David et Orphée, *Institut de France* 1964, no. 20; *idem*, *Semitica* 14, 1964, 37-40; M. Philonenko, David-Orphée sur une mosaïque de Gaza, *RHPR* 1967, 355-357; J. Magne, Seigneur de l'univers ou David-Orphée, *Revue de Qumran* 34, 1977, 189ff.; see, however, Sister Charles Murray, *art. cit.*, 20, n. 5, for a convincing criticism of this view.

be stated that the bird as such became a symbol of life after death and the renewal of life often connected with the concept of the Great Year whose beginning and end mark the beginning and end of the world.[40] Might we suppose that this concept is indicated by the phrase *lywmt 'lm'* = till the days of eternity, which is part of the Syriac inscription on the mosaic? The Phoenix also symbolizes the human soul, its eternity and imperishableness and this concept fits in very well with the representation on our mosaic: a standing Phoenix on a funerary stele with a tomb in front of it. Since the Phoenix itself has various symbolical connotations not hinted at on our mosaic or the inscription on it, once again solid conclusions cannot be reached. What is certain is that it bears upon the concept of life after death. This concept is likely connected with the idea of periodicity in world history that has a beginning and an end.

The Orpheus Mosaic represents a common theme in pagan iconography: Orpheus playing the lyre and charming the beasts. It has paradisiac connotations and therefore was taken over by the Christians in their literature and art from the second century A.D. on.[41] It is not surprising that the Orpheus theme also became a motif in pagan as well as Christian funerary art. The descent of Orpheus into the underworld is a funerary image par excellence and Orpheus charming the beasts evokes a paradisiac existence that one wants for the dead. Both motifs together occur on two steles from Pannonia and in a tomb in Libya. A stele from Intercisa in Pannonia and two funerary mosaics at Cherchel and Constantine in Algeria only depict Orpheus charming the beasts.[42] None of the known steles and mosaics refers to the doctrines of Orphism; on the contrary, they all—however vague the symbolical meanings

---

[40] cf. Van den Broek, *The Myth of the Phoenix*, 414f.; for other symbolical connotations of the Phoenix see M. Tardieu, Pour un phénix gnostique, *RHR* 183, 1973, 117-142.

[41] cf. Sister Charles Murray, *art. cit.*; H. Stern, *art. cit.*; A. Wrzésniowski, *art. cit.*; the literature on Orpheus mosaics is enormous, *cf. e.g.* Ch. Picard, Sur l'Orphée de la fontaine monumentale de Byblos, *Misc. Jerphanion* I, Rome 1947, 266-281; H. Stern, La mosaïque d'Orphée de Blanzy-les-Fismes, *Gallia* 13, 1955, 41-77; M. Ponsich, Une mosaïque d'Orphée, *Bulletin d'Archéologie marocaine* 6, 1966, 479-481.

[42] cf. H. Stern, La mosaïque d'Orphée, 67, no's 29 and 30 of his catalogue of Orpheus mosaics.

they bear may be—breathe an atmosphere of peace that even encompasses the world of animals and plants, and therefore the most appropriate places of Orpheus mosaics used to be courtyards or fountains.[43] There is, consequently, no reason to interpret the Orpheus mosaic from Edessa as evidence of an Orphic cult or sect at Edessa, of which the members observed a moral self-abnegation in order to purify the soul from all the uncleanness of the world.[44] Since Orpheus' lyre on the Edessan mosaic has only three strings, it does not lend itself to a symbolical interpretation either.

Both mosaics from the first half of the third century express the expectation of an after-life for the human soul that will even go beyond the existence of this world. The Orpheus mosaic stresses the paradisiac character of this after-life. Both are in all likelihood non-Christian, although the concepts they convey are related to Christian ideas, as we will see. They attest to the spread at Edessa of motifs and ideas from the Greco-Roman world which became part of local culture. The inscriptions on the mosaics are written in Syriac and not in Greek, so that—at least at Edessa—an artificially drawn border-line between Greco-Roman and local culture does not coincide with the distinction between speakers of Greek and of the local Aramaic dialect.

Another instance of influence from the West on Edessan concepts of after-life might be the two reliefs of what J. B. Segal calls an embracing couple (Pl. V). They are each other's reflection and probably were intended to decorate a niche or arcosolium in a tomb. Both represent a female figure, the lower part of whose body is dressed, and the upper part nude, and a completely nude male figure, embracing and kissing each other. Parallels to this scene in the field of funerary art seem to be non-existent. It may be suggested here that both reliefs express the idea of the nude soul freed from the body and from all worldly aspirations returning to its origin. The relief breathes a nearly heavenly serenity and might convey this idea. The return of the soul to its heavenly place of origin is, in fact, a journey through the spheres of the planets. At

---

[43] Stern, *art. cit.*, 64f.; on symbolical interpretations of Orpheus' lyre with seven strings see Cumont, *Symbolisme funéraire*, 18, n. 4, 499.

[44] So Segal, *Edessa*, 55f.

each sphere the soul crosses it leaves behind the quality the planet gave it when the soul descended for a temporary sojourn in a human body. At the end of its journey the soul is completely emptied, ethereal, nude, and then finds eternal rest.

If the tentative interpretation offered here might claim to have some truth in it, then the closest parallel to this concept of after-life of the soul is to be found in the doctrine of Bardaiṣan, the Aramaic philosopher from Edessa (154-222 A.D.). The soul, in his view, crosses the planet spheres during its journey back to its origin and in the end enters the 'Bridal Chamber of Light,' where the heavenly wedding is celebrated, the final union of the soul with its origin, the return to the womb of the Mother of Life.[45] This idea might be envisaged in both reliefs!

In the person of Bardaiṣan early Christianity enters into the discussion of pagan religion at Edessa. It arrived there at the end of the first or the beginning of the second century A.D., but its earliest history is practically unknown. Marcion seems to have had many followers in that area since Bardaiṣan wrote dialogues against their dualistic world-view, but the philosopher at the court of King Abgar the Great is, in fact, the first personality in the history of Christianity at Edessa whose contours can be sketched relatively faithfully.[46] It is of high importance that his doctrine on creation and salvation has all kinds of contacts with pagan religion and philosophy. He actually was a man of syntheses and harmony and this was probably the main reason why he opposed the radical Marcionites who said good-bye to this world and its creator.

---

[45] cf. Drijvers, *Bardaiṣan of Edessa*, 151-160 based on Ephrem Syrus' polemics against Bardaiṣan, cf. e.g. Ephrem Syrus, *Prose Refutations of Mani, Marcion and Bardaiṣan*, ed. Mitchell, II, lxxvii (transl.), 164, 32-40 (syr. text).

[46] cf. Drijvers, *Bardaiṣan of Edessa*; later publications; *idem*, Mani und Bardaiṣan. Ein Beitrag zur Vorgeschichte des Manichäismus, *Mélanges H.-Ch. Puech*, Paris 1974, 459ff.; *idem*, Bardaiṣan von Edessa als Repräsentant des syrischen Synkretismus im 2. Jahrhundert n. Chr., *Synkretismus im syrisch-persischen Kulturbereich*, *AAWG.PH* 96, 1975, 109ff.; B. Aland, Mani und Bardesanes. Zur Entstehung des manichäischen Systems, *Synkretismus*, 123ff.; E. Beck, Ephraems Brief an Hypatios, *OrChr* 58, 1974, 76ff.; E. Beck, Ephräms Rede gegen eine philosophische Schrift des Bardaiṣan, *OrChr* 60, 1976, 24ff.; Drijvers, art. *Bardesanes*, TRE (in print)

The introduction of Christianity into the cultural and religious
pattern of Edessa constituted, however, not only the addition of
a new tessera to the variegated religious mosaic, but at last a
seemingly complete change of the existing pattern by the introduction of doctrinal controversies into the body social of Edessa.
The pagan religions aimed at a consolidation of the existing order
by strengthening its solidarity on the one hand and giving a certain
identity to the various groups in the population on the other. This
complicated pattern of centripetal and centrifugal forces never led
to doctrinal controversies splitting the population up into sharply
confined groups whose identity only consisted of having a religion
of their own, although there surely were all kinds of tensions. The
pattern of ancient Christianity at Edessa shows various groups
with different views who fought against and complained about
each other. This remark is not meant as a depreciation of Christianity as such, but only as an indication of what the social results of
bringing the Gospel could be.

The period during which in its various forms Christianity and
paganism existed side by side at Edessa is of particular interest
for the study of the functioning of different religions within one
city, the influences they exercised upon each other, and the various
ways they shaped the city and its life. The history of Christianity
at Edessa and remaining Syria as a social and cultural movement
still needs to be written, although many publications have contributed a good deal of material to it.[47] In the context of this study
we will restrict ourselves to some remarks on possible influences
exercised by pagan religions on early Christianity. A key position
is again held by Bardaiṣan, who combined philosophical and
astrological concepts with local religious traditions as well as part
of the message of the Gospel. In the historical process of the development of Christian doctrine at Edessa its famous philosopher was
more and more charged with heresy and that process went parallel
with the extirpation of pagan religions. This is an indication that

---

[47] cf. Introduction p. 2, n. 5; cf. at last J. Fiey, *Jalons pour une histoire de
l'église en Iraq*, *CSCO* Subs. 36, Louvain 1970; the present author intends
in the near future to publish a history of ancient Syrian Christianity up to
the end of the fourth century,

Christian belief and paganism co-existed rather peacefully in the beginning. Pagan and Christian held different views, but they did not fight each other. The predominant position of Nebo, god of wisdom and human fate, son of the god of heaven Bel, has its counterpart in the Christian Jesus, son of God and the incarnation of His Wisdom. The accent on the healing capacities of Christ and His Wisdom in Christian doctrine at Edessa might have some relations to pagan views and practice. The same holds true, e.g., for concepts of after-life. The ideas expressed by the Orpheus mosaic are rather similar to concepts of after-life in the Syriac Odes of Solomon and related literature.[48]

Besides religious doctrine there is religious practice. It is rather revealing that Ephrem Syrus at the end of the fourth century not only combats pagan views, especially those represented by Marcion, Bardaiṣan and Mani, but also pagan practices having to do with astrology, magic, the use of amulets, etc.[49] It seems that paganism and Christianity had such practices in common in spite of their doctrinal differences. It is after all much easier to change certain opinions than human behaviour!

Our main document of the shift of religion at Edessa is still the *Doctrina Addai*, however tendentious and apologetic it may be. It does not inform us about historical events during the first, second and third century A.D., but champions a kind of orthodoxy that must be considered the preliminary final phase of a long development of Christian and pagan controversies and doctrinal discussions and fights in the Christian community of Edessa. The

---

[48] A systematic study of concepts of the after-life in Early Syriac Christian literature is not available; the topic will be dealt with in the monograph announced in the foregoing note. Generally speaking the main concept of the after-life according to Christian doctrine in Syria is a return to man's original abode, Paradise, to which he is guided by Christ. It is of interest to note that the concept of the Divine Singer is to be found also in the Odes of Solomon.

[49] Ephrem's *Hymni contra Haereses* are full of polemics against such pagan practices which are identified by him with heterodoxy; *cf.* for a striking example E. Peterson, Die geheimen Praktiken eines syrischen Bischofs, *Frühkirche, Judentum und Gnosis*, Freiburg 1959, 333-345; see also Ephrem Syrus, *Carmina Nisibina* (ed. E. Beck), *CSCO, Script. Syri* 92, 9, 6; 11, 16; Ephrem Syrus, *Hymnen de Fide* (ed. E. Beck), *CSCO, Script. Syri* 73, 37, 15.

various layers that can be detected in the *Doctrina* itself shed some
vague light on underlying historical processes without making
them completely clear.[50] The aim of this treatise is, however,
perfectly clear; in its attacks on paganism, in its claim that King
Abgar and his nobles had converted to Christian belief, in its
elaboration of a complete ecclesiastical hierarchy, and a daily
liturgy, a religious reorganisation of the whole city and its population is the very aim. This is why Addai holds its long sermon for
the gathered population at the very religious and social center of
the city, where processions started and ended, and where the
city's identity was shown. When Christianity had won the battle
against paganism, it fulfilled exactly the same unifying and centralizing function in urban life that its antagonist once did. It held
processions, had an elaborate liturgy and a vast ecclesiastical
hierarchy; it shaped time by the feast of its saints, and urban space
by transforming former temples into churches or by building new
ones. Then it became evident to what extent Christianity was the
real heir of classical culture and pagan religion, how much the
world had changed during the foregoing centuries when both
religions existed peacefully side by side or persecuted each other
in a long process of mutual influence. The best qualities of a loser
are often taken over by the victor. To elucidate these qualities is,
therefore, the only aim of this description of the cults and beliefs
at Edessa.

---

[50] I hope to demonstrate this in a forthcoming publication *Studies in the
Doctrina Addai*; it is *e.g.* noteworthy that Addai's relation to King Abgar
has an exact counterpart in Mani's relation to the Sassanid king!

INDEX

LIST OF PLATES

with pediment. After A. R. Bellinger, *The Syrian Tetradrachms of Caracalla and Macrinus, NS* 3, N.Y. 1940, Pl. XI, 7

5. Tetradrachm of Caracalla from Edessa; the reverse shows an eagle, head r., between legs, shrine with pediment. After Bellinger, *The Syrian Tetradrachms*, Pl. X, 17

6. Tetradrachm of Macrinus from Edessa; the reverse shows an eagle, head r., between legs, shrine with pediment. After Bellinger, *The Syrian Tetradrachms*, Pl. XI, 11

7. Tetradrachm of Elagabal from Edessa; the reverse shows an eagle, head l., between legs, shrine with pediment. After Bellinger, *The Syrian Tetradrachms*, Pl. XII, 2

PLATES I-XXXIV

PLATE I

Plate II

PLATE III

PLATE IV

PLATE V

PLATE VI

PLATE VII

Plate VIII

PLATE IX

PLATE X

PLATE XI

PLATE XII

PLATE XIII

Plate XIV

PLATE XV

PLATE XVI

PLATE XVII

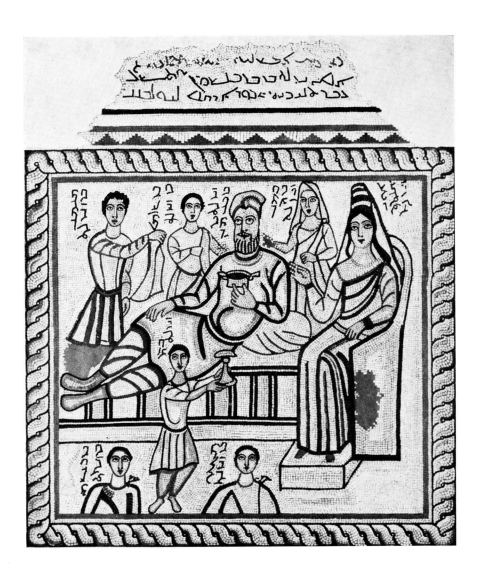

PLATE XVIII

PLATE XIX

PLATE XX

PLATE XXI

PLATE XXII

PLATE XXIII

Plate XXIV

Plate XXV

Plate XXVI

PLATE XXVII

PLATE XXVIII

PLATE XXIX

PLATE XXX

PLATE XXXI

PLATE XXXII

1

2

3

4

5